Flying Witch

Chihiro Ishizuka

Contents

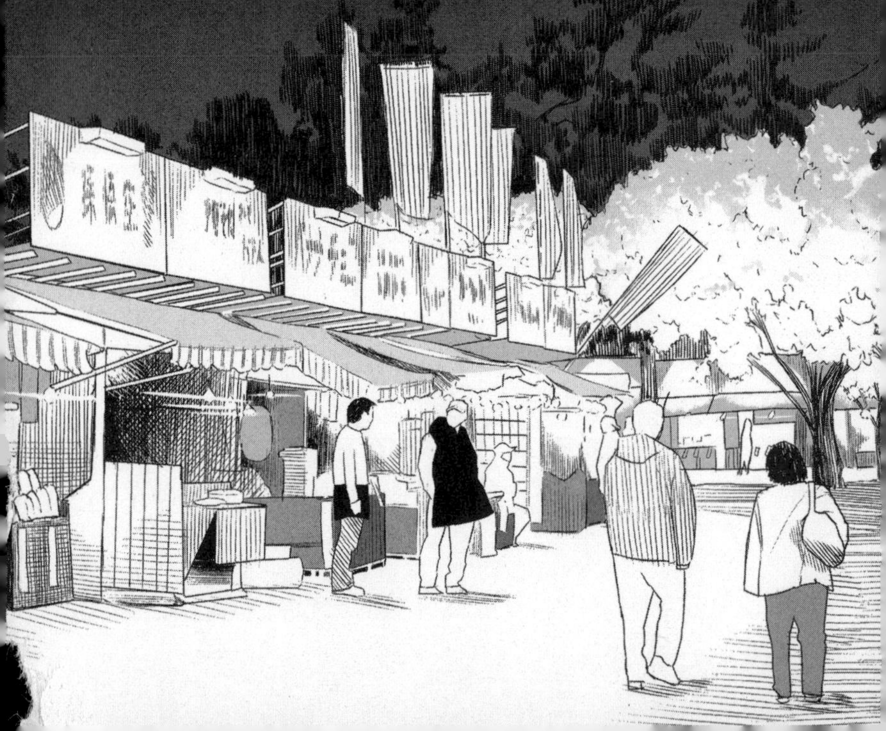

Chapter 7
A Dream, and Good Fortune on the Roadside

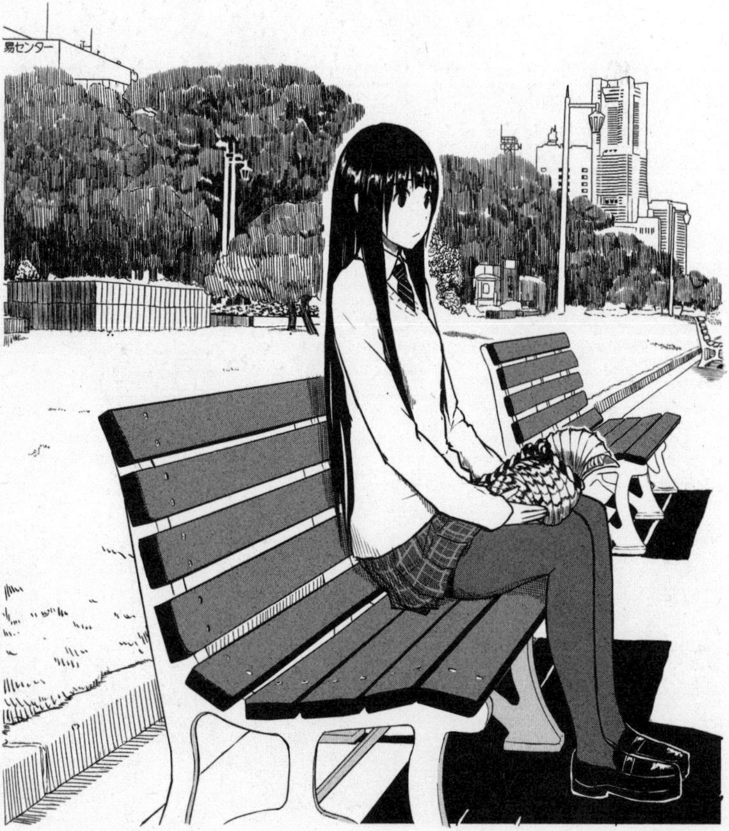
易センター

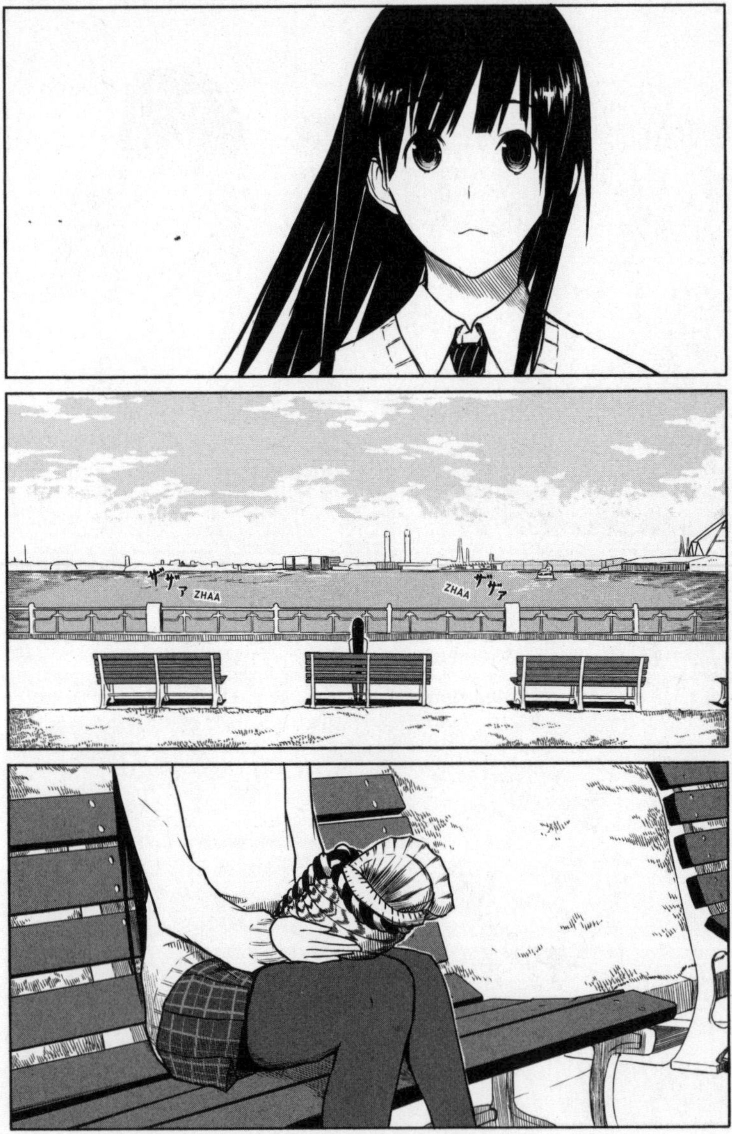
ザザァ
ZHAA
ザザァ
ZHAA

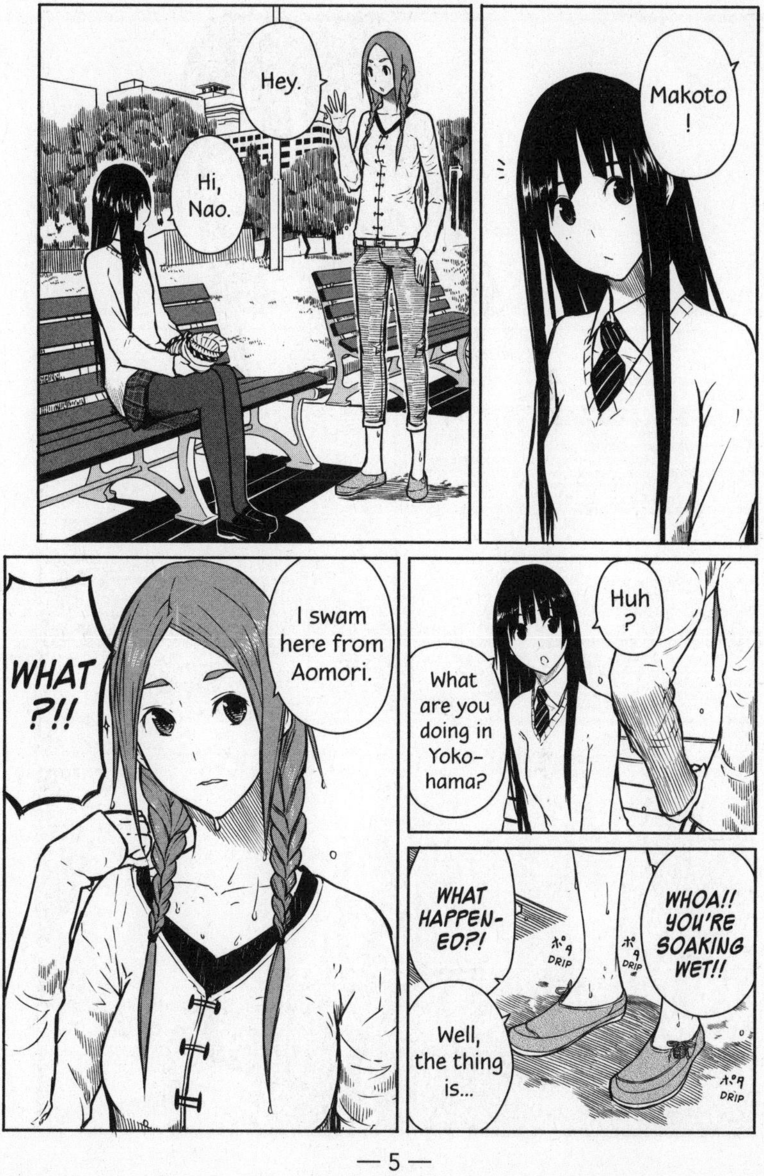
Makoto!
Hey.
Hi, Nao.
Huh?
What are you doing in Yokohama?
WHOA!! YOU'RE SOAKING WET!!
WHAT HAPPENED?!
ポタ DRIP
ポタ DRIP
ポタ DRIP
Well, the thing is...
I swam here from Aomori.
WHAT?!!

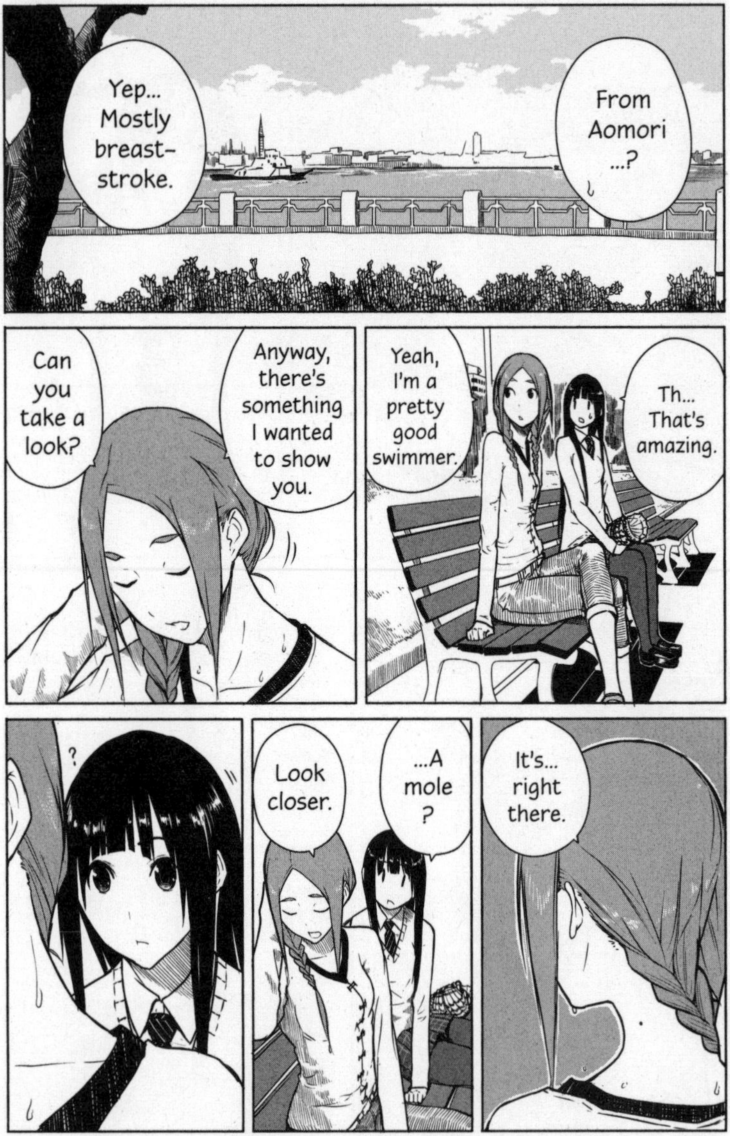
From Aomori ...?
Yep... Mostly breast-stroke.
Th... That's amazing.
Yeah, I'm a pretty good swimmer.
Anyway, there's something I wanted to show you.
Can you take a look?
It's... right there.
...A mole ?
Look closer.
?

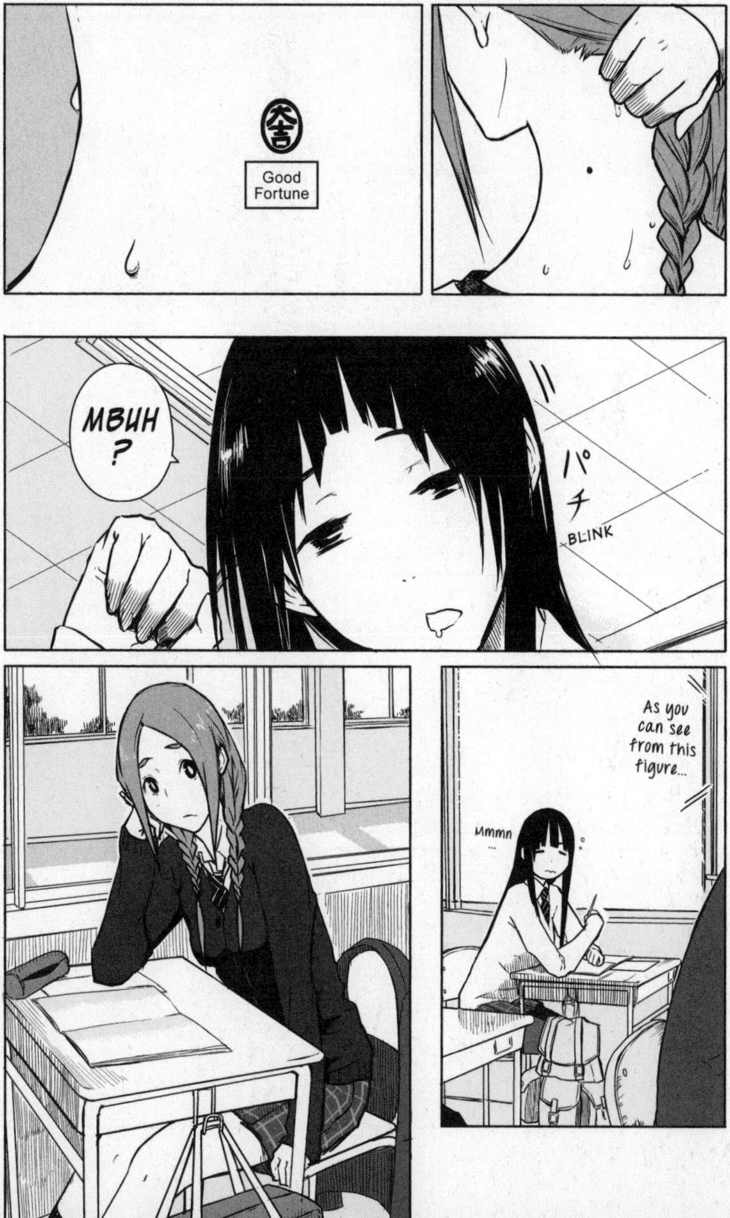
大吉
Good Fortune
パチ
BLINK
MBUH?
As you can see from this figure...
Mmmn...

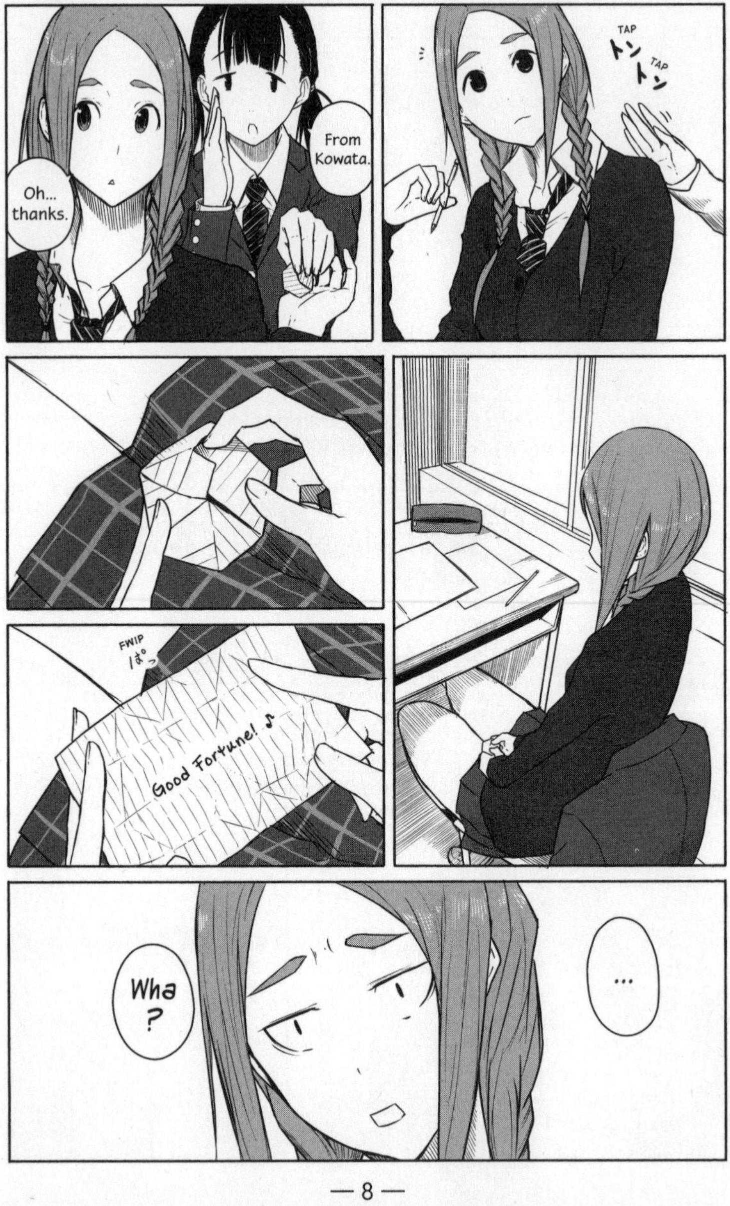
TAP
トン
TAP
トン
From Kowata.
Oh... thanks.
FWIP
ぱっ
Good Fortune! ♪
...
Wha?

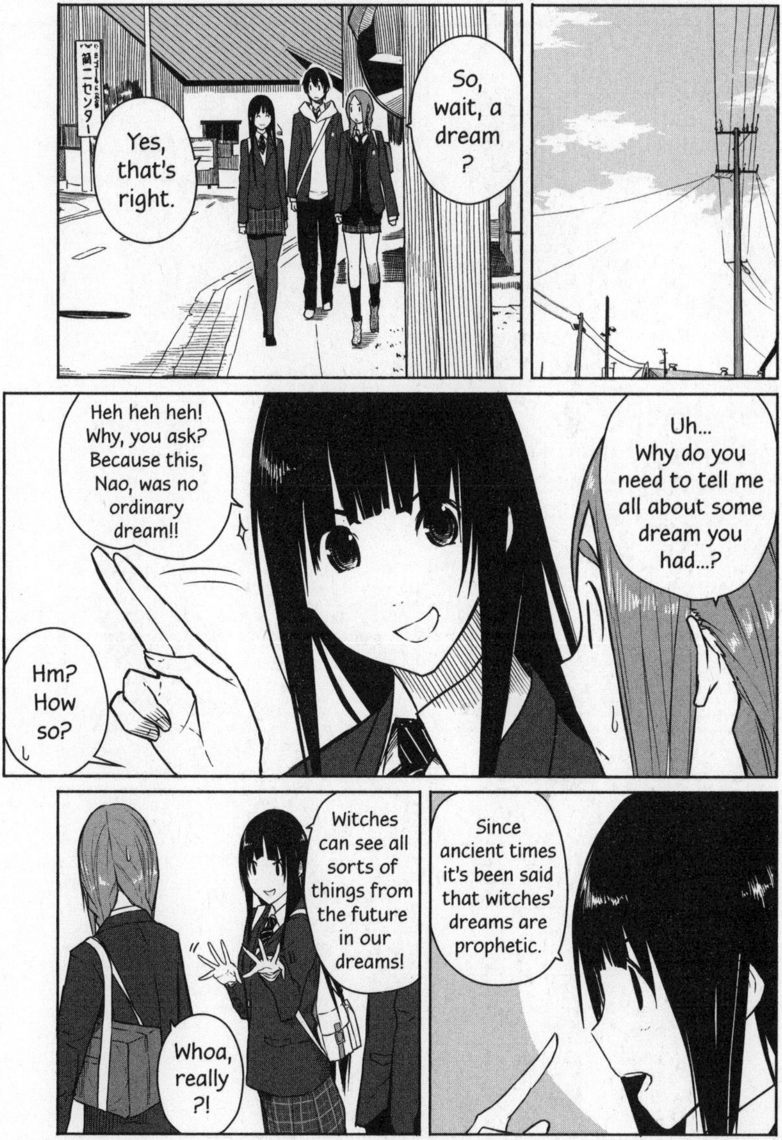
So, wait, a dream?
Yes, that's right.
Uh... Why do you need to tell me all about some dream you had...?
Heh heh heh! Why, you ask? Because this, Nao, was no ordinary dream!!
Hm? How so?
Since ancient times it's been said that witches' dreams are prophetic.
Witches can see all sorts of things from the future in our dreams!
Whoa, really?!

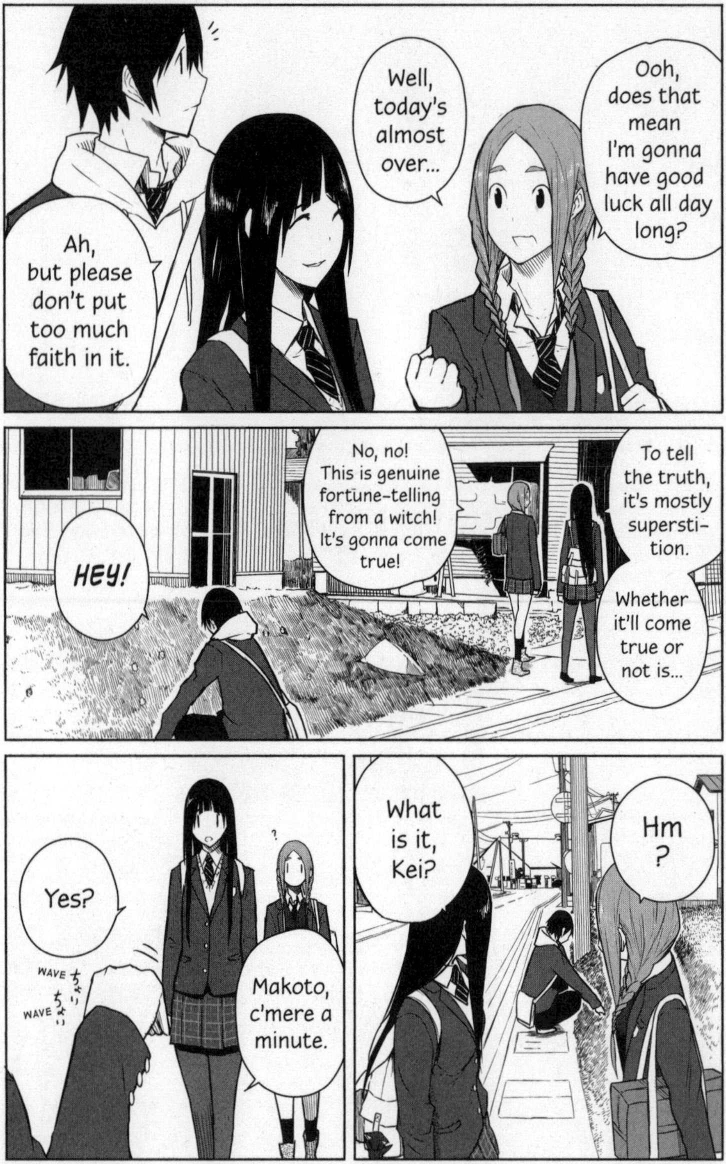
Ooh, does that mean I'm gonna have good luck all day long?
Well, today's almost over...
Ah, but please don't put too much faith in it.
To tell the truth, it's mostly supersti-tion.
No, no! This is genuine fortune-telling from a witch! It's gonna come true!
Whether it'll come true or not is...
HEY!
Hm ?
What is it, Kei?
Makoto, c'mere a minute.
Yes?
WAVE ちょい
WAVE ちょい

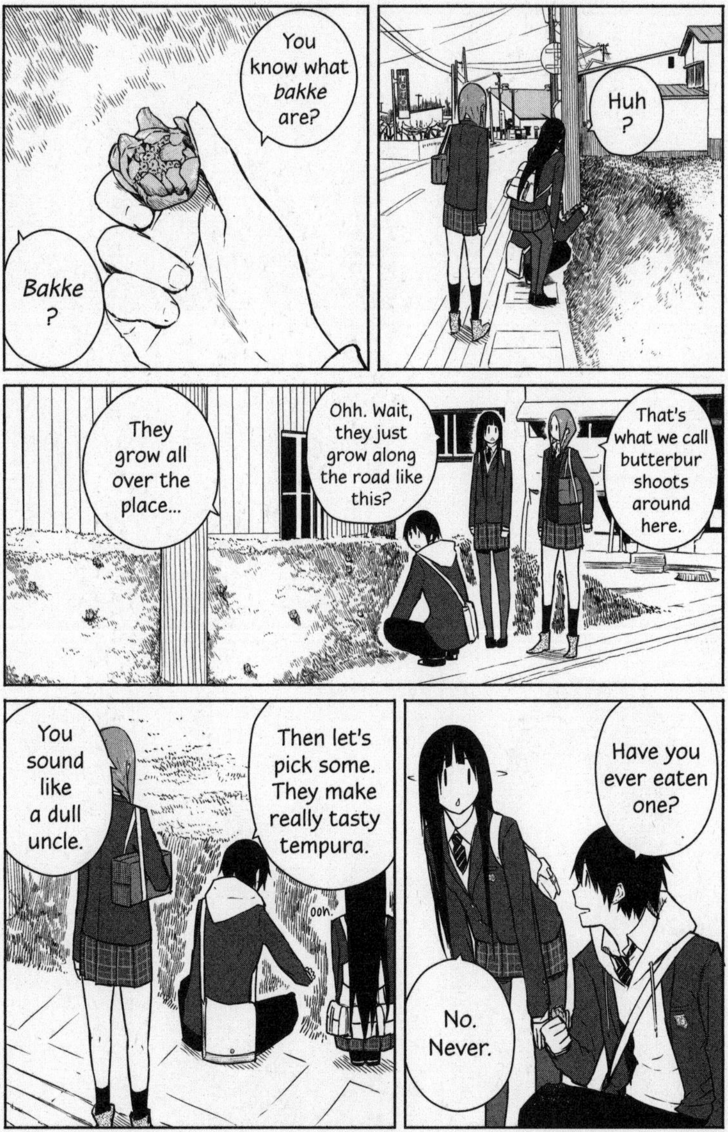
Huh
?
You know what *bakke* are?
Bakke
?
That's what we call butterbur shoots around here.
Ohh. Wait, they just grow along the road like this?
They grow all over the place...
Have you ever eaten one?
No. Never.
Then let's pick some. They make really tasty tempura.
ooh.
You sound like a dull uncle.

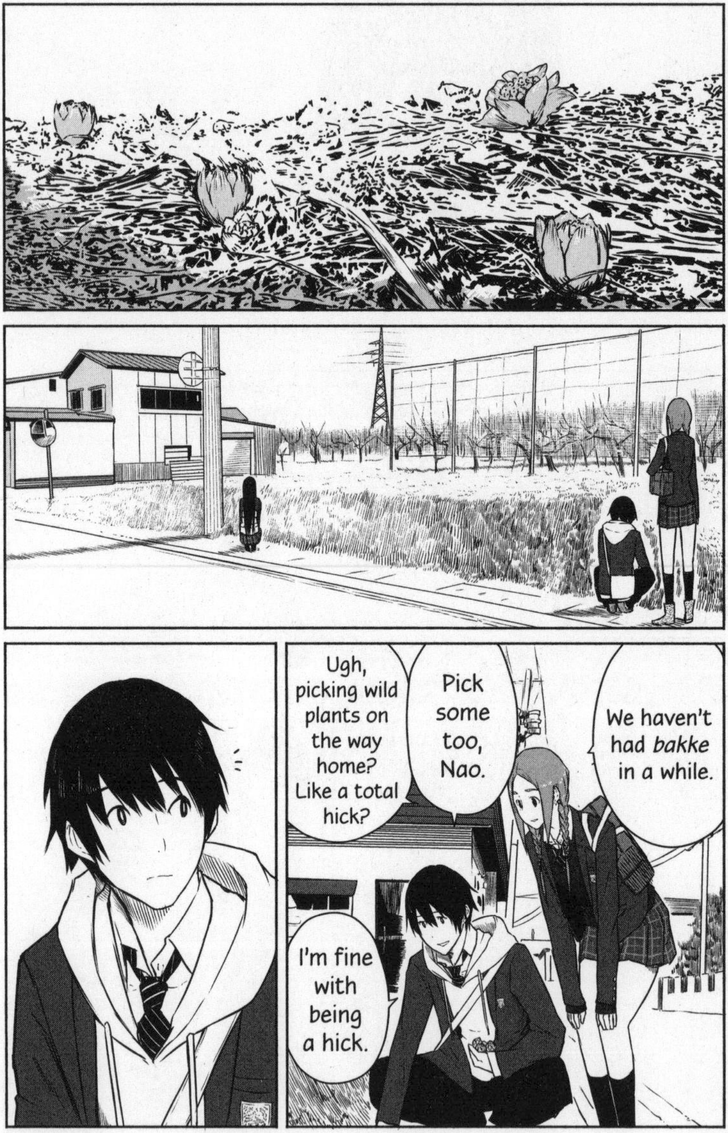
We haven't had *bakke* in a while.
Pick some too, Nao.
Ugh, picking wild plants on the way home? Like a total hick?
I'm fine with being a hick.

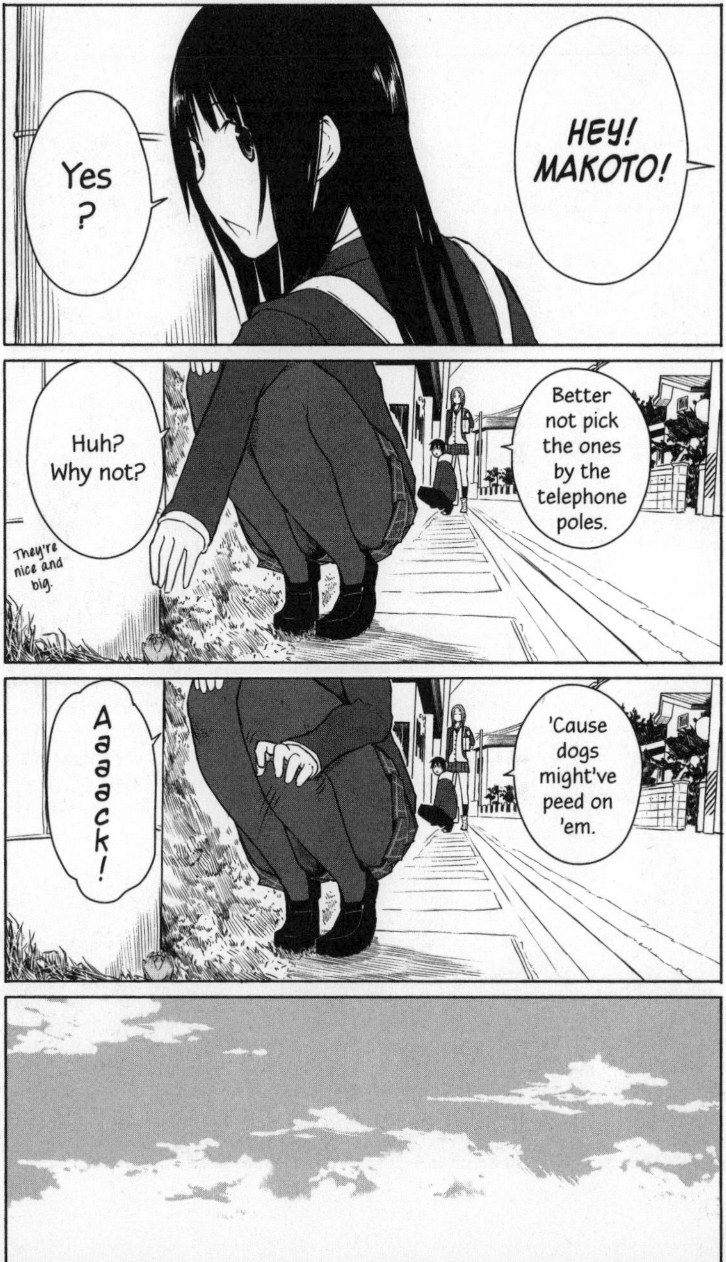
HEY! MAKOTO!
Yes?
Better not pick the ones by the telephone poles.
Huh? Why not?
They're nice and big.
'Cause dogs might've peed on 'em.
Aaaack!

Oh, this is a pretty good haul.

You don't have any school stuff in your bag at all.

She's right...

Huh? Yeah... I leave it all in my desk.

WHAT THE ?!!

What ?!

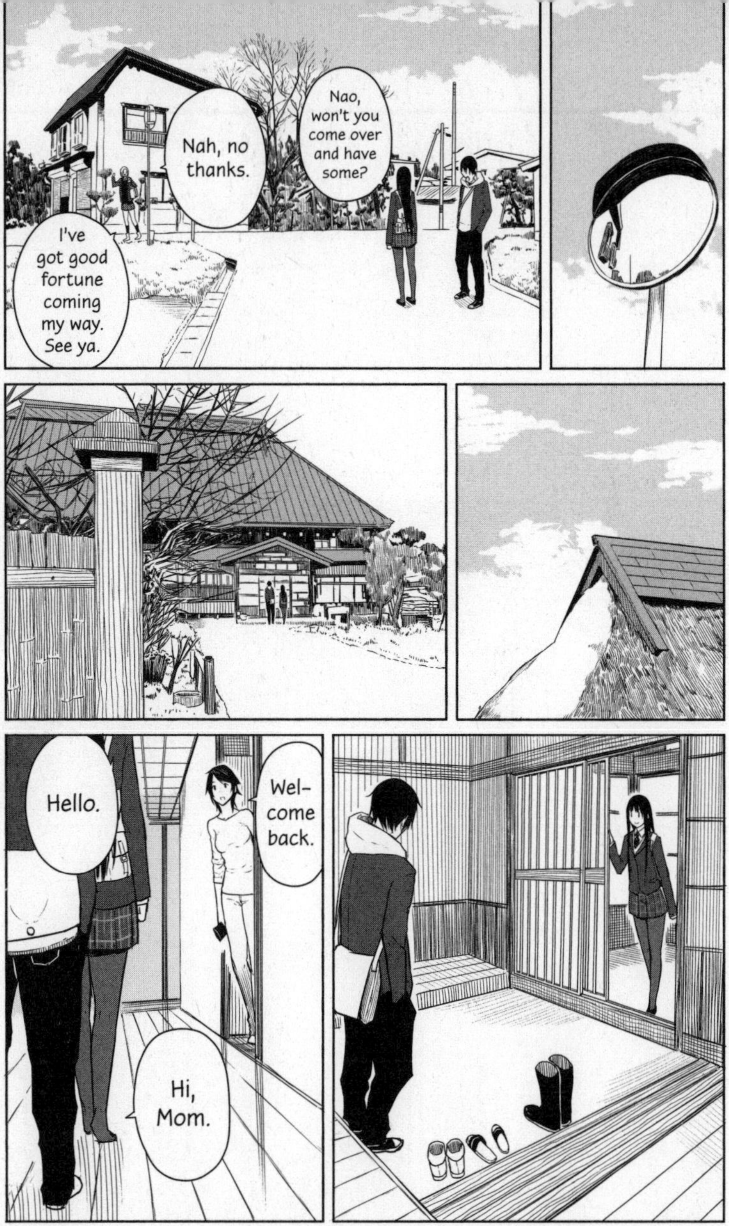
Nao, won't you come over and have some?
Nah, no thanks.
I've got good fortune coming my way. See ya.
Wel-come back.
Hello.
Hi, Mom.

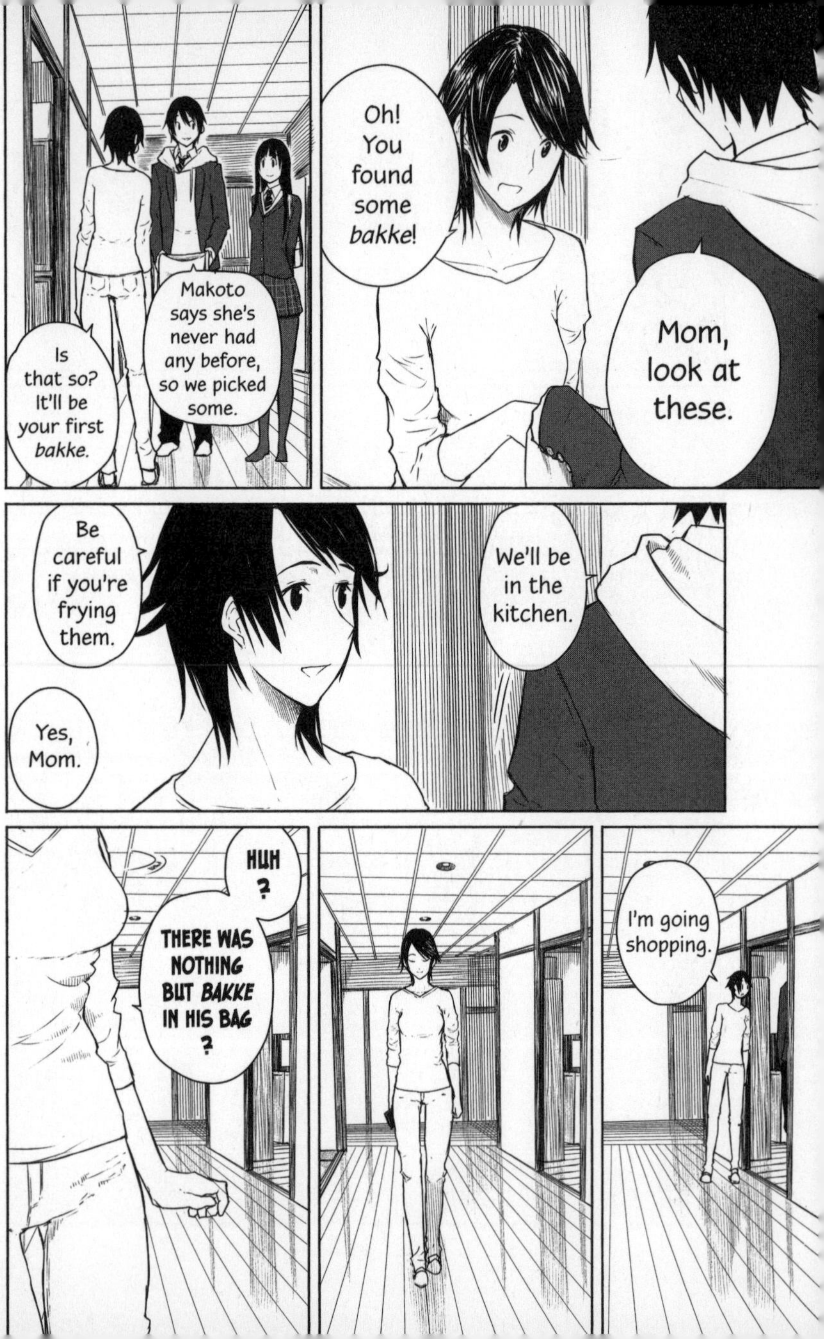
Mom, look at these.
Oh! You found some *bakke*!
Makoto says she's never had any before, so we picked some.
Is that so? It'll be your first *bakke*.
We'll be in the kitchen.
Be careful if you're frying them.
Yes, Mom.
I'm going shopping.
HUH?
THERE WAS NOTHING BUT *BAKKE* IN HIS BAG?

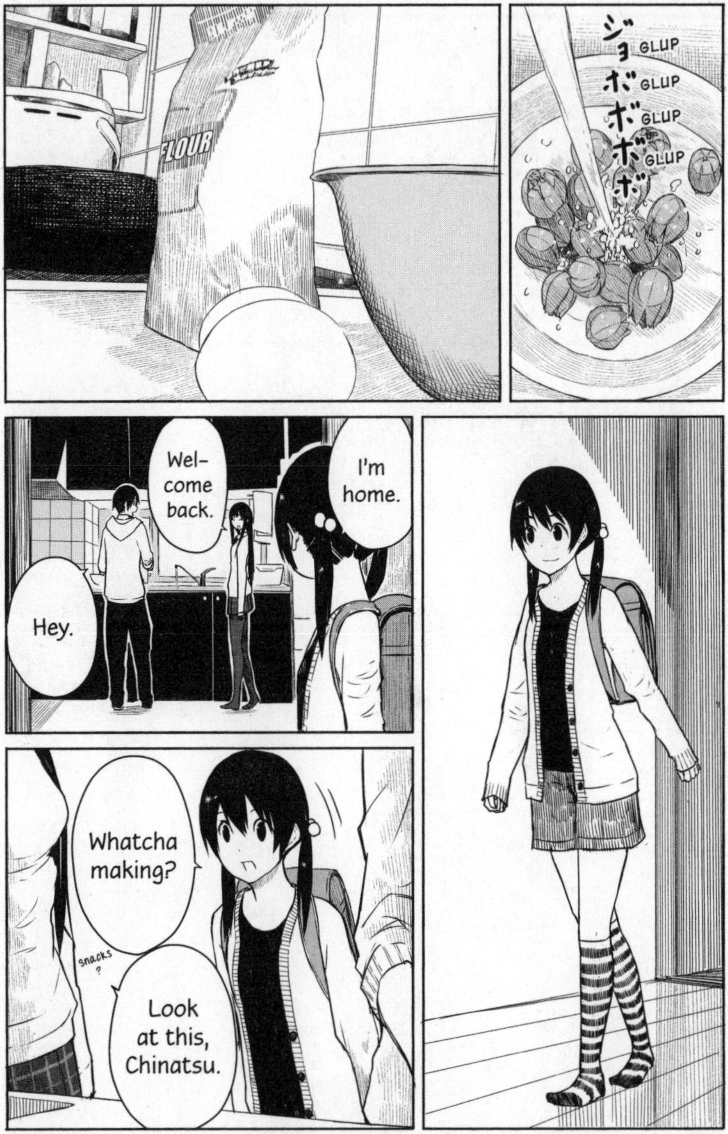
ジョボボボボ
GLUP
GLUP
GLUP
GLUP
FLOUR
I'm home.
Wel-come back.
Hey.
Whatcha making?
snacks ?
Look at this, Chinatsu.

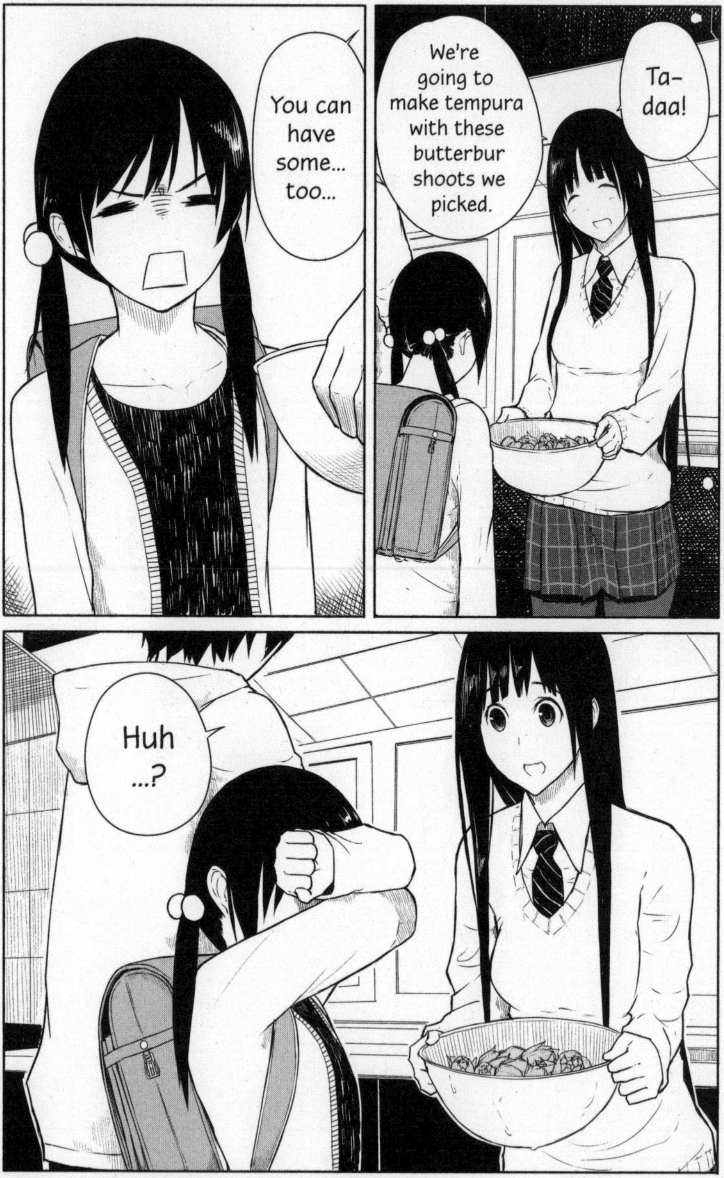
Ta-daa!
We're going to make tempura with these butterbur shoots we picked.
You can have some... too...
Huh ...?

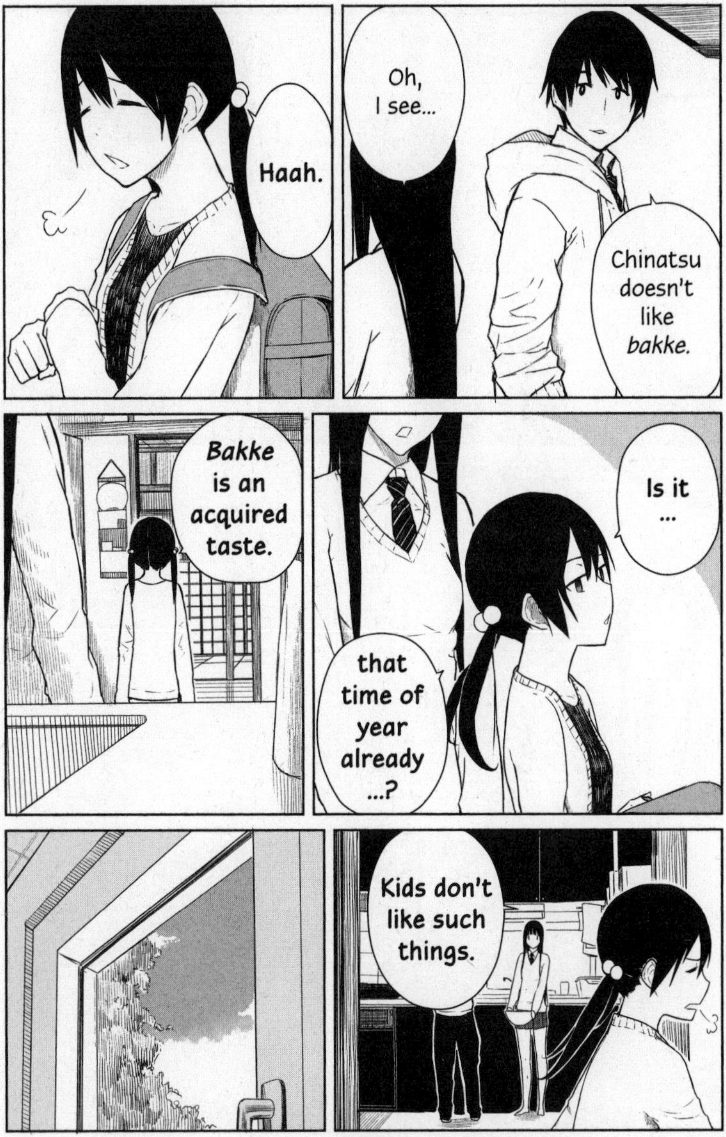

Oh, I see...
Chinatsu doesn't like *bakke.*
Haah.
Is it ...
that time of year already ...?
Bakke is an acquired taste.
Kids don't like such things.

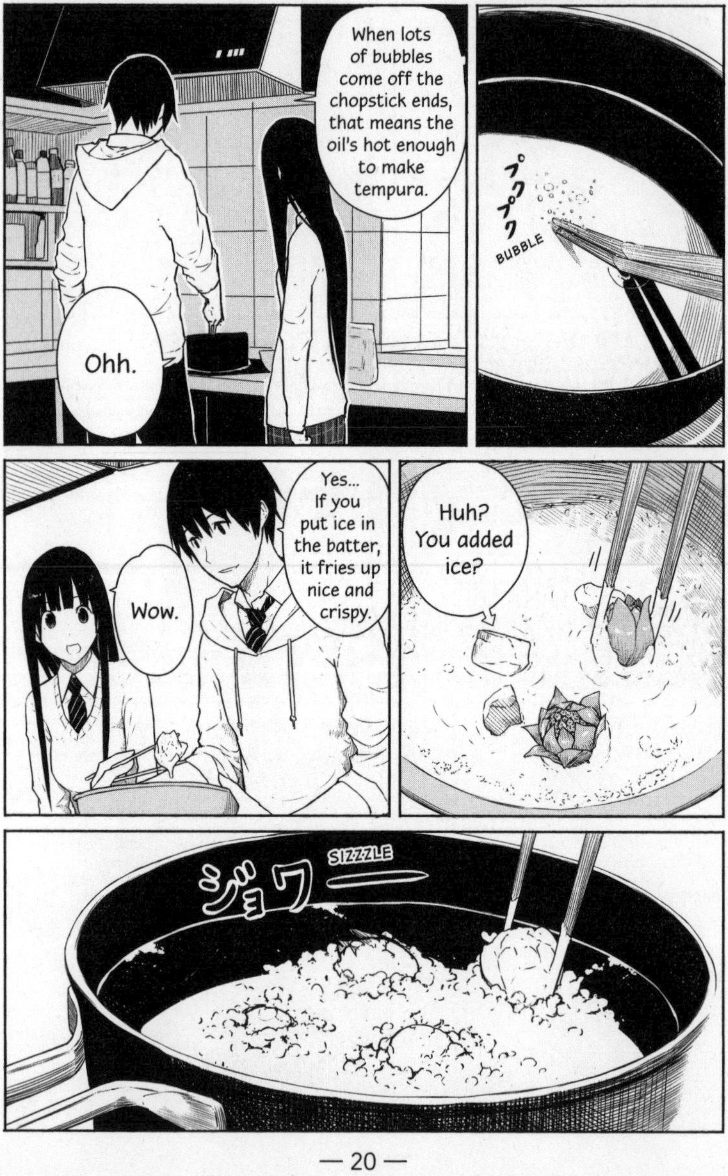
プクプク
BUBBLE
When lots of bubbles come off the chopstick ends, that means the oil's hot enough to make tempura.
Ohh.
Huh? You added ice?
Yes... If you put ice in the batter, it fries up nice and crispy.
Wow.
ジョワー
SIZZZLE

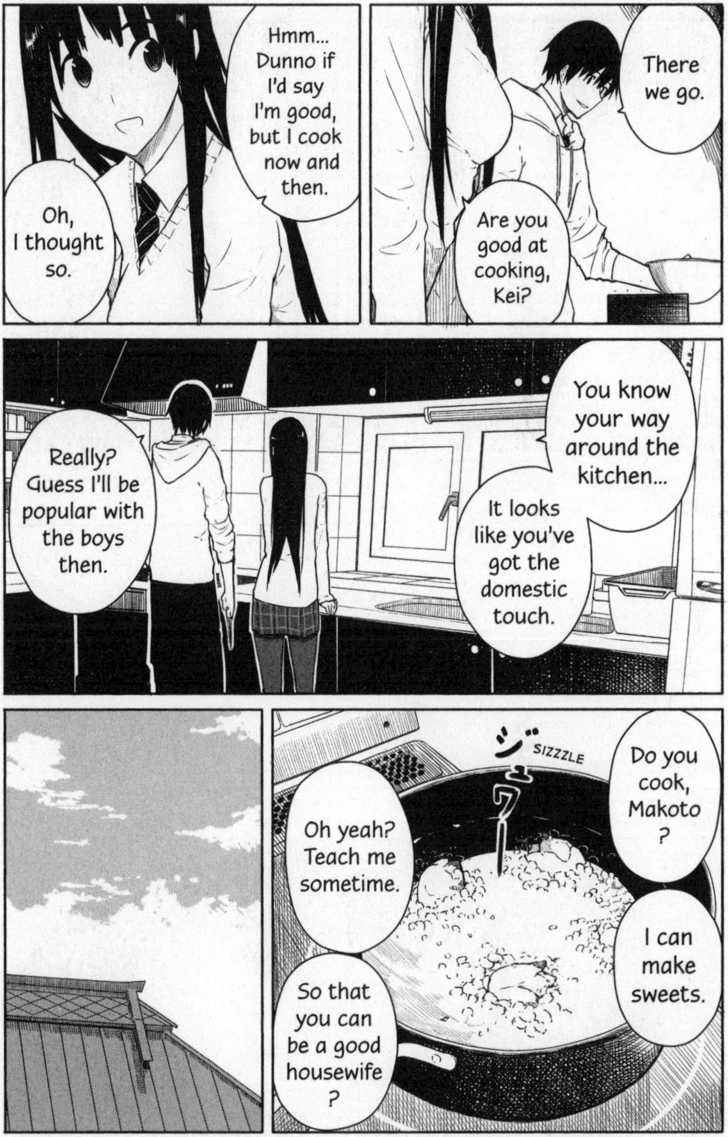
There we go.
Are you good at cooking, Kei?
Hmm... Dunno if I'd say I'm good, but I cook now and then.
Oh, I thought so.
You know your way around the kitchen...
It looks like you've got the domestic touch.
Really? Guess I'll be popular with the boys then.
ジュワ
SIZZZLE
Do you cook, Makoto?
I can make sweets.
Oh yeah? Teach me sometime.
So that you can be a good housewife?

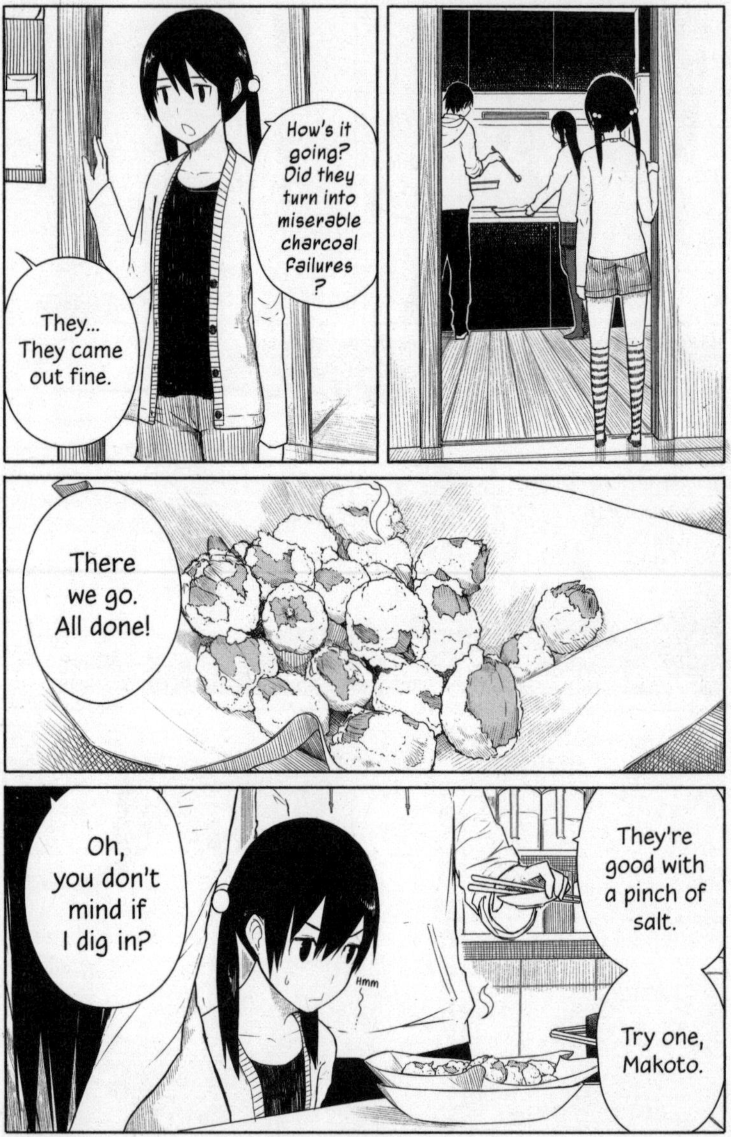
How's it going? Did they turn into miserable charcoal failures?
They... They came out fine.
There we go. All done!
They're good with a pinch of salt.
Try one, Makoto.
Hmm
Oh, you don't mind if I dig in?

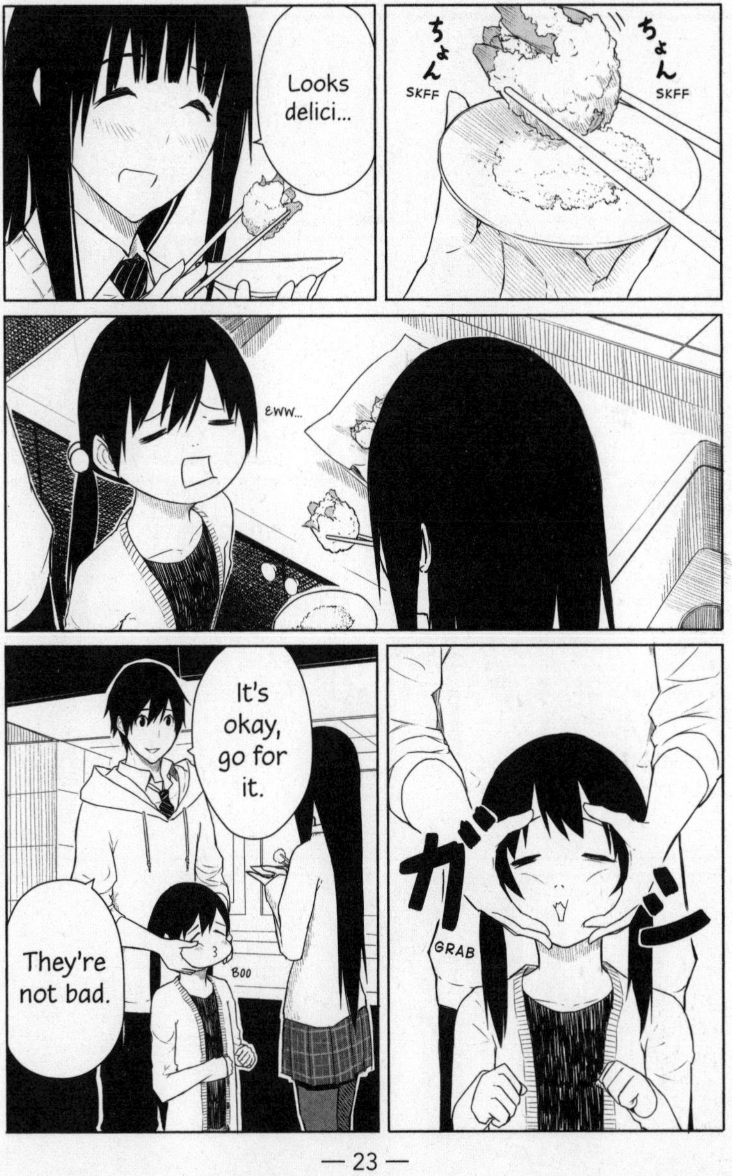
ちょん
SKFF
ちょん
SKFF
Looks delici...
EWW...
ガシ
GRAB
It's okay, go for it.
BOO
They're not bad.

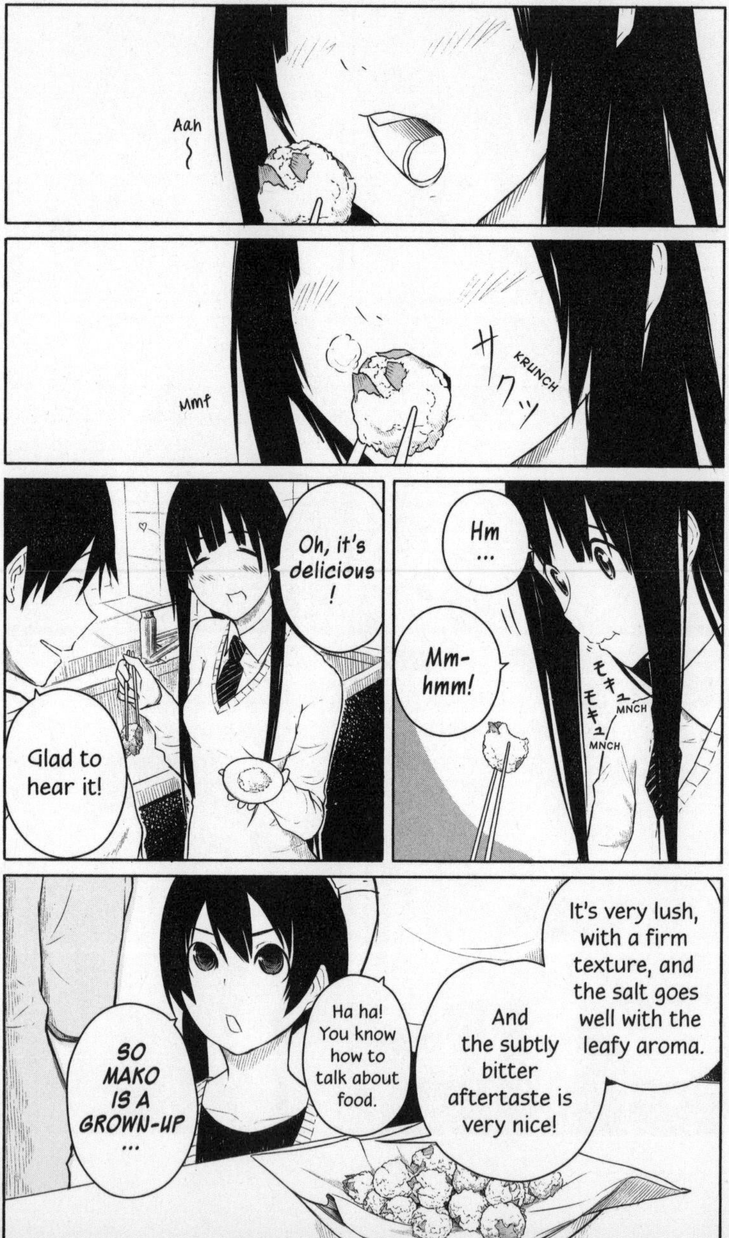
Aah ~
サクッ
KRUNCH
Mmf
Hm ...
Mm-hmm!
モキュ
MNCH
モキュ
MNCH
Oh, it's delicious!
Glad to hear it!
It's very lush, with a firm texture, and the salt goes well with the leafy aroma.
And the subtly bitter aftertaste is very nice!
Ha ha! You know how to talk about food.
SO MAKO IS A GROWN-UP ...

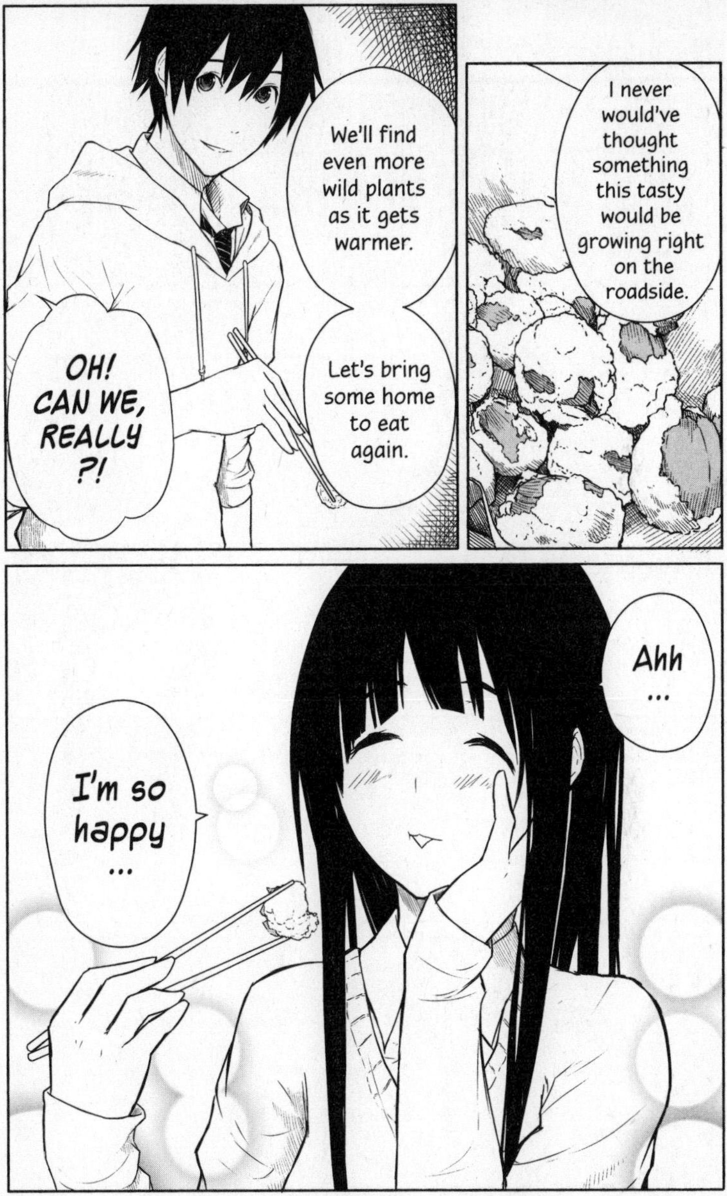
I never would've thought something this tasty would be growing right on the roadside.
We'll find even more wild plants as it gets warmer.
Let's bring some home to eat again.
OH! CAN WE, REALLY ?!
Ahh ...
I'm so happy ...

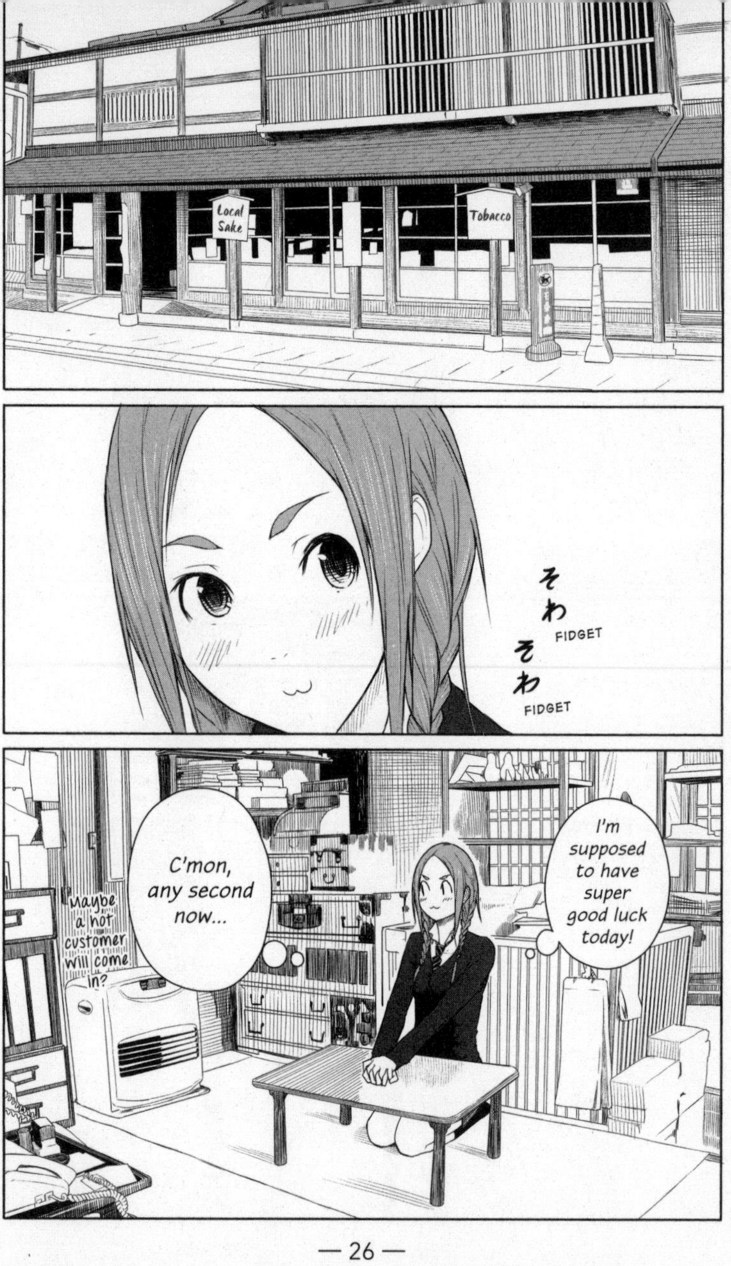
Tobacco
Local Sake
そわ
FIDGET
そわ
FIDGET
I'm supposed to have super good luck today!
C'mon, any second now...
Maybe a hot customer will come in?

Flying
Witch

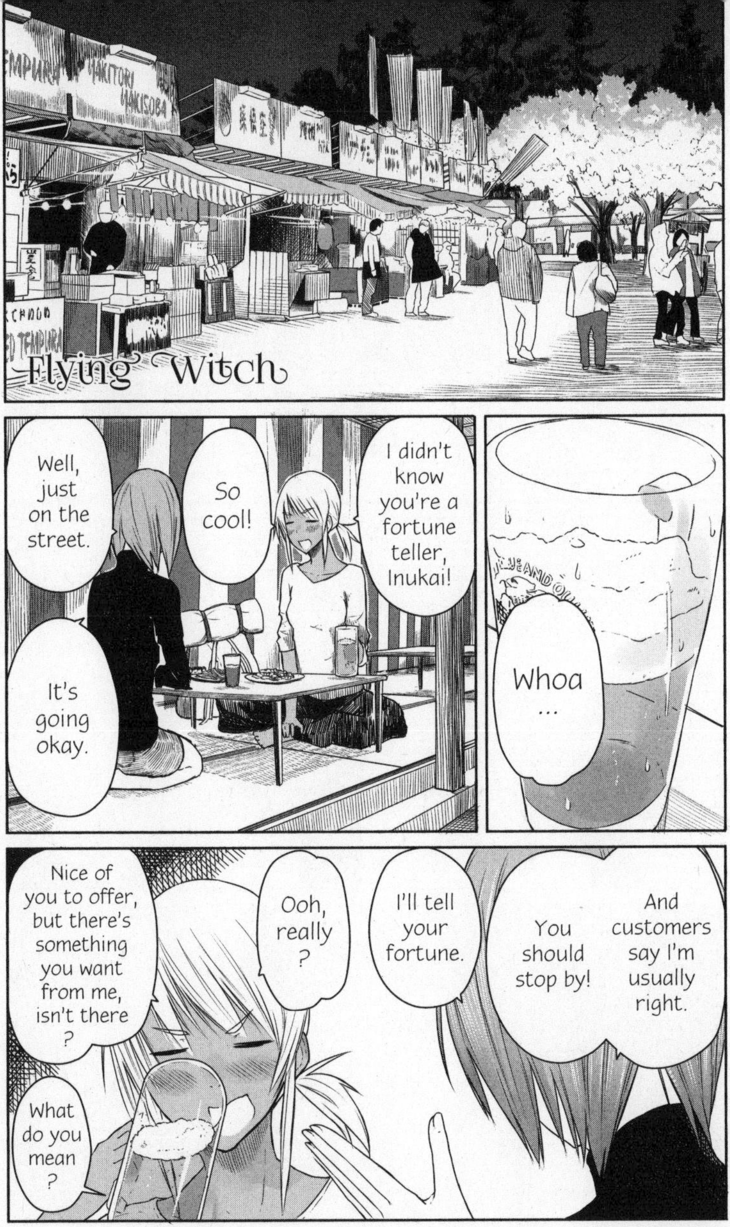
Flying Witch
Whoa ...
I didn't know you're a fortune teller, Inukai!
So cool!
Well, just on the street.
It's going okay.
And customers say I'm usually right.
You should stop by!
I'll tell your fortune.
Ooh, really?
Nice of you to offer, but there's something you want from me, isn't there?
What do you mean?

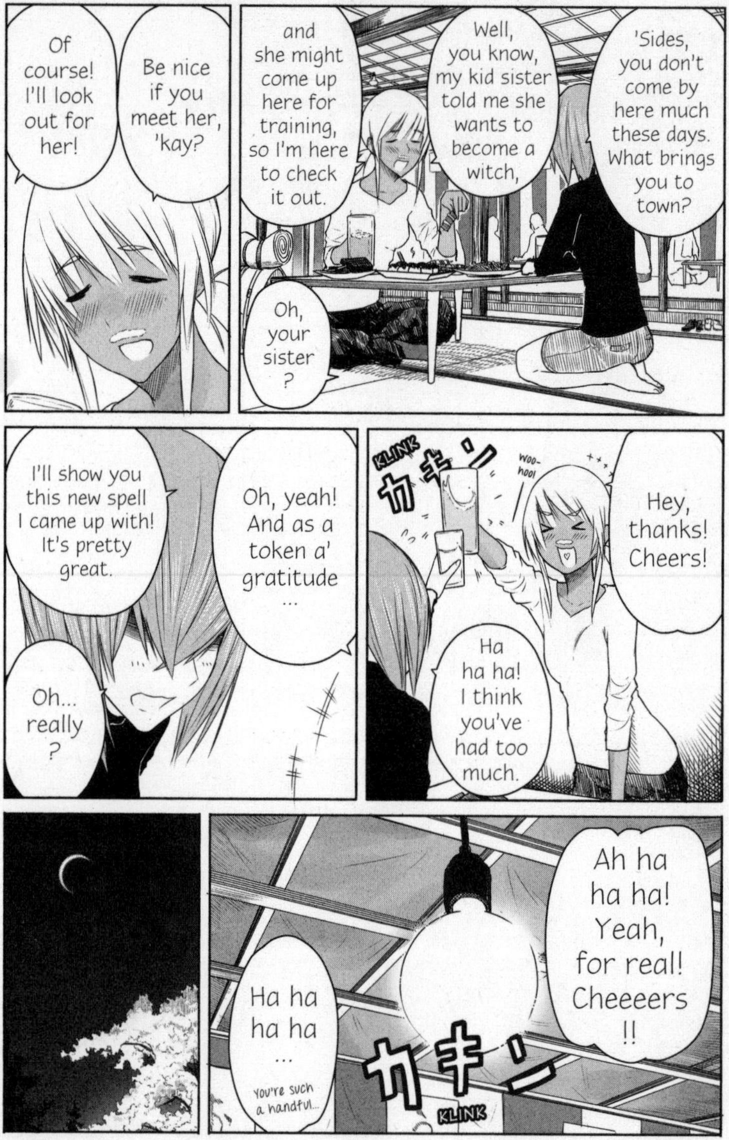
'Sides, you don't come by here much these days. What brings you to town?
Well, you know, my kid sister told me she wants to become a witch,
and she might come up here for training, so I'm here to check it out.
Oh, your sister ?
Be nice if you meet her, 'kay?
Of course! I'll look out for her!
Hey, thanks! Cheers!
Woo-hoo!
カキン
KLINK
Ha ha ha! I think you've had too much.
Oh, yeah! And as a token a' gratitude ...
I'll show you this new spell I came up with! It's pretty great.
Oh... really ?
Ah ha ha ha! Yeah, for real! Cheeeers !!
Ha ha ha ha ...
You're such a handful...
カキン
KLINK

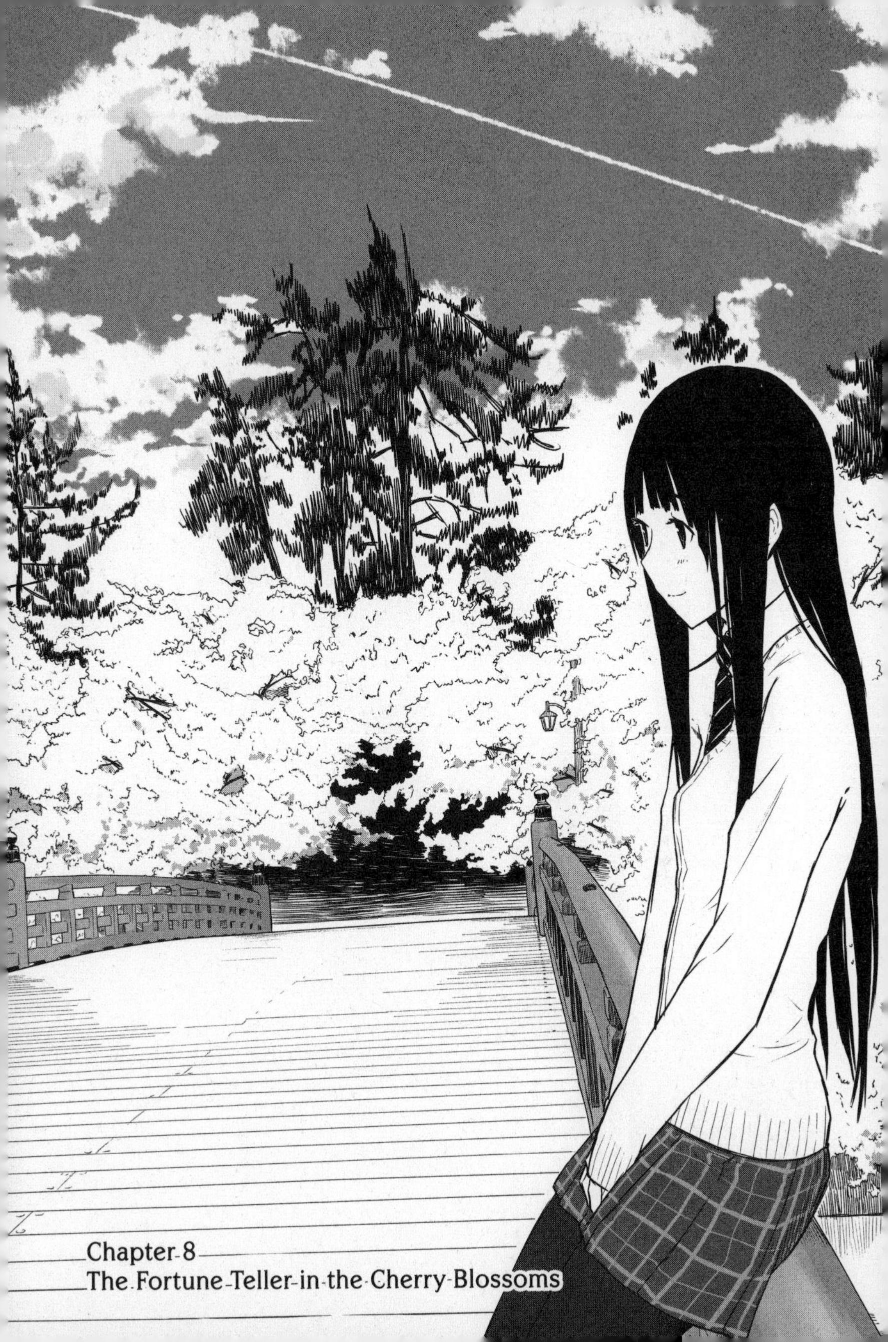

Chapter 8
The Fortune Teller in the Cherry Blossoms

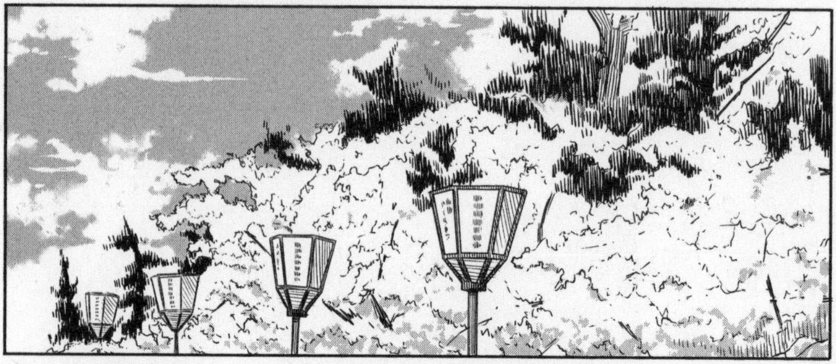

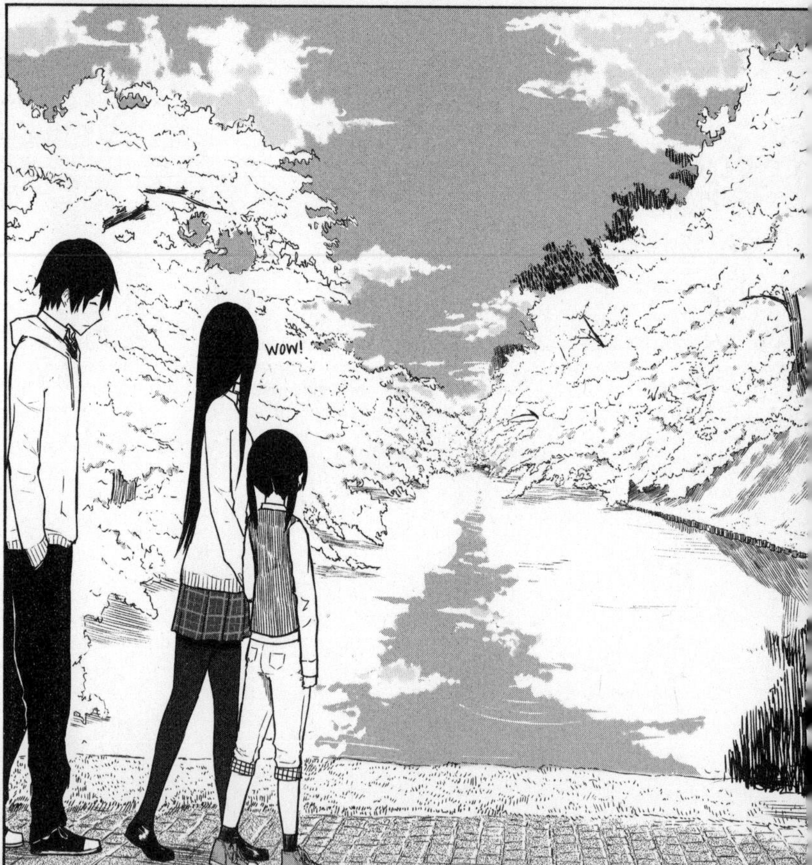
WOW!

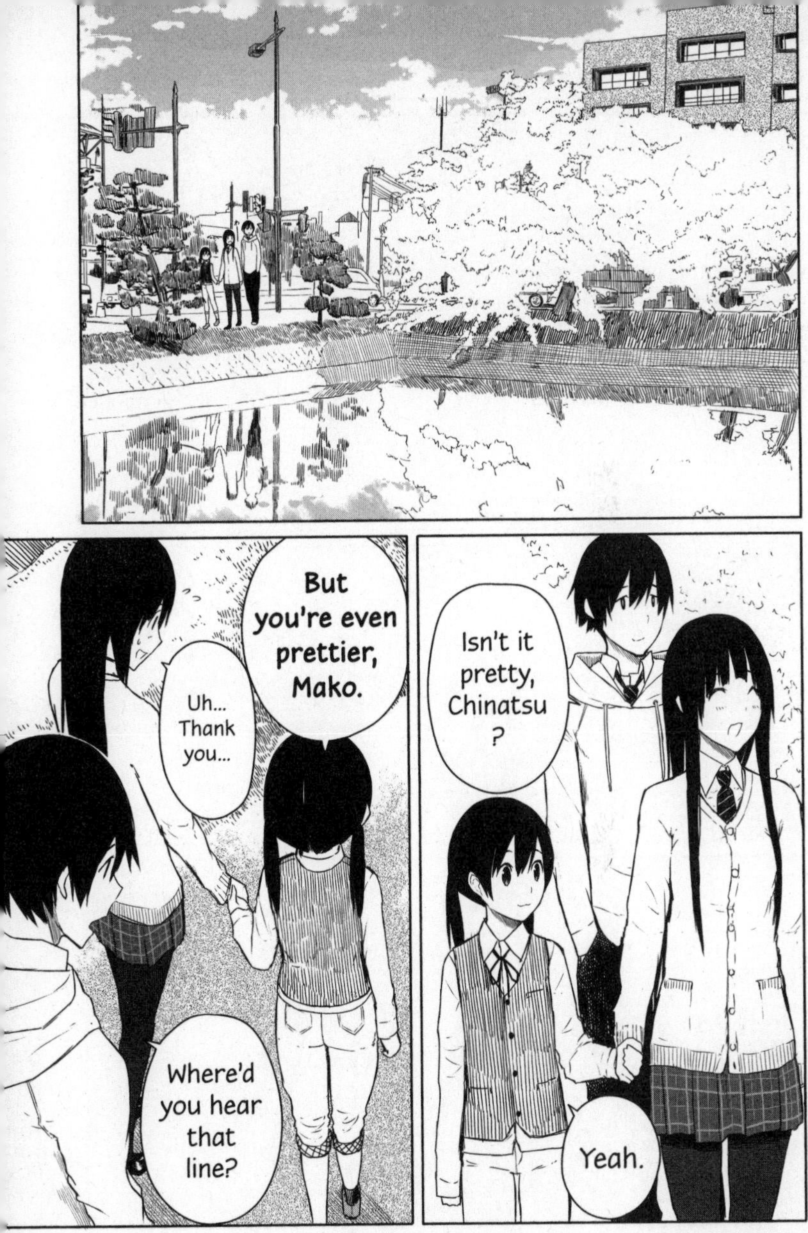
Isn't it pretty, Chinatsu?
Yeah.
But you're even prettier, Mako.
Uh... Thank you...
Where'd you hear that line?

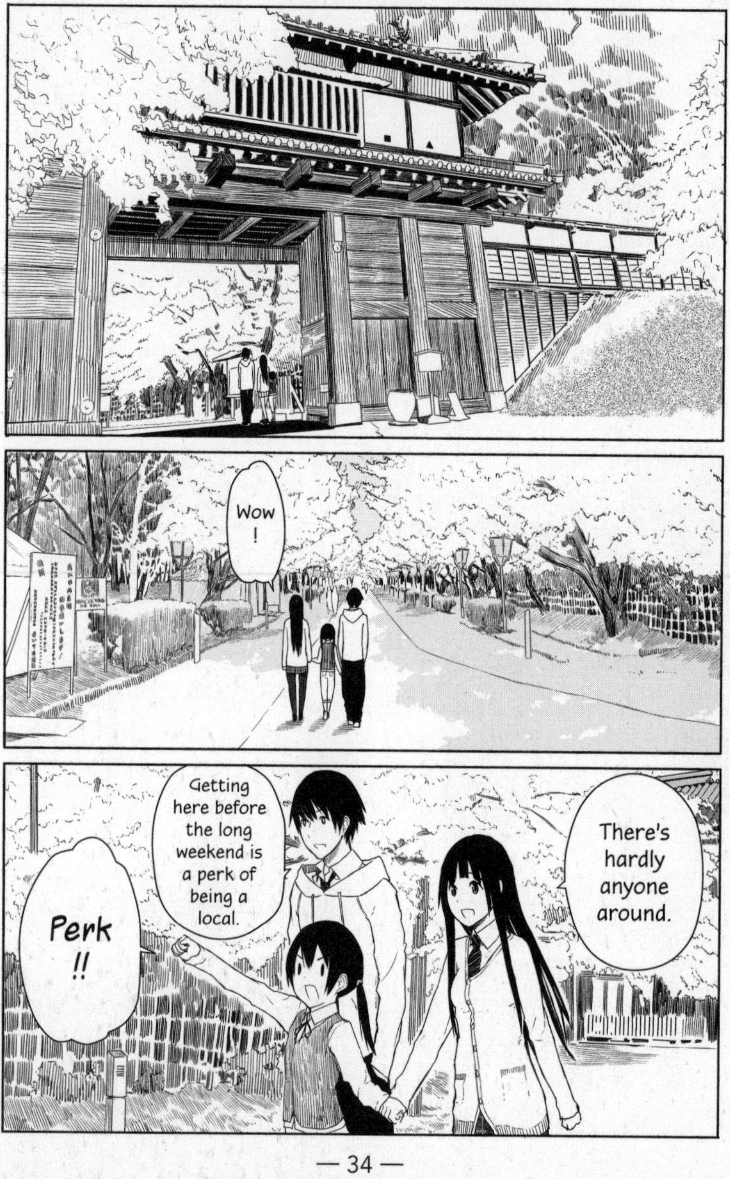
Wow!
There's hardly anyone around.
Getting here before the long weekend is a perk of being a local.
Perk!!

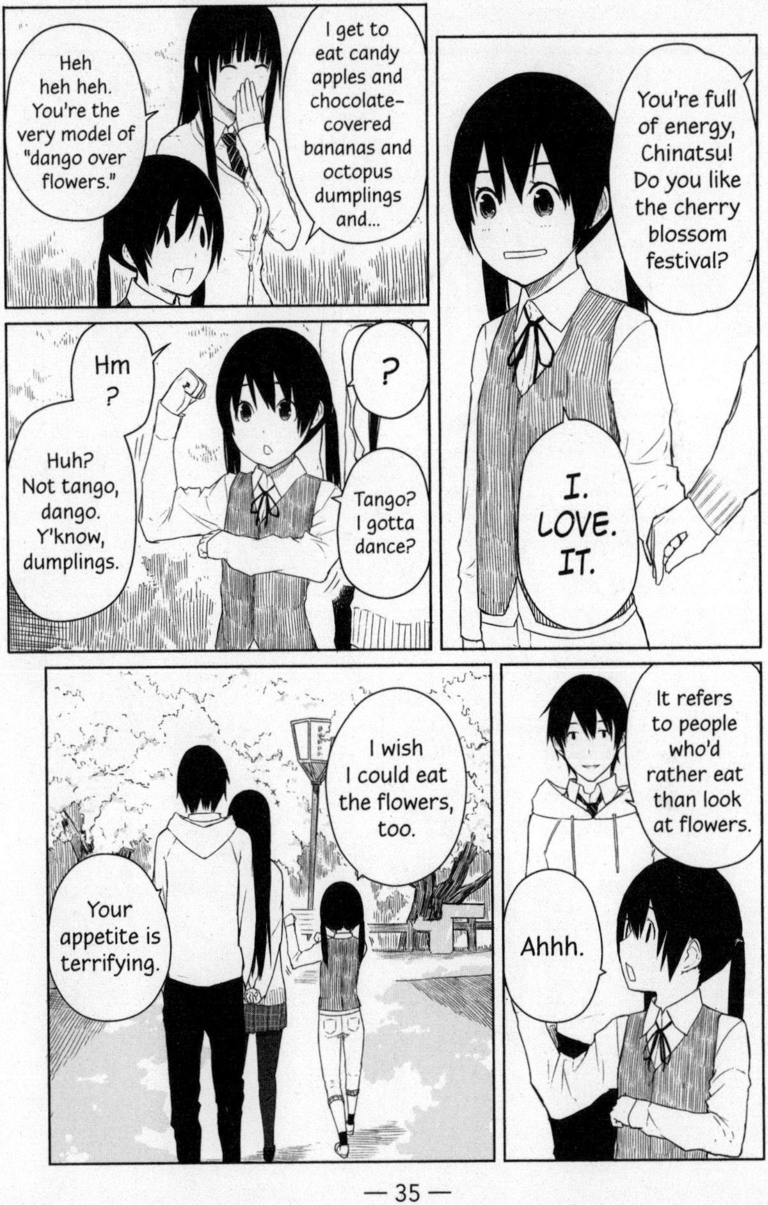
You're full of energy, Chinatsu! Do you like the cherry blossom festival?
I. LOVE. IT.
I get to eat candy apples and chocolate-covered bananas and octopus dumplings and...
Heh heh heh. You're the very model of "dango over flowers."
?
Hm ?
Tango? I gotta dance?
Huh? Not tango, dango. Y'know, dumplings.
It refers to people who'd rather eat than look at flowers.
Ahhh.
I wish I could eat the flowers, too.
Your appetite is terrifying.

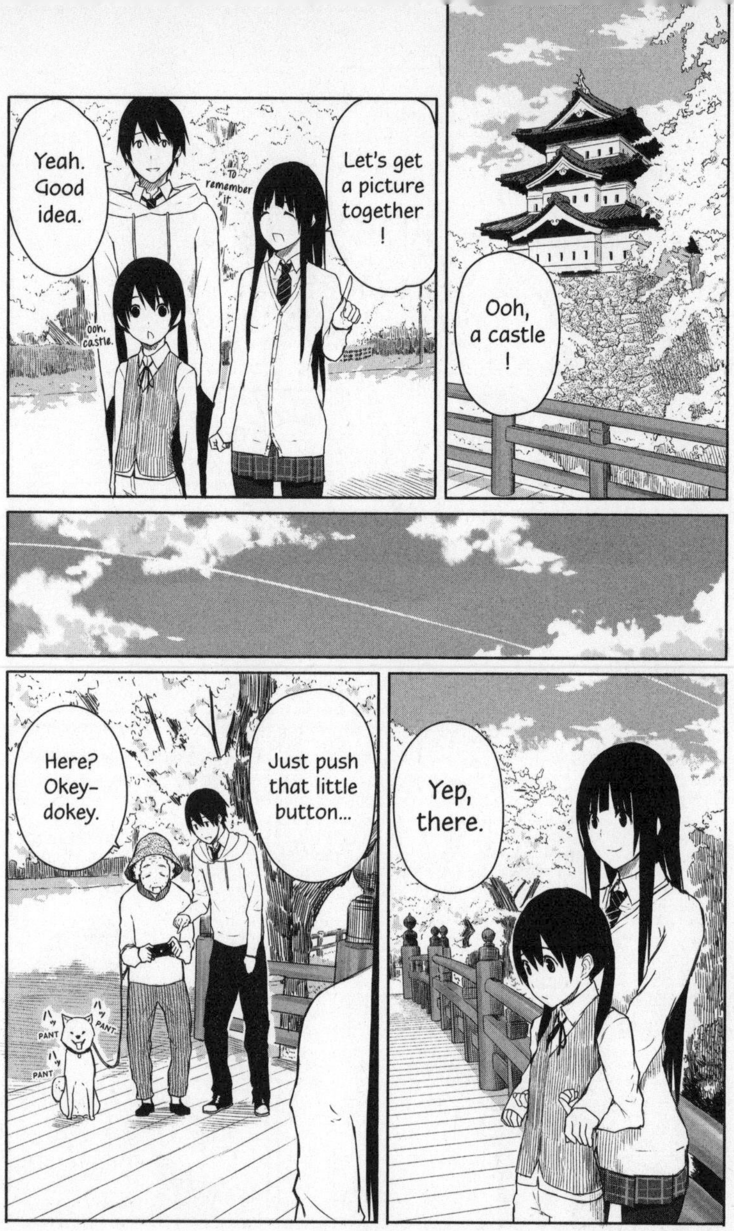
Ooh, a castle!
Let's get a picture together!
To remember it.
Yeah. Good idea.
Ooh, castle.
Yep, there.
Just push that little button...
Here? Okey-dokey.
ハッ PANT
ハッ PANT
ハッ PANT

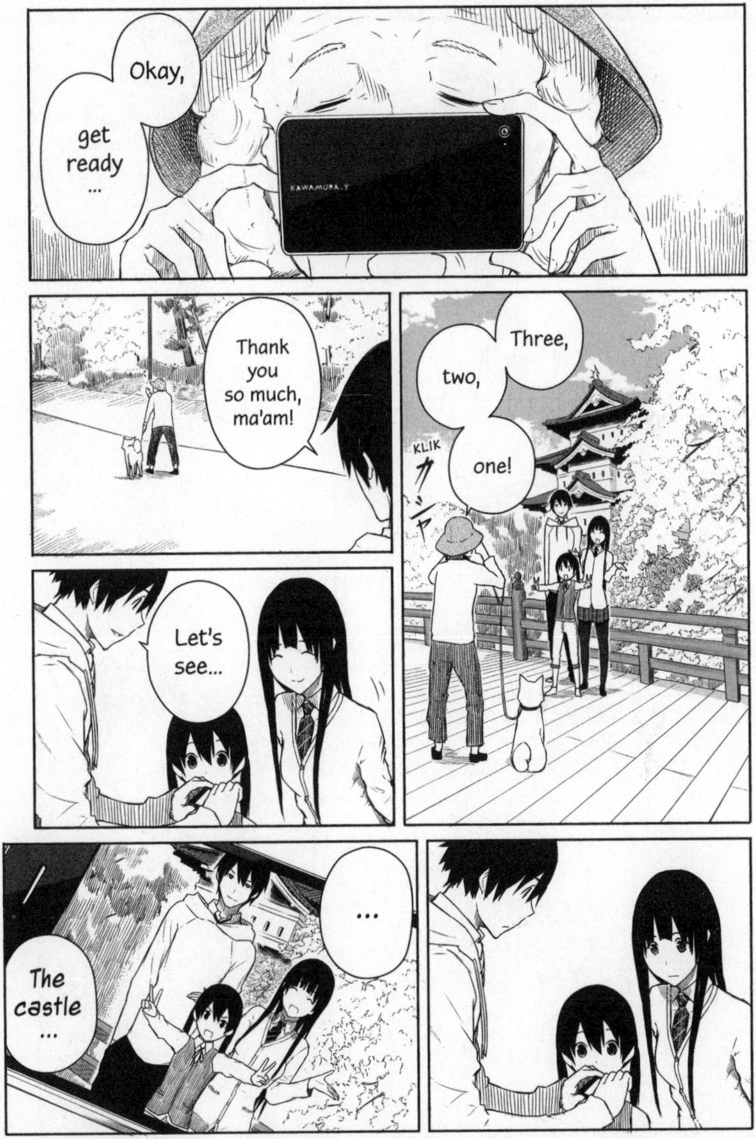
Okay,
get ready ...
Three,
two,
one!
KLIK
カシャ
Thank you so much, ma'am!
Let's see...
...
The castle ...

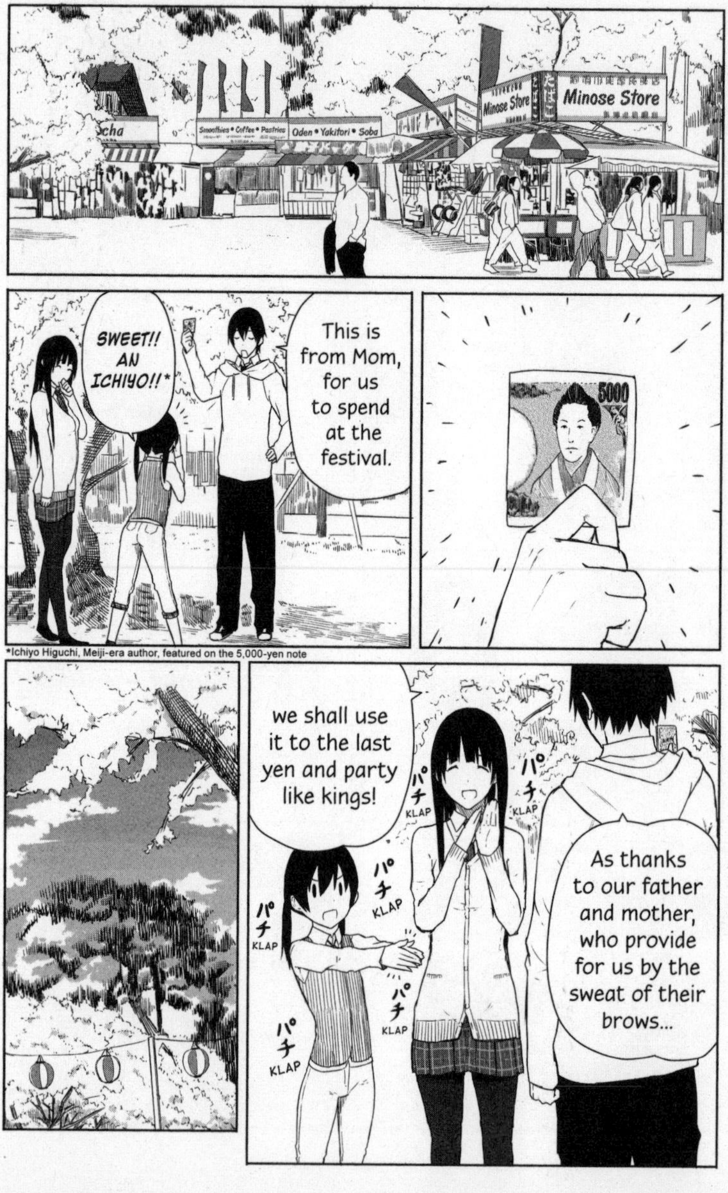
Minose Store
Minose Store
Smoothies • Coffee • Pastries
Oden • Yakitori • Soba
cha
5000
This is from Mom, for us to spend at the festival.
SWEET!! AN ICHIYO!!*
As thanks to our father and mother, who provide for us by the sweat of their brows...
we shall use it to the last yen and party like kings!
パチ KLAP
パチ KLAP
パチ KLAP
パチ KLAP
パチ KLAP
パチ KLAP

*Ichiyo Higuchi, Meiji-era author, featured on the 5,000-yen note

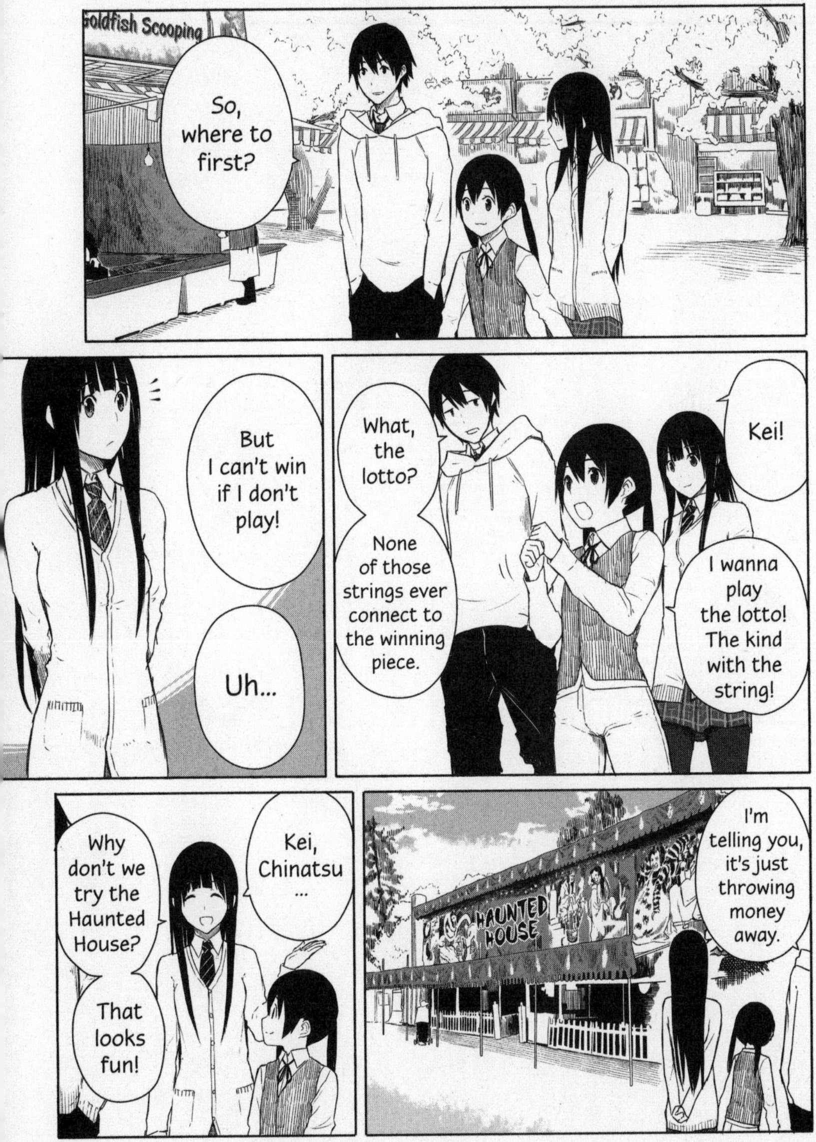
Goldfish Scooping
So, where to first?
Kei!
I wanna play the lotto! The kind with the string!
What, the lotto?
None of those strings ever connect to the winning piece.
But I can't win if I don't play!
Uh...
I'm telling you, it's just throwing money away.
HAUNTED HOUSE
Kei, Chinatsu ...
Why don't we try the Haunted House?
That looks fun!

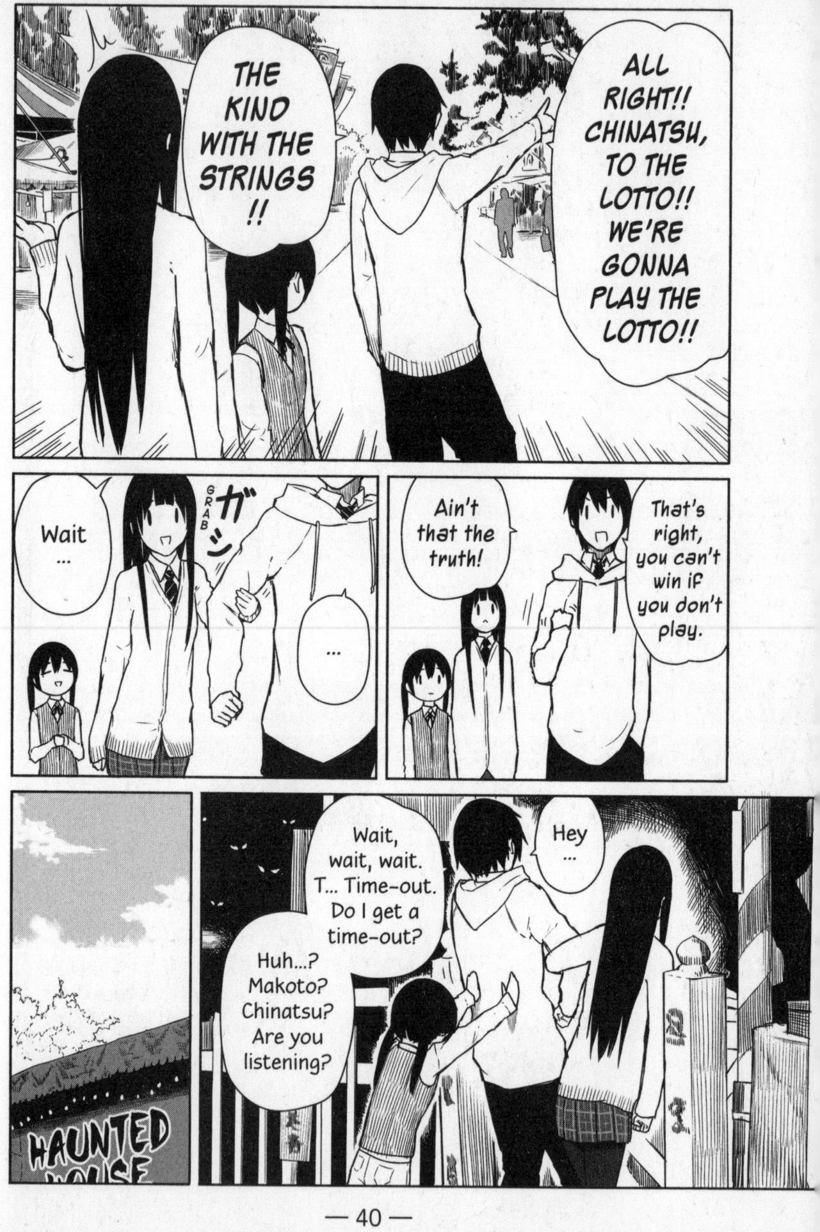
ALL RIGHT!! CHINATSU, TO THE LOTTO!! WE'RE GONNA PLAY THE LOTTO!!
THE KIND WITH THE STRINGS !!
That's right, you can't win if you don't play.
Ain't that the truth!
GRAB
ガシ
Wait ...
...
Hey ...
Wait, wait, wait. T... Time-out. Do I get a time-out?
Huh...? Makoto? Chinatsu? Are you listening?
HAUNTED

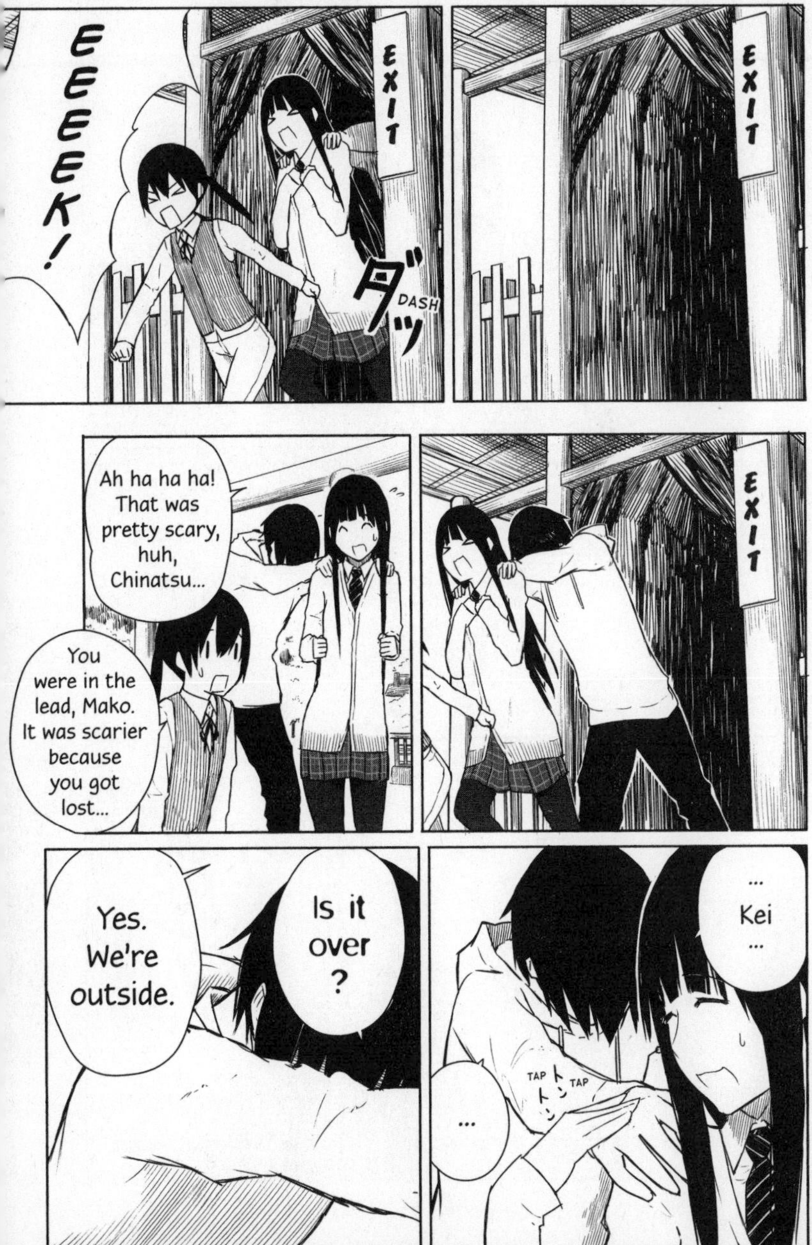
EXIT
EXIT
EEEEEK!
ダッ DASH
EXIT
Ah ha ha ha! That was pretty scary, huh, Chinatsu...
You were in the lead, Mako. It was scarier because you got lost...
... Kei ...
トン トン TAP TAP
...
Is it over?
Yes. We're outside.

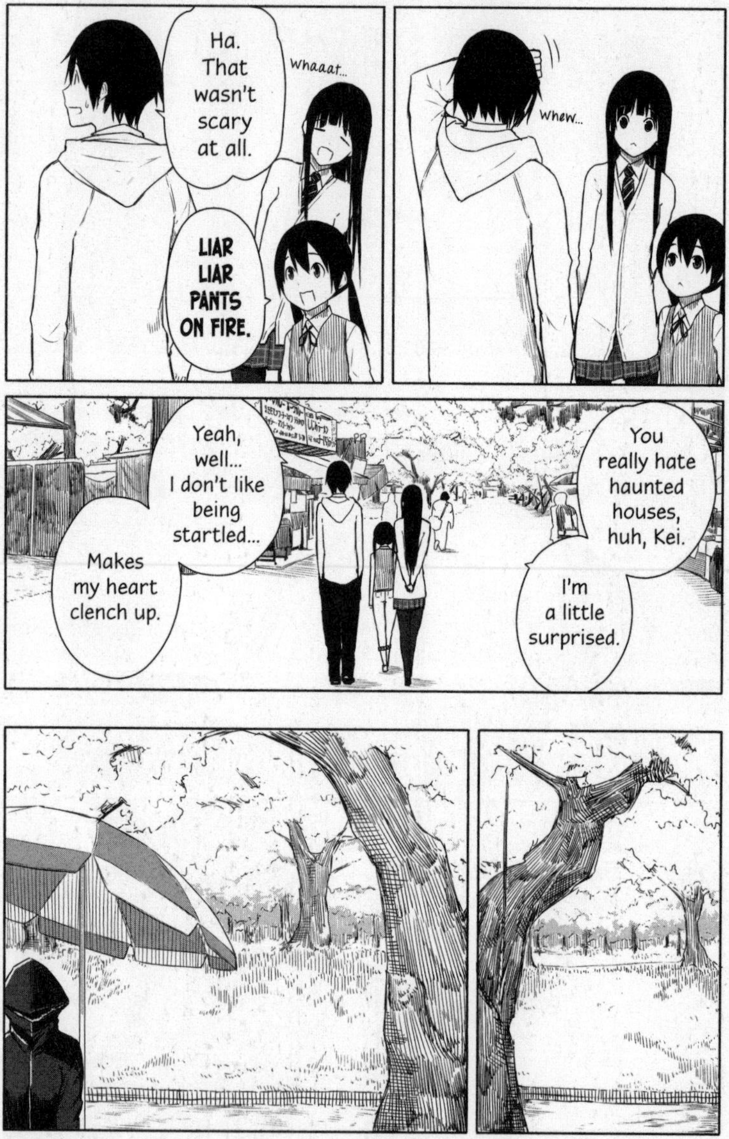
Whew...
Ha. That wasn't scary at all.
Whaaat...
LIAR LIAR PANTS ON FIRE.
You really hate haunted houses, huh, Kei.
I'm a little surprised.
Yeah, well... I don't like being startled...
Makes my heart clench up.

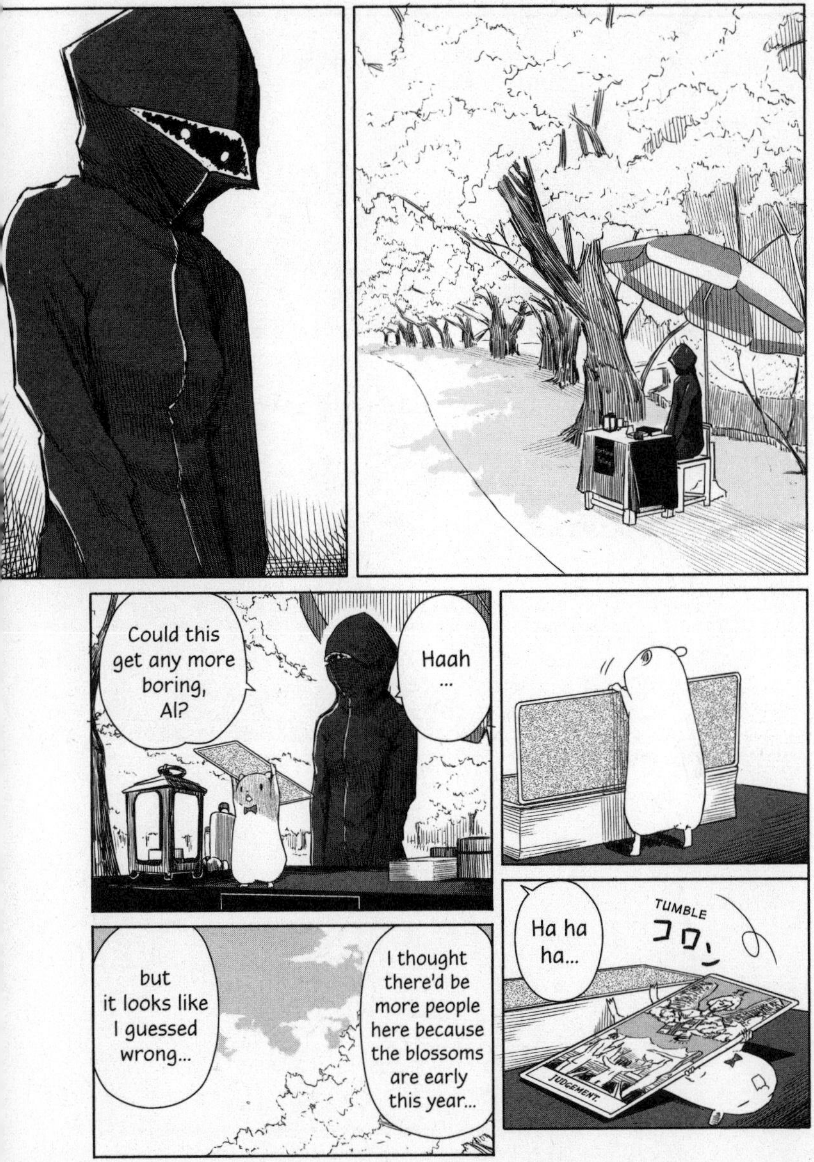
Haah ...
Could this get any more boring, Al?
TUMBLE
コロン
Ha ha ha...
I thought there'd be more people here because the blossoms are early this year...
but it looks like I guessed wrong...
JUDGEMENT.

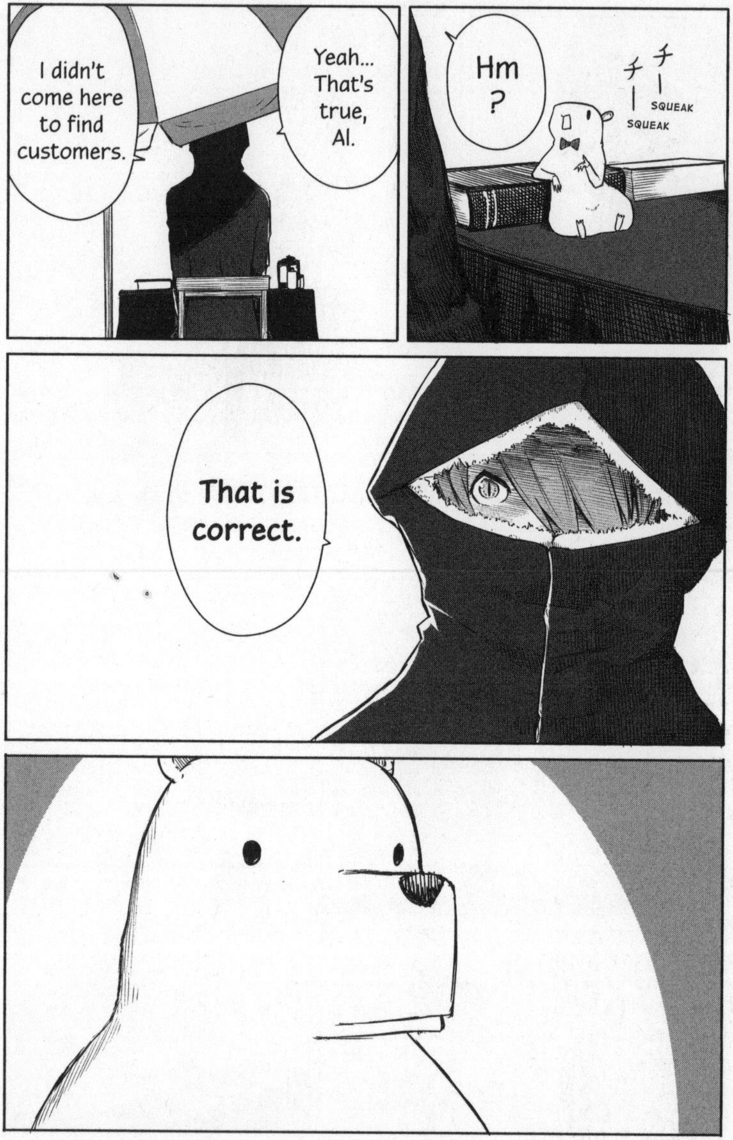
Hm?
チー
SQUEAK
チー
SQUEAK
Yeah... That's true, Al.
I didn't come here to find customers.
That is correct.

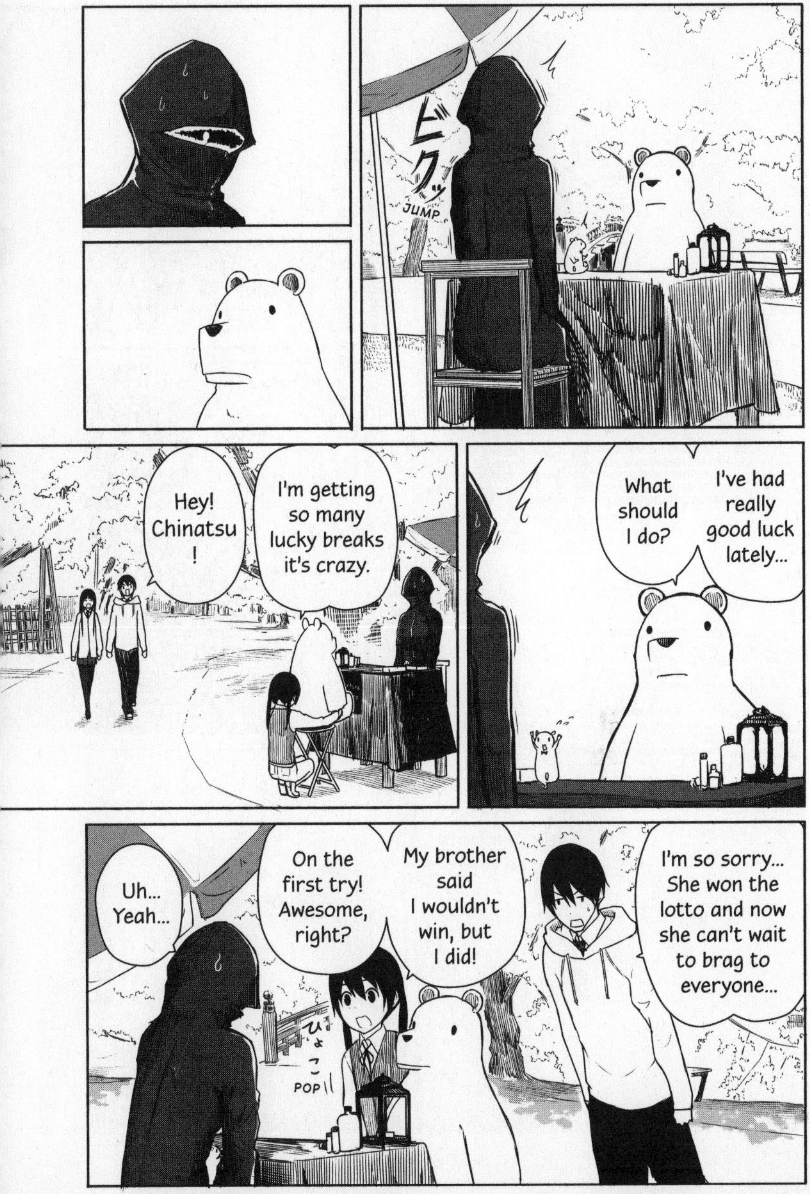
ビクッ
JUMP
I've had really good luck lately...
What should I do?
I'm getting so many lucky breaks it's crazy.
Hey! Chinatsu!
I'm so sorry... She won the lotto and now she can't wait to brag to everyone...
My brother said I wouldn't win, but I did!
On the first try! Awesome, right?
ひょこ
POP
Uh... Yeah...

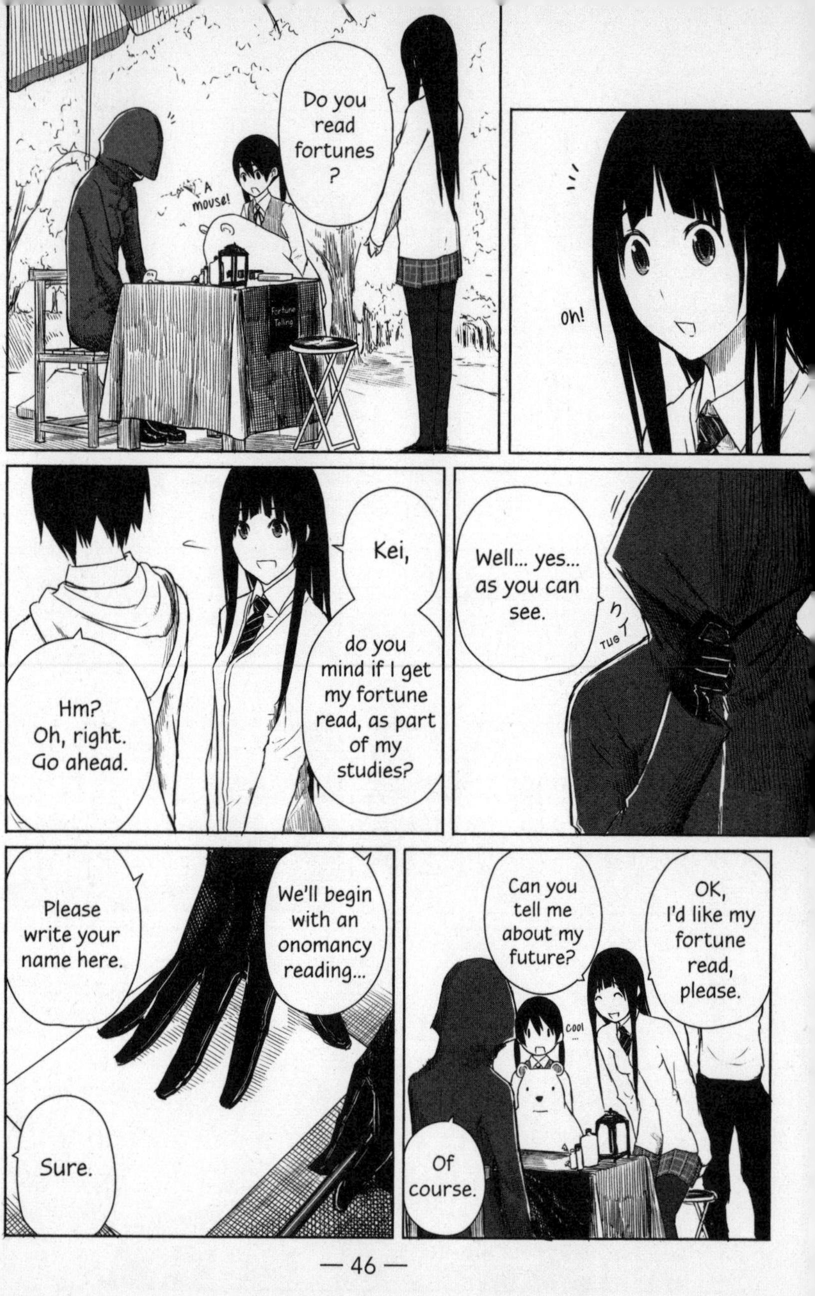
Oh!
Do you read fortunes?
A mouse!
Fortune Telling
Well... yes... as you can see.
TUG
Kei,
do you mind if I get my fortune read, as part of my studies?
Hm? Oh, right. Go ahead.
OK, I'd like my fortune read, please.
Can you tell me about my future?
Cool...
Of course.
We'll begin with an onomancy reading...
Please write your name here.
Sure.

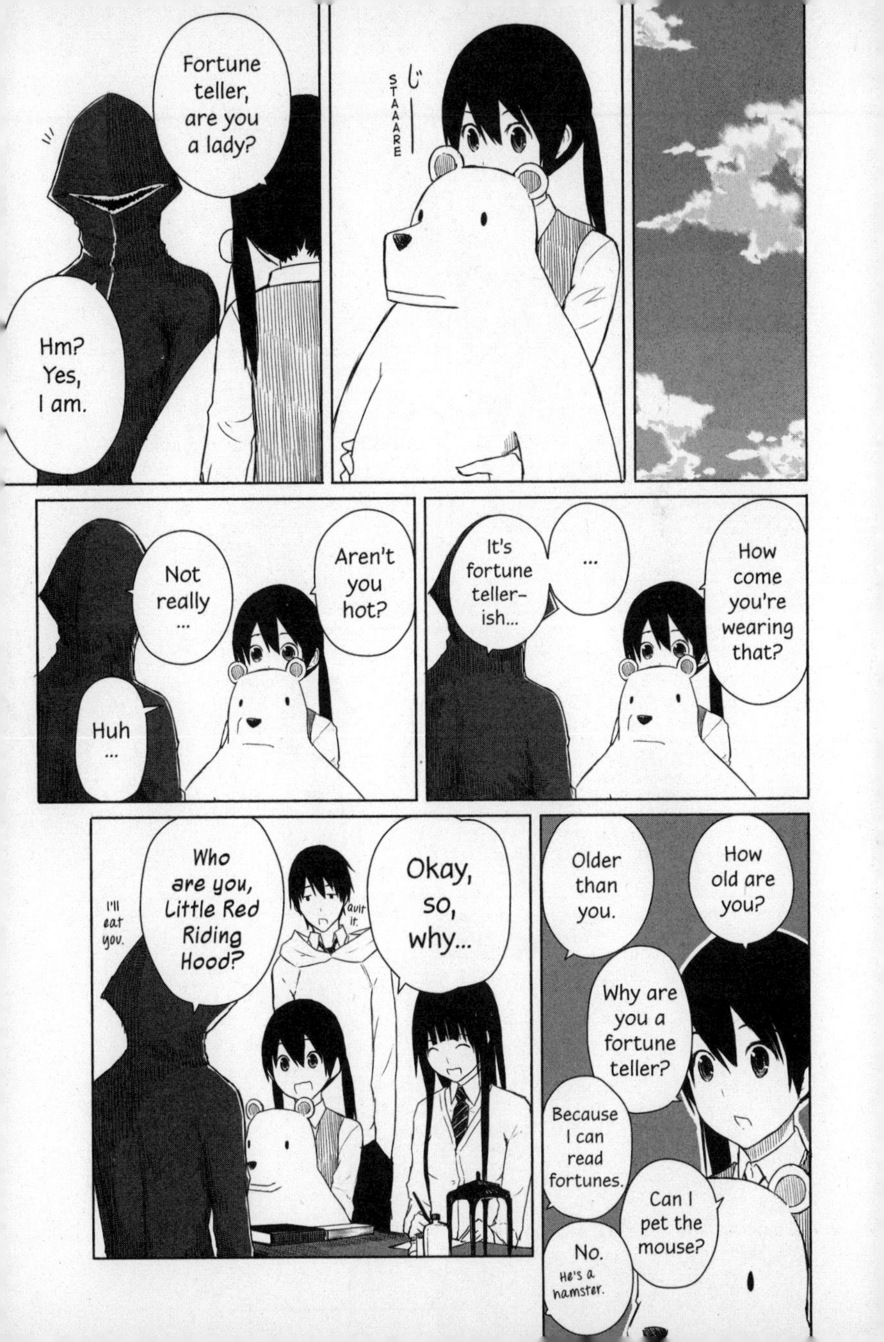

じ
STAAARE
Fortune teller, are you a lady?
Hm? Yes, I am.
How come you're wearing that?
...
It's fortune teller-ish...
Aren't you hot?
Not really ...
Huh ...
How old are you?
Older than you.
Why are you a fortune teller?
Because I can read fortunes.
Can I pet the mouse?
No.
He's a hamster.
Okay, so, why...
Quit it.
Who are you, Little Red Riding Hood?
I'll eat you.

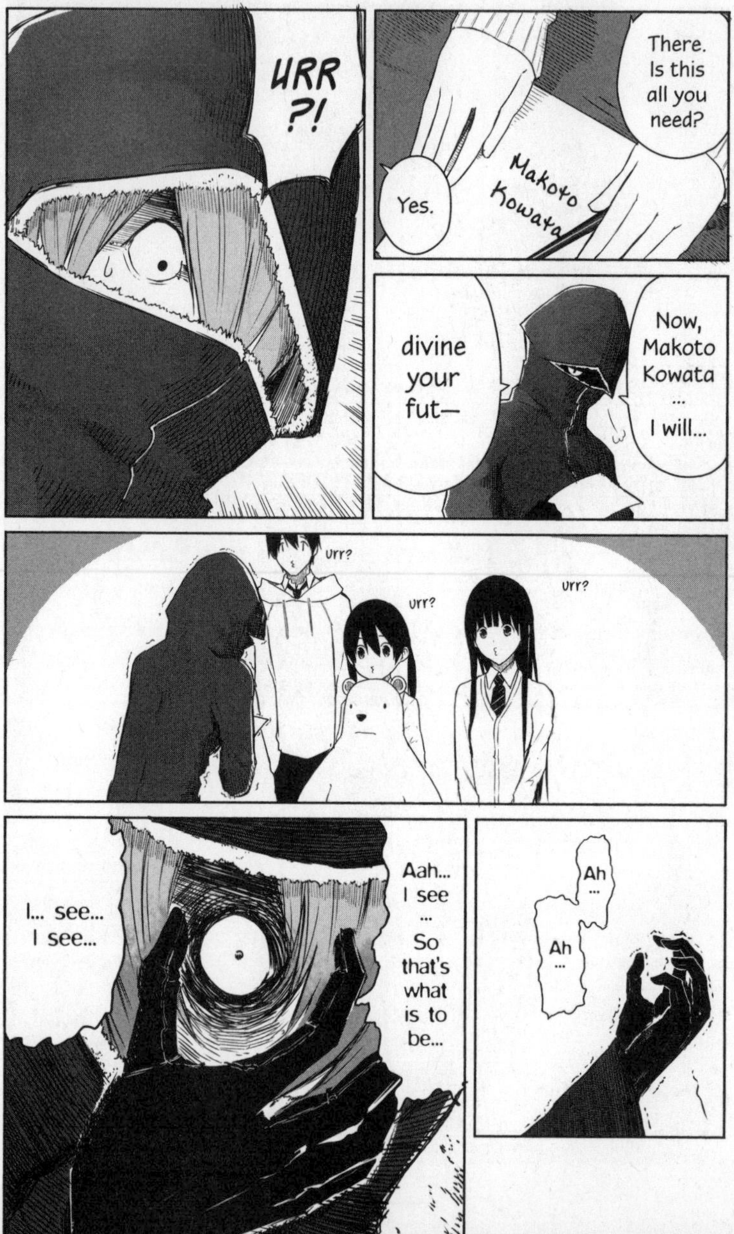
There. Is this all you need?
Makoto Kowata
Yes.
Now, Makoto Kowata ... I will...
divine your fut—
URR ?!
Urr?
Urr?
Urr?
Ah ...
Ah ...
Aah... I see ... So that's what is to be...
I... see... I see...

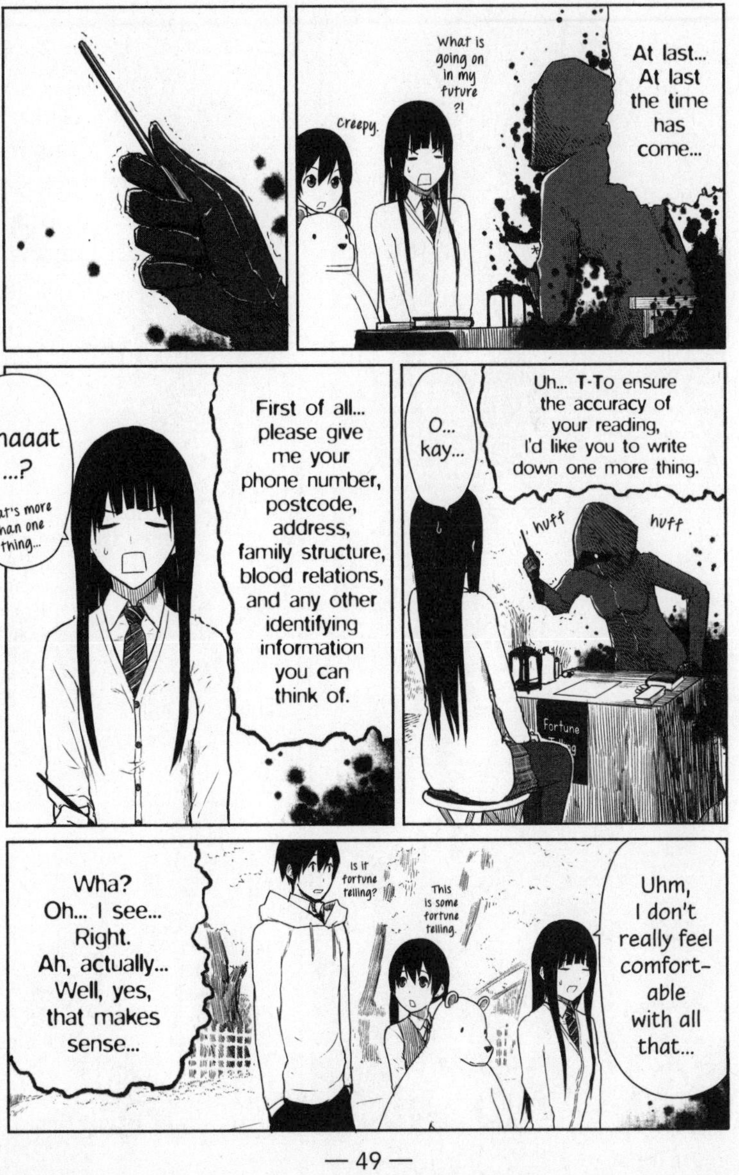
At last... At last the time has come...
What is going on in my future ?!
Creepy.
Uh... T-To ensure the accuracy of your reading, I'd like you to write down one more thing.
O... kay...
huff
huff
First of all... please give me your phone number, postcode, address, family structure, blood relations, and any other identifying information you can think of.
Whaaat ...?
That's more than one thing...
Uhm, I don't really feel comfort-able with all that...
This is some fortune telling.
Is it fortune telling?
Wha? Oh... I see... Right. Ah, actually... Well, yes, that makes sense...

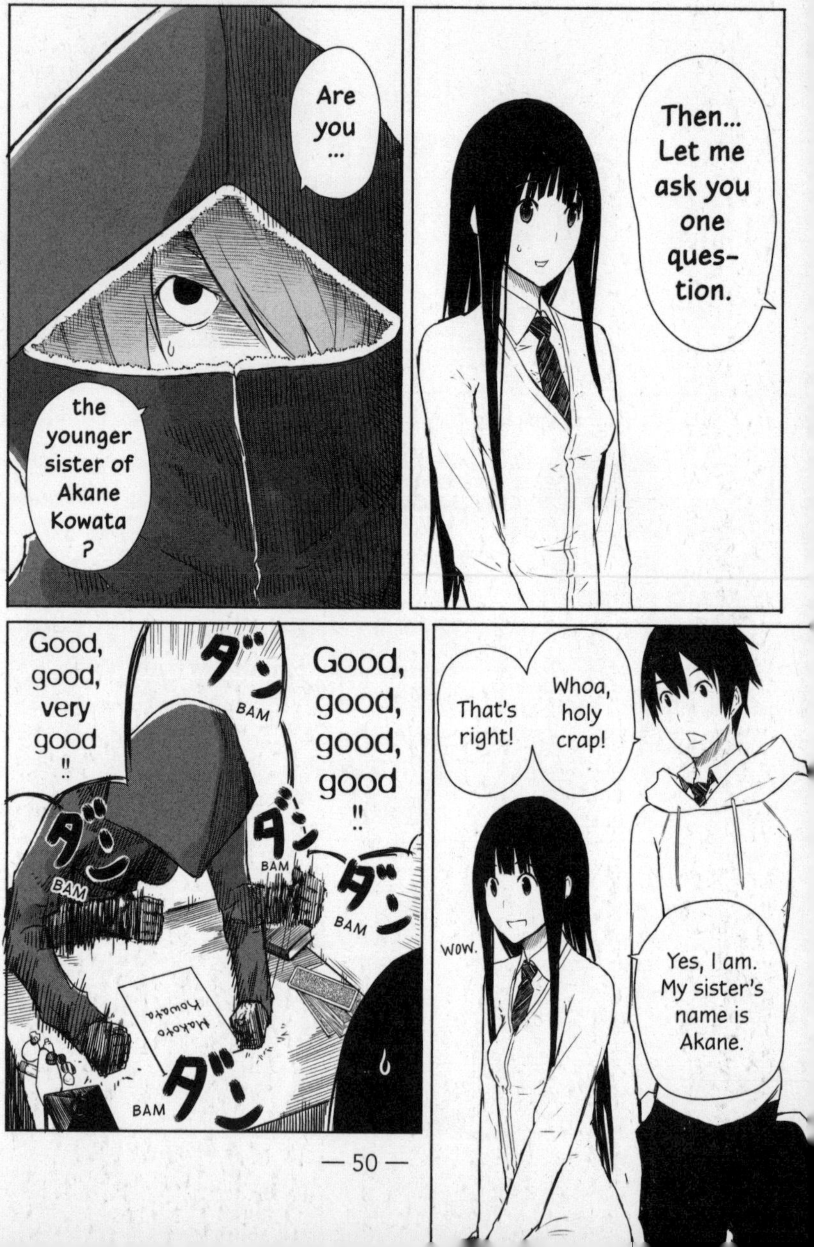
Then... Let me ask you one question.
Are you ...
the younger sister of Akane Kowata?
Yes, I am. My sister's name is Akane.
Whoa, holy crap!
That's right!
WOW.
ダン BAM
Good, good, good, good!!
Good, good, very good!!
ダン BAM
ダン BAM
ダン BAM
Makoto Kowata
ダン BAM

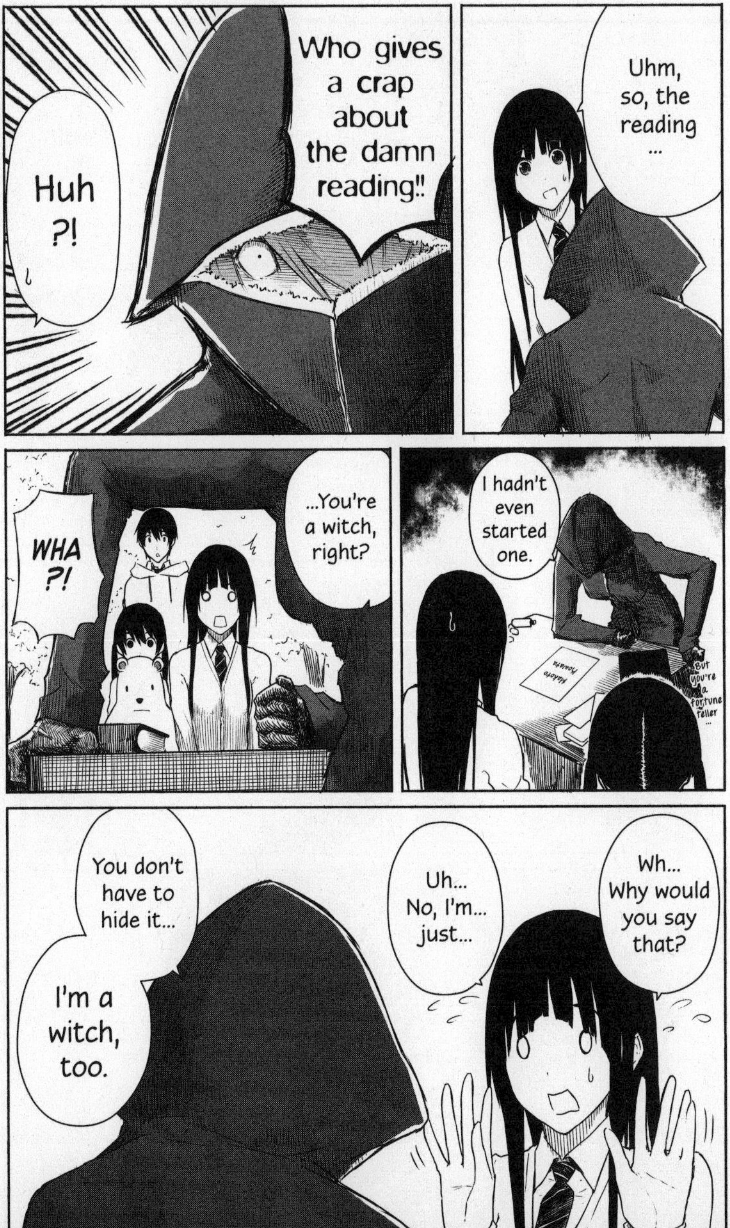
Uhm, so, the reading ...
Who gives a crap about the damn reading!!
Huh ?!
I hadn't even started one.
But you're a fortune teller ...
...You're a witch, right?
WHA ?!
Wh... Why would you say that?
Uh... No, I'm... just...
You don't have to hide it...
I'm a witch, too.

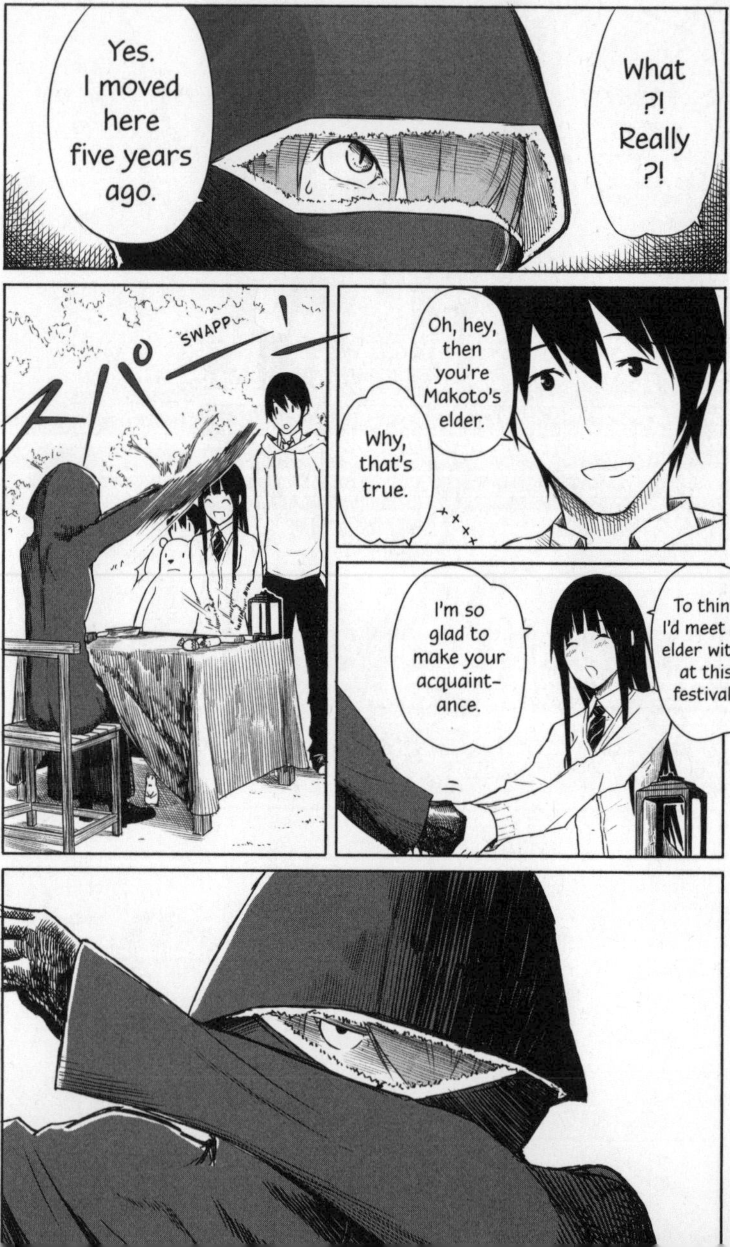
What ?! Really ?!
Yes. I moved here five years ago.
Oh, hey, then you're Makoto's elder.
Why, that's true.
To think I'd meet an elder witch at this festival...
I'm so glad to make your acquaintance.
SWAPP

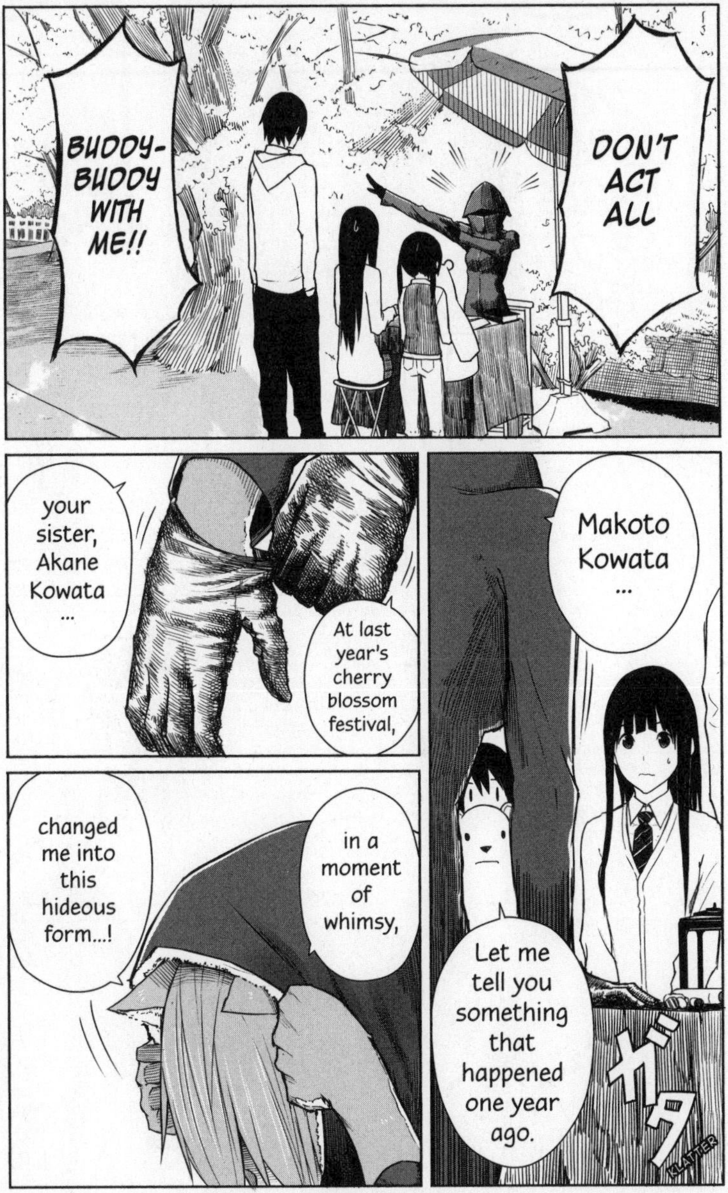
DON'T ACT ALL
BUDDY-BUDDY WITH ME!!
Makoto Kowata ...
Let me tell you something that happened one year ago.
ガタ
KLATTER
At last year's cherry blossom festival,
your sister, Akane Kowata ...
in a moment of whimsy,
changed me into this hideous form...!

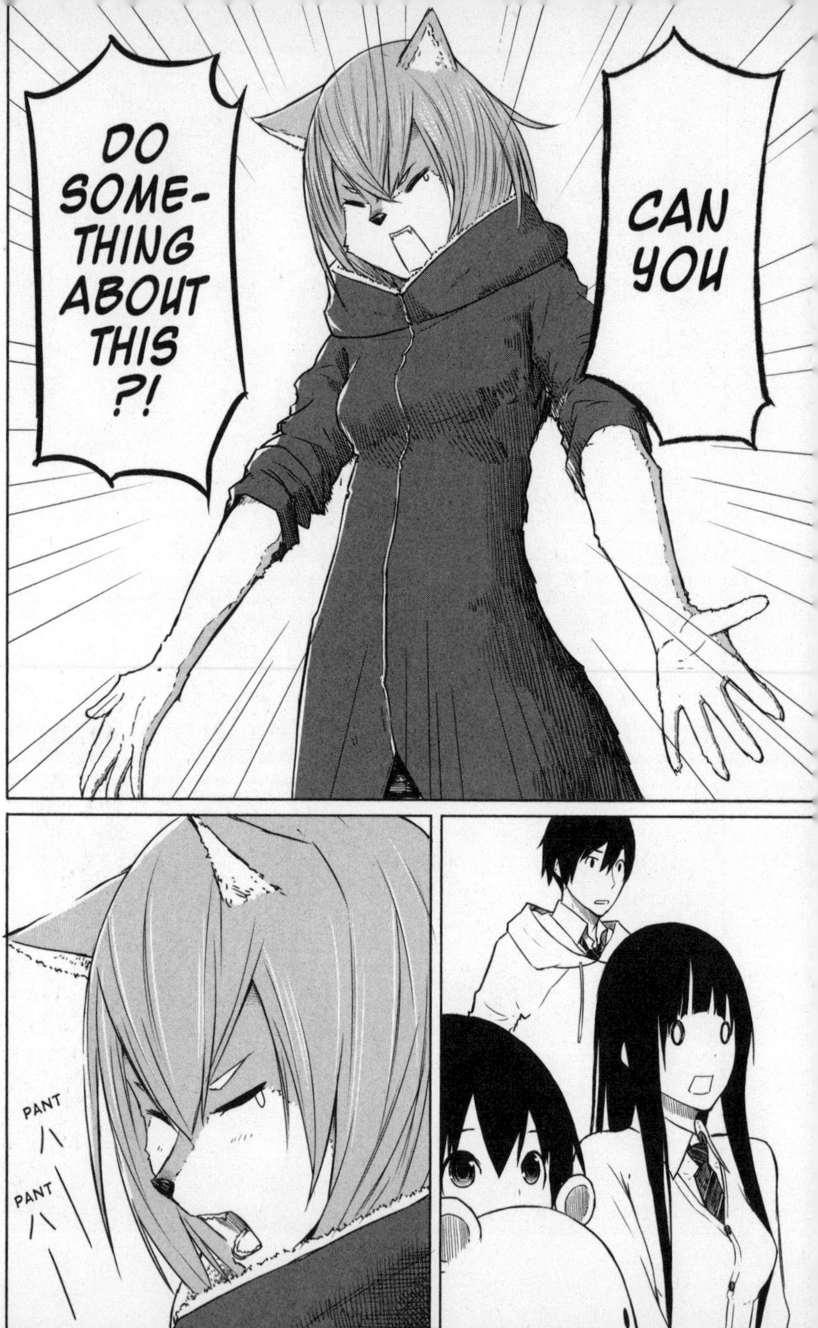
CAN YOU
DO SOMETHING ABOUT THIS?!
PANT
PANT

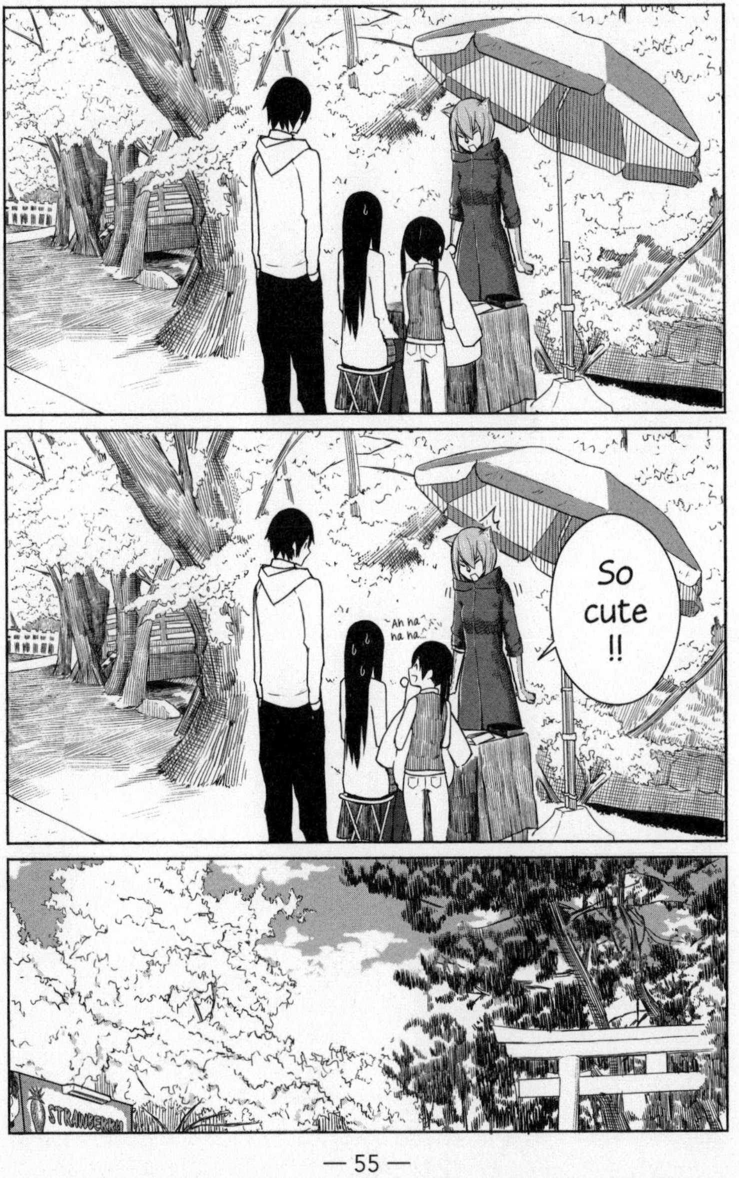
So cute !!
~Ah ha ha ha...

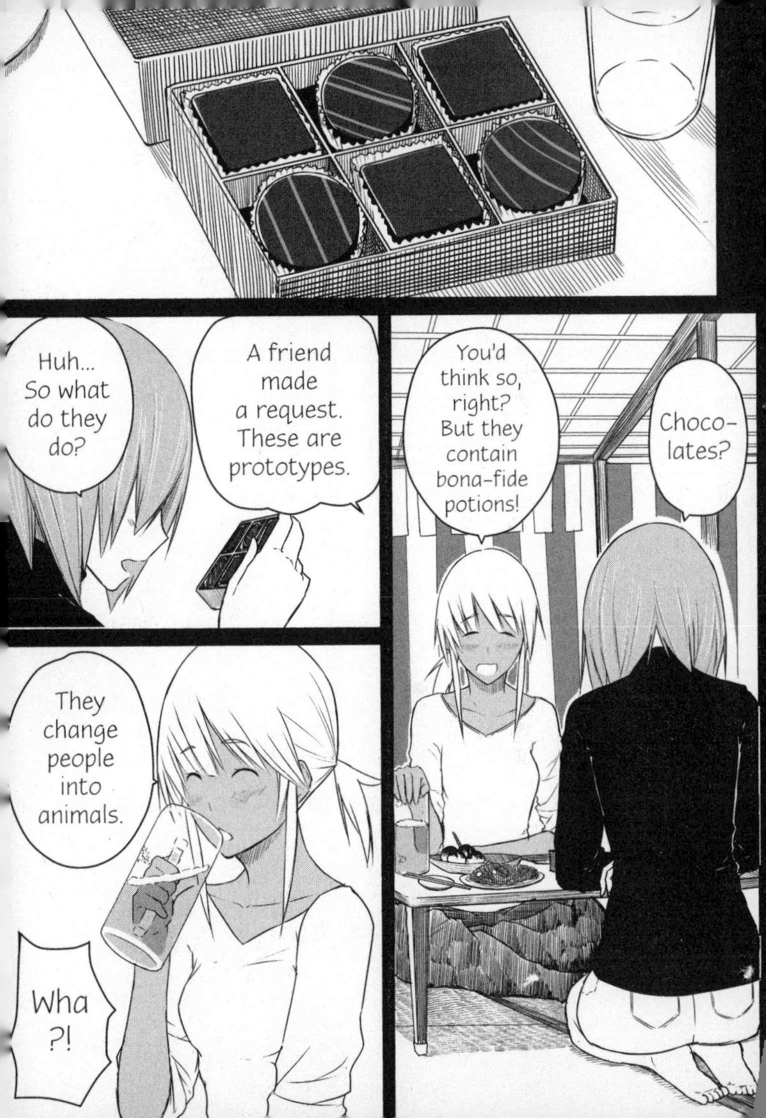
Chocolates?
You'd think so, right? But they contain bona-fide potions!
A friend made a request. These are prototypes.
Huh... So what do they do?
They change people into animals.
Wha?!

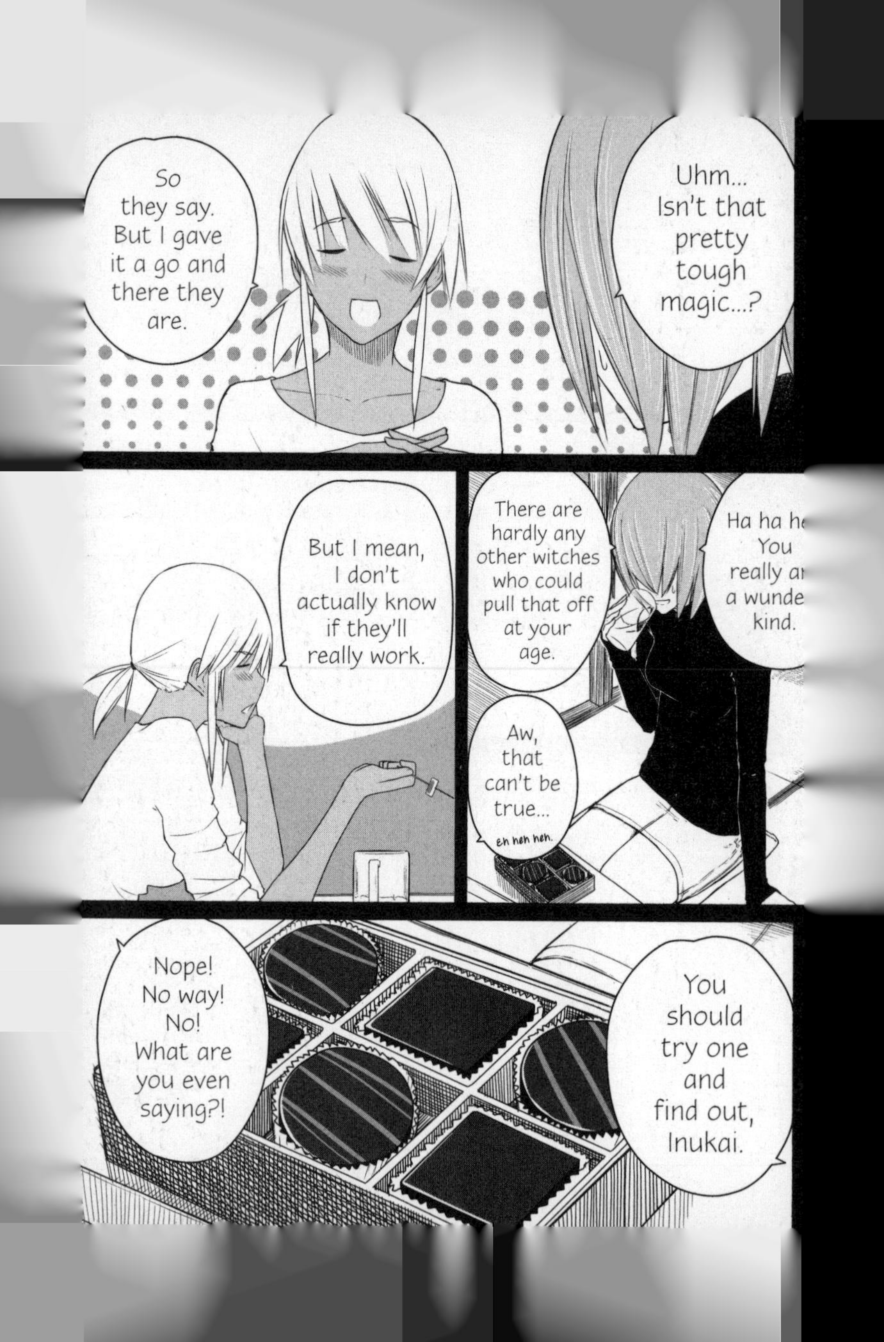
Uhm... Isn't that pretty tough magic...?
So they say. But I gave it a go and there they are.
Ha ha he You really ar a wunde kind.
There are hardly any other witches who could pull that off at your age.
Aw, that can't be true...
Eh heh heh.
But I mean, I don't actually know if they'll really work.
You should try one and find out, Inukai.
Nope! No way! No! What are you even saying?!

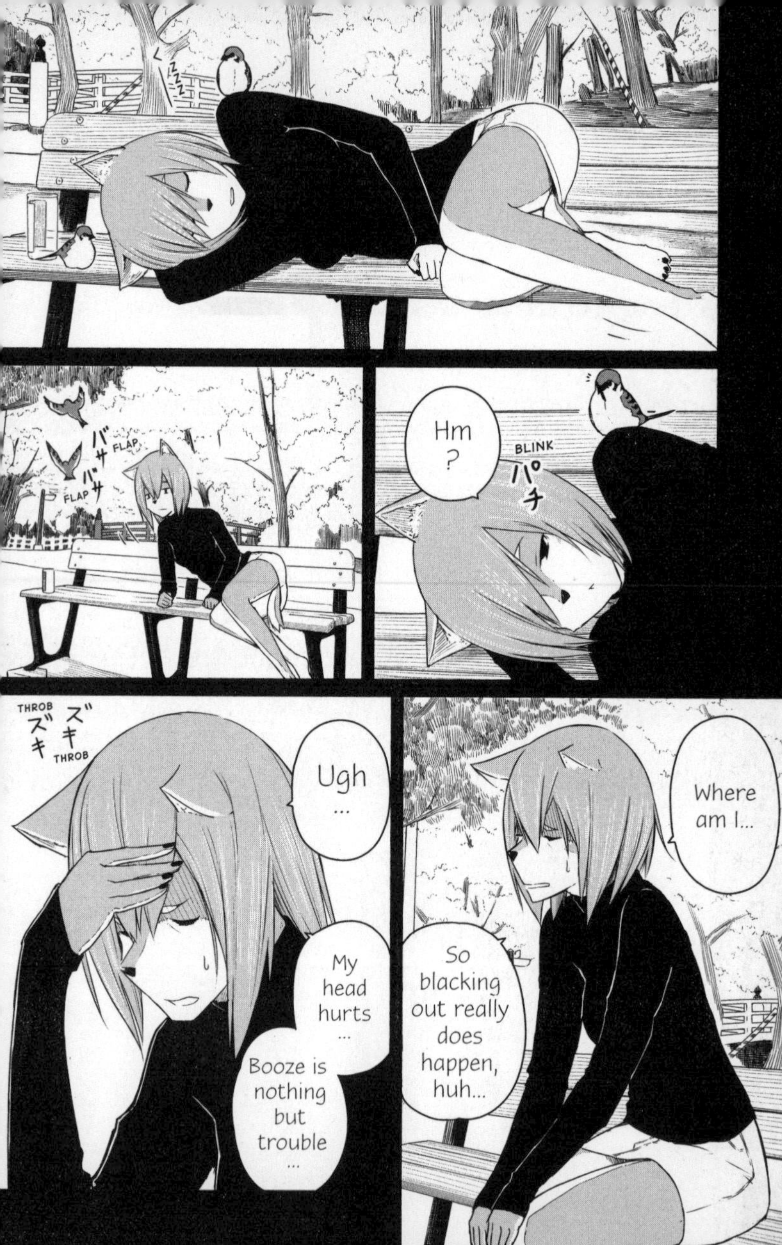
Hm ?
BLINK
パチ
バサ FLAP
バサ FLAP
Where am I...
So blacking out really does happen, huh...
THROB
ズキ ズキ
THROB
Ugh ...
My head hurts ...
Booze is nothing but trouble ...

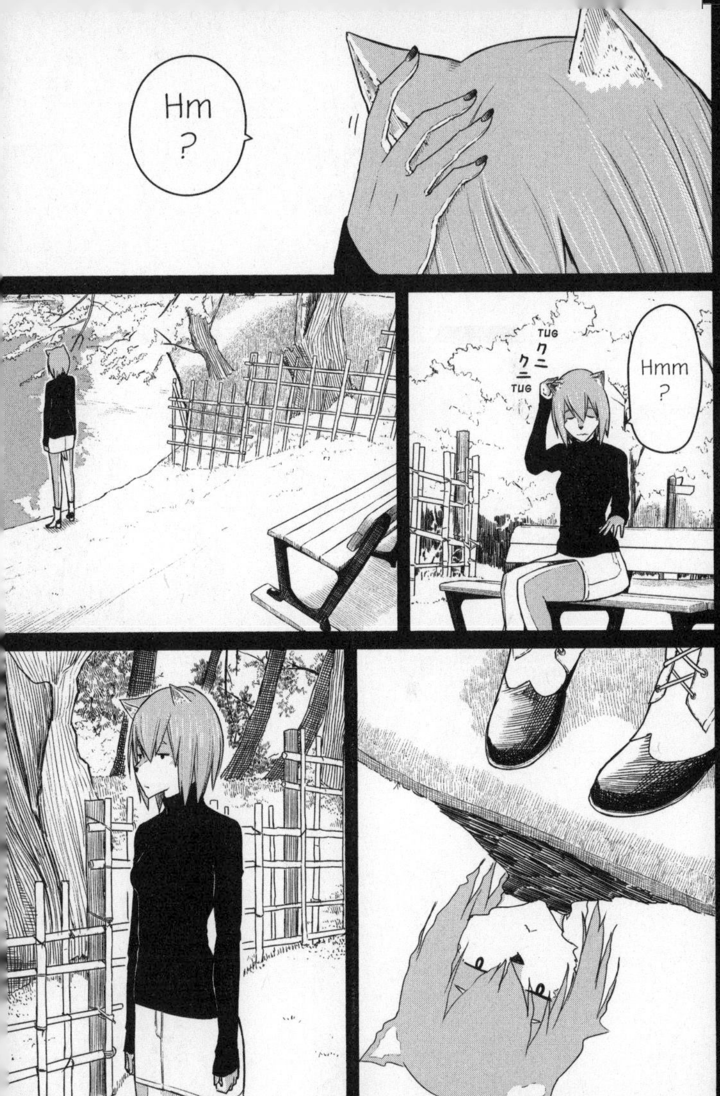
Hm ?
クニ TUG
クニ TUG
Hmm ?

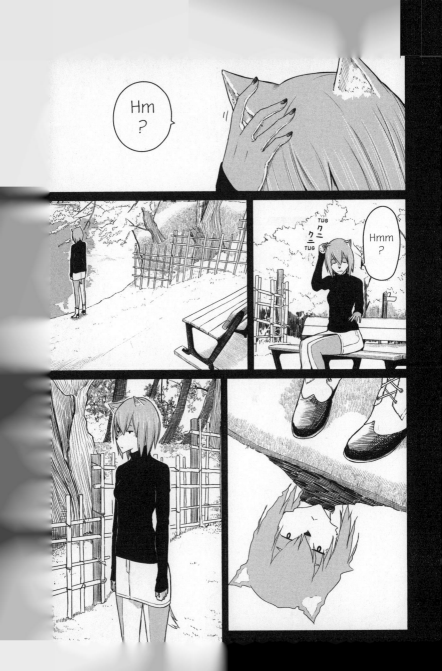

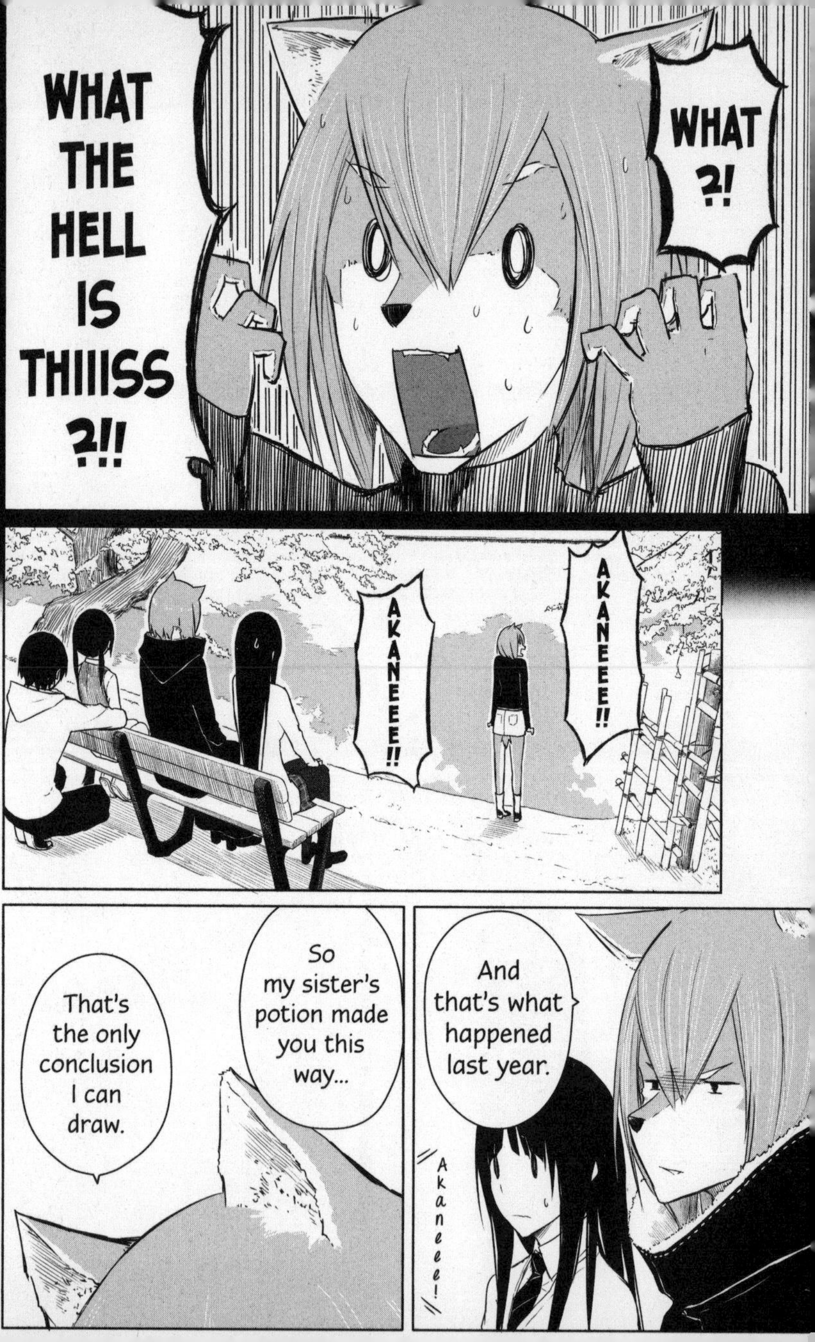
WHAT ?!
WHAT THE HELL IS THIIISS ?!!
AKANEEE!!
AKANEEE!!
And that's what happened last year.
Akaneee!
So my sister's potion made you this way...
That's the only conclusion I can draw.

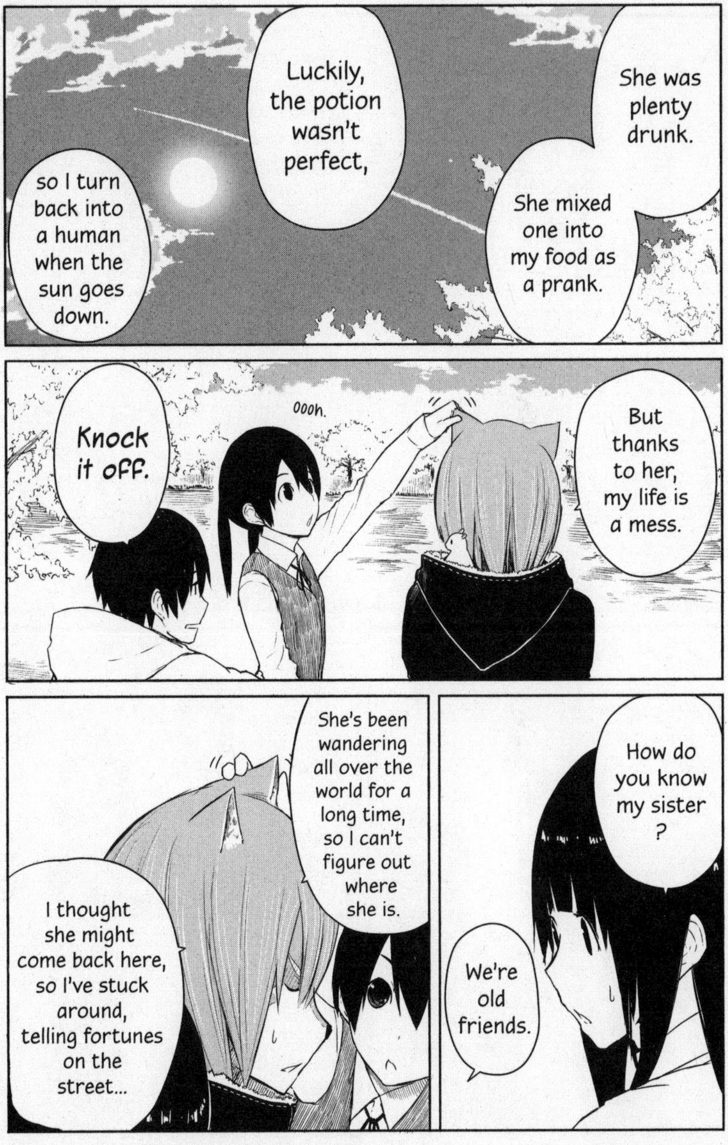
She was plenty drunk.
She mixed one into my food as a prank.
Luckily, the potion wasn't perfect,
so I turn back into a human when the sun goes down.
But thanks to her, my life is a mess.
Oooh.
Knock it off.
How do you know my sister?
We're old friends.
She's been wandering all over the world for a long time, so I can't figure out where she is.
I thought she might come back here, so I've stuck around, telling fortunes on the street...

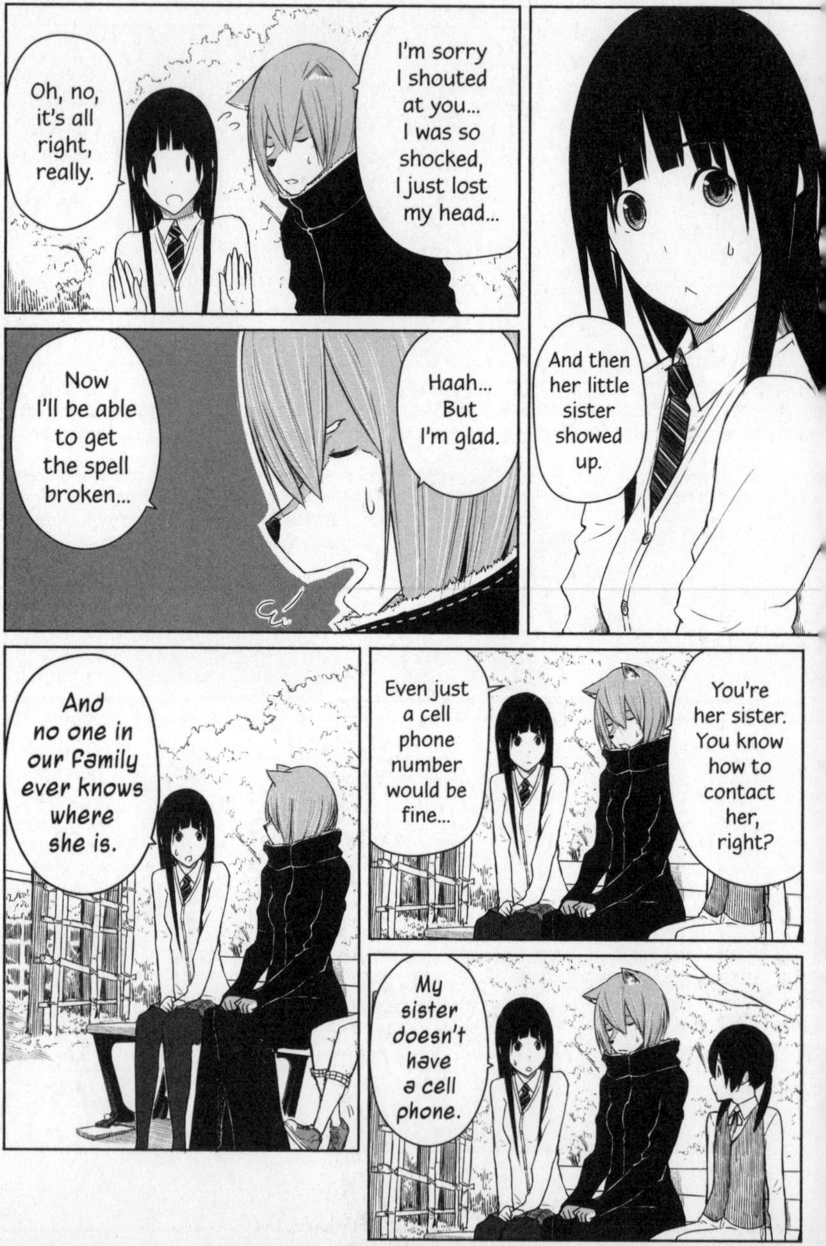
And then her little sister showed up.
I'm sorry I shouted at you... I was so shocked, I just lost my head...
Oh, no, it's all right, really.
Haah... But I'm glad.
Now I'll be able to get the spell broken...
You're her sister. You know how to contact her, right?
Even just a cell phone number would be fine...
My sister doesn't have a cell phone.
And no one in our family ever knows where she is.

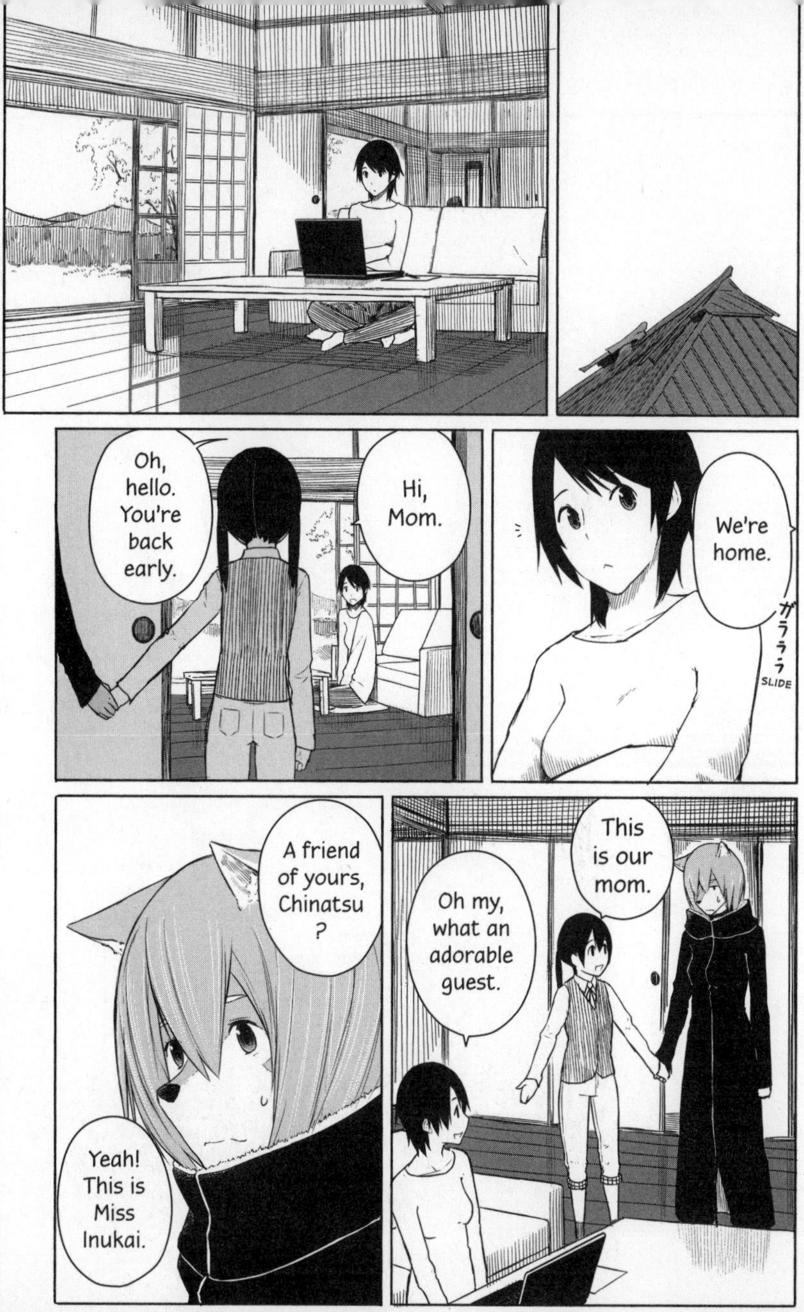
We're home.
ガラララ
SLIDE
Hi, Mom.
Oh, hello. You're back early.
This is our mom.
Oh my, what an adorable guest.
A friend of yours, Chinatsu?
Yeah! This is Miss Inukai.

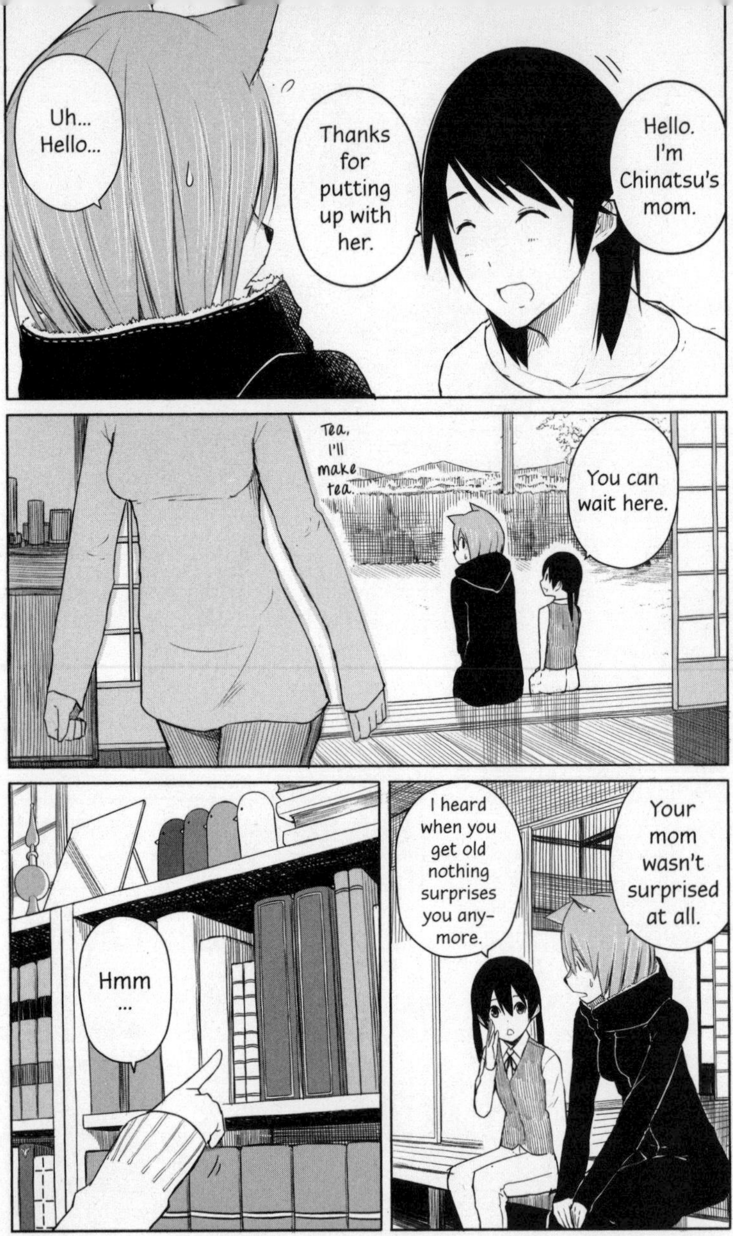
Hello. I'm Chinatsu's mom.
Thanks for putting up with her.
Uh... Hello...
You can wait here.
Tea, I'll make tea.
Your mom wasn't surprised at all.
I heard when you get old nothing surprises you any-more.
Hmm ...

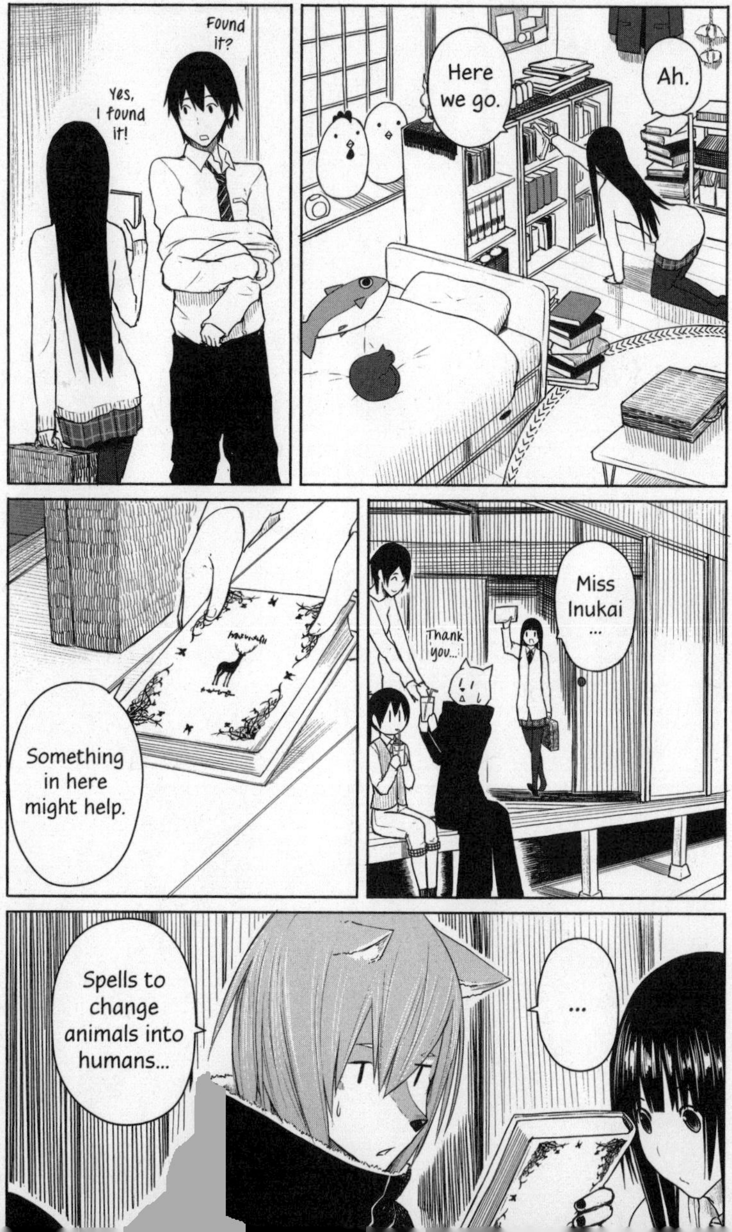
Ah.
Here we go.
Found it?
Yes, I found it!
Miss Inukai ...
Thank you...
Something in here might help.
...
Spells to change animals into humans...

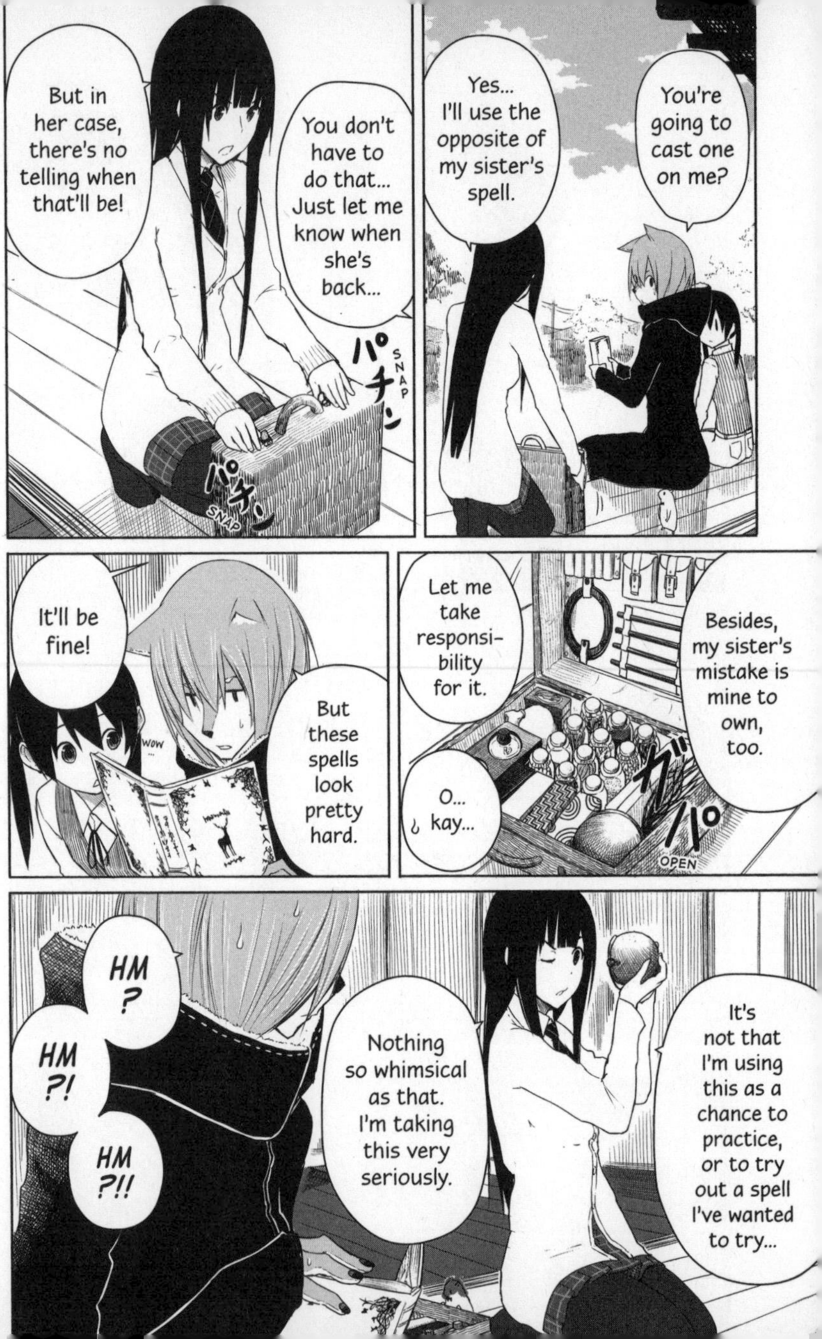
You're going to cast one on me?
Yes... I'll use the opposite of my sister's spell.
You don't have to do that... Just let me know when she's back...
But in her case, there's no telling when that'll be!
パチン
SNAP
パチン
SNAP
Besides, my sister's mistake is mine to own, too.
Let me take responsibility for it.
ガパ
OPEN
O... kay...
But these spells look pretty hard.
It'll be fine!
WOW...
It's not that I'm using this as a chance to practice, or to try out a spell I've wanted to try...
Nothing so whimsical as that. I'm taking this very seriously.
HM?
HM?!
HM?!!

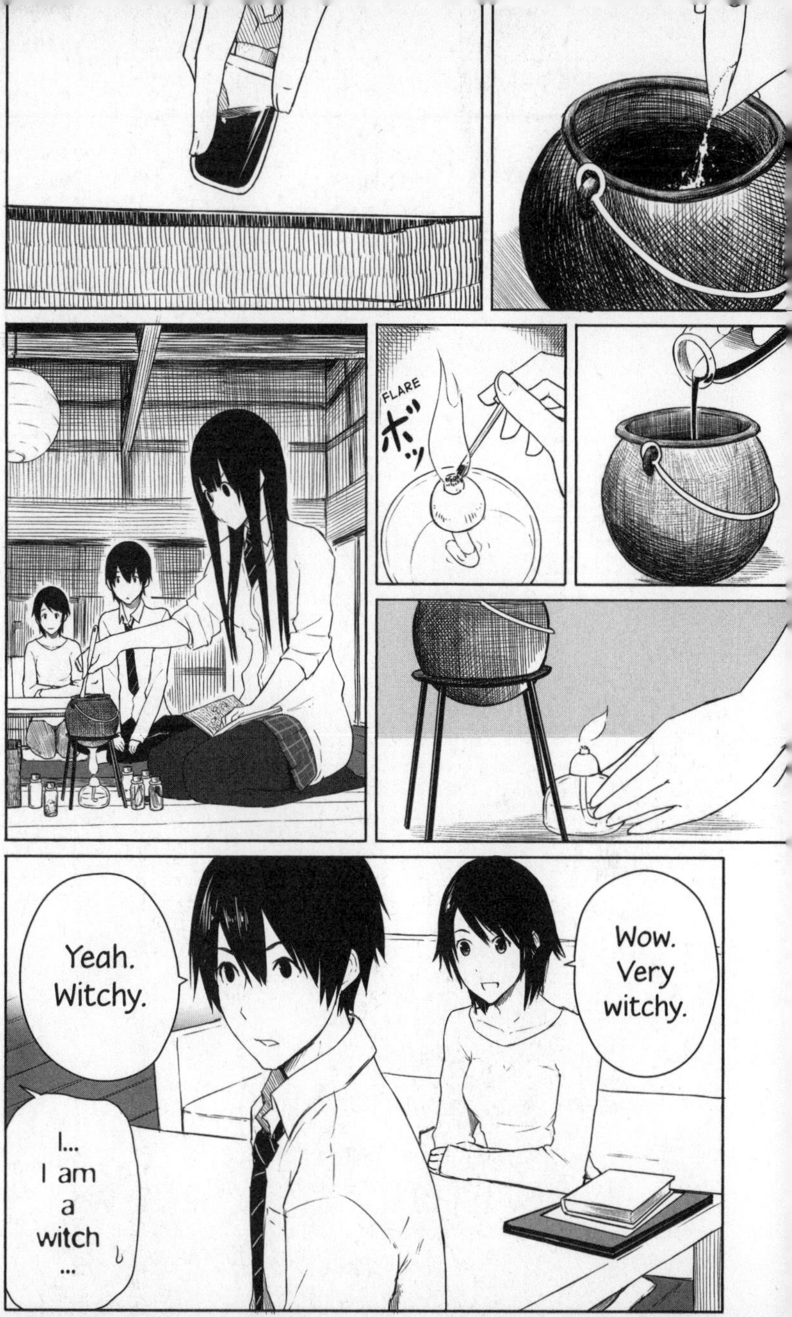
FLARE
ボッ
Wow. Very witchy.
Yeah. Witchy.
I... I am a witch ...

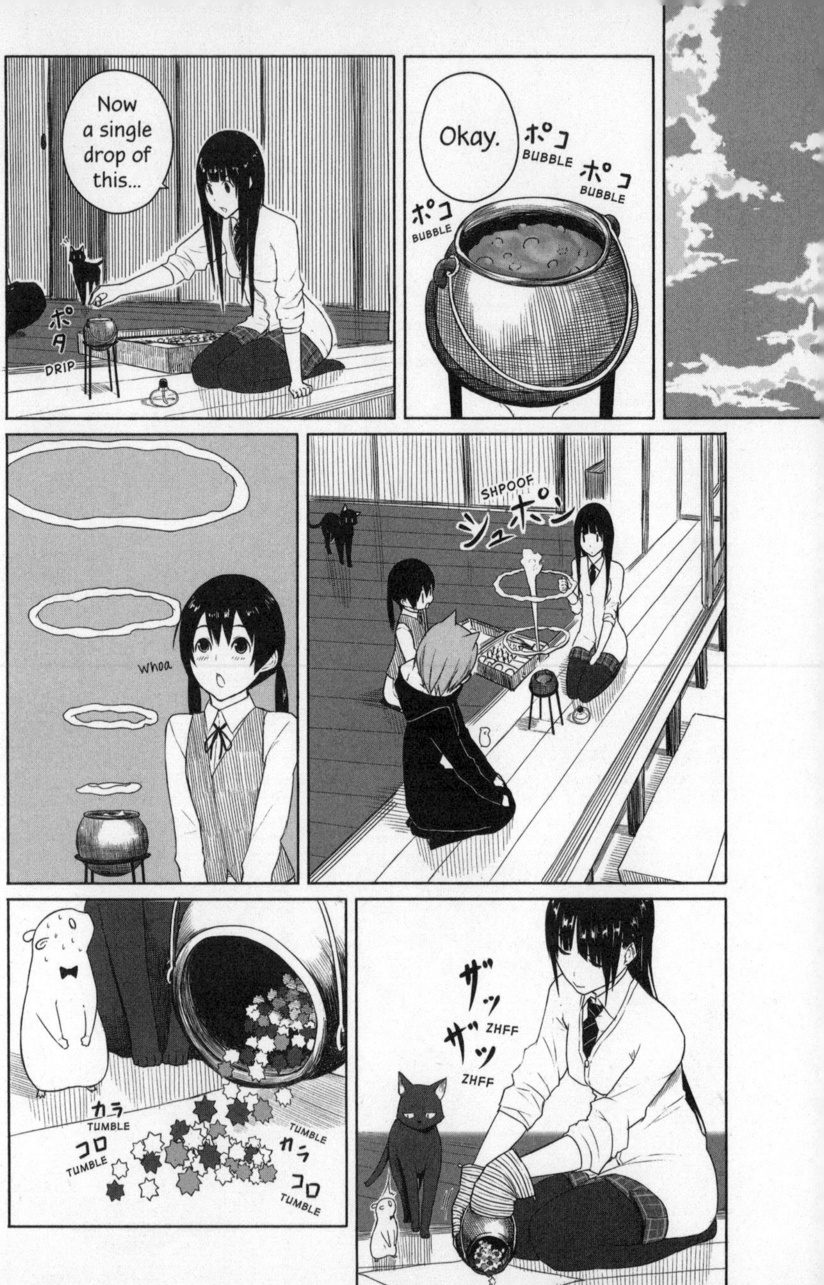

Okay.
ポコ
BUBBLE
ポコ
BUBBLE
ポコ
BUBBLE
Now a single drop of this...
ポタ
DRIP
SHPOOF
シュポン
whoa
ザッ
ZHFF
ザッ
ZHFF
カラ
TUMBLE
コロ
TUMBLE
カラ
TUMBLE
コロ
TUMBLE

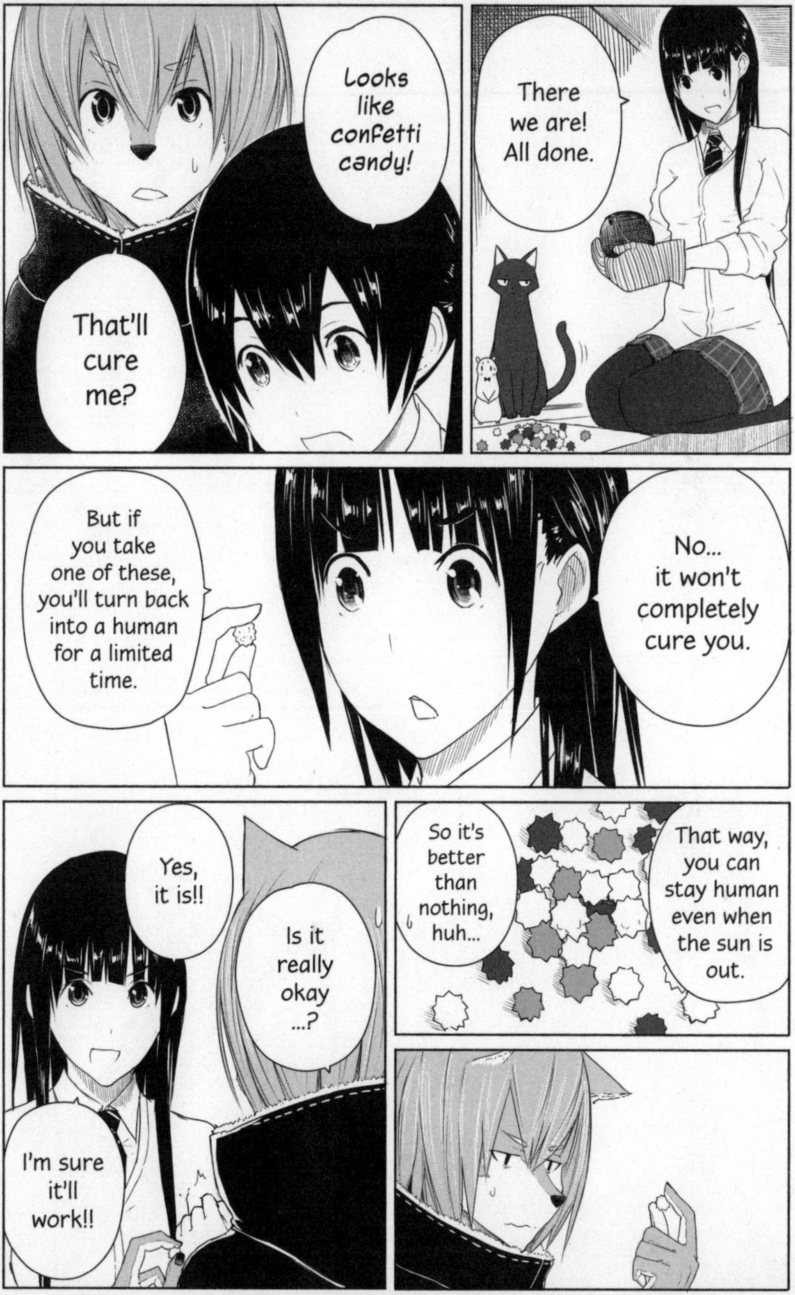
There we are! All done.
Looks like confetti candy!
That'll cure me?
No... it won't completely cure you.
But if you take one of these, you'll turn back into a human for a limited time.
That way, you can stay human even when the sun is out.
So it's better than nothing, huh...
Is it really okay ...?
Yes, it is!!
I'm sure it'll work!!

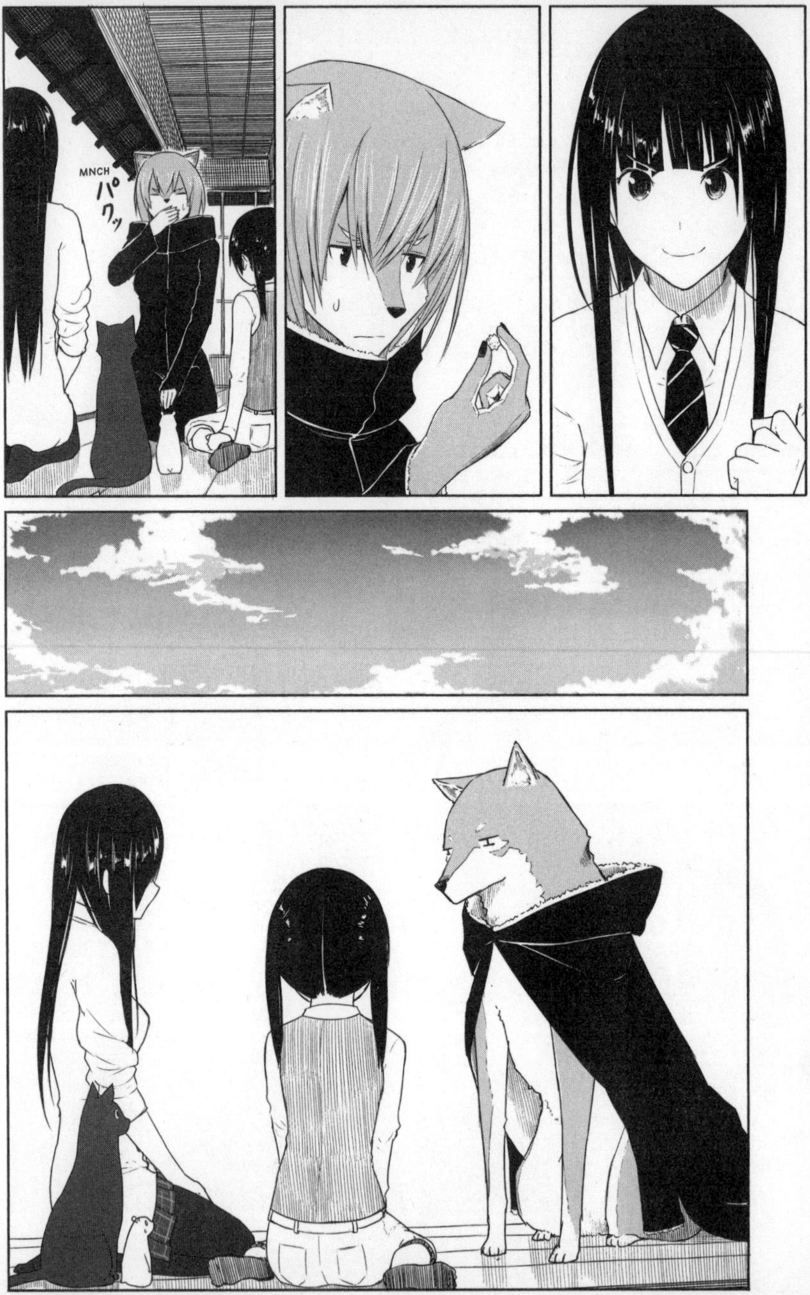
MNCH
パクッ

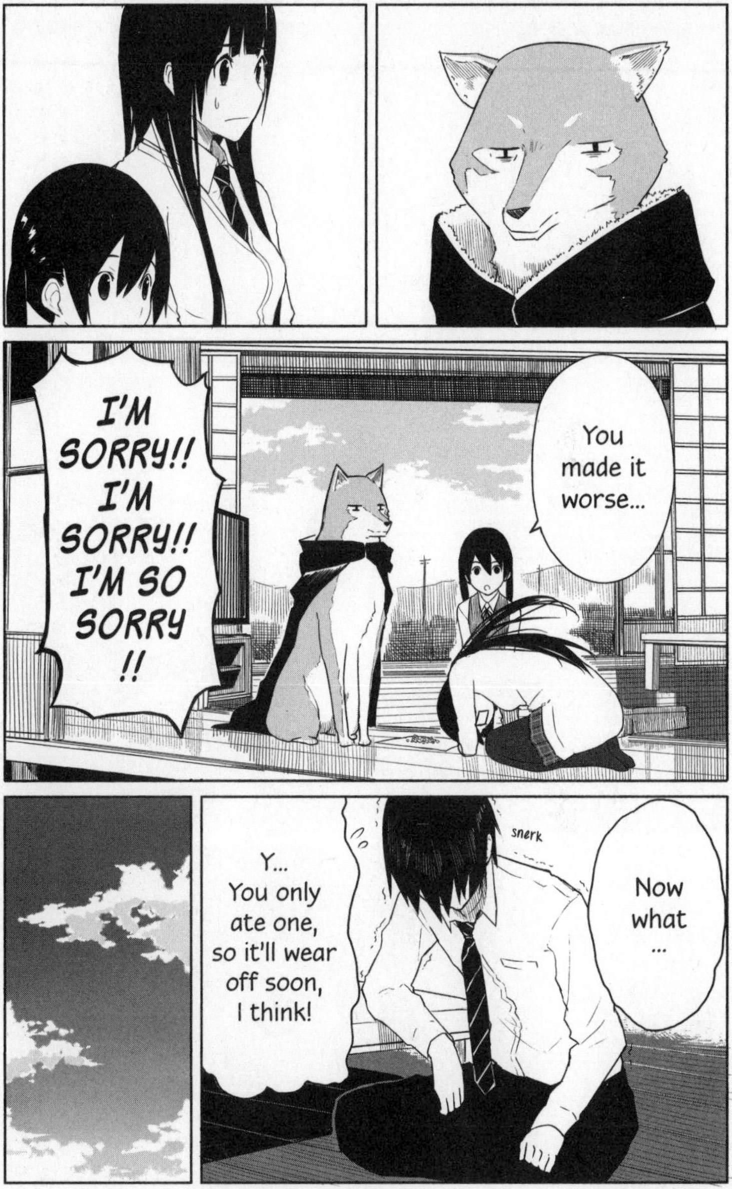
You made it worse...
I'M SORRY!! I'M SORRY!! I'M SO SORRY !!
Now what ...
snerk
Y... You only ate one, so it'll wear off soon, I think!

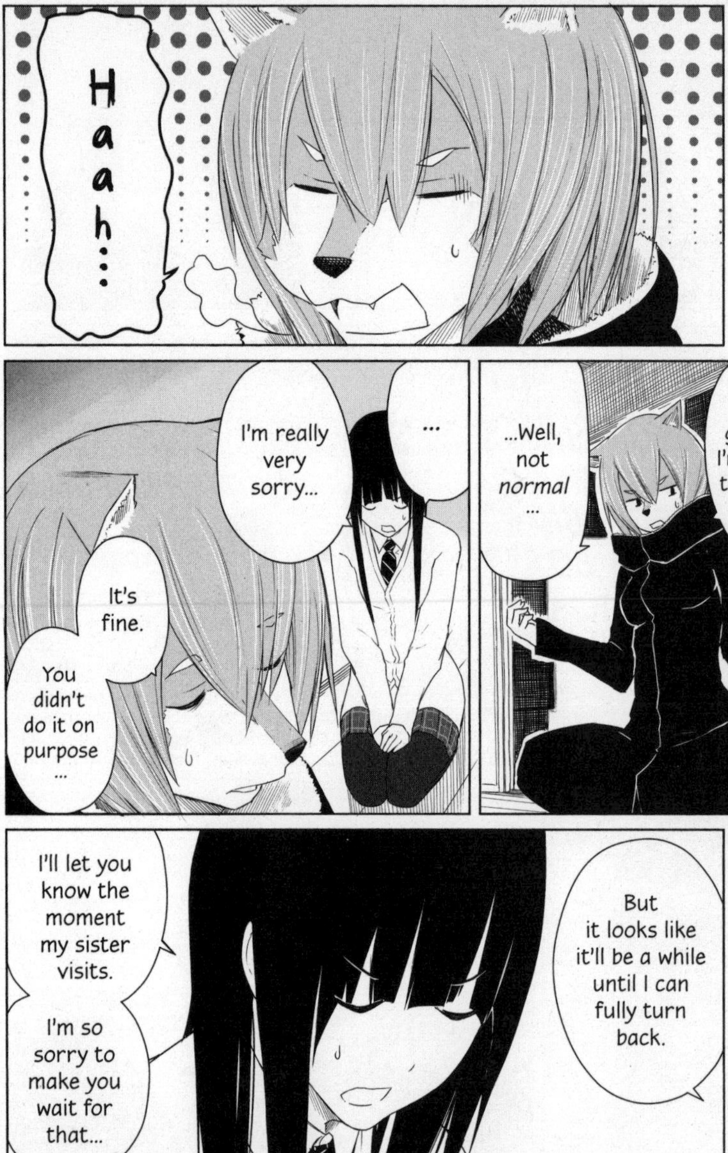
Haah...
Oh, good... I'm back to nor-mal.
...Well, not *normal* ...
...
I'm really very sorry...
It's fine.
You didn't do it on purpose ...
But it looks like it'll be a while until I can fully turn back.
I'll let you know the moment my sister visits.
I'm so sorry to make you wait for that...

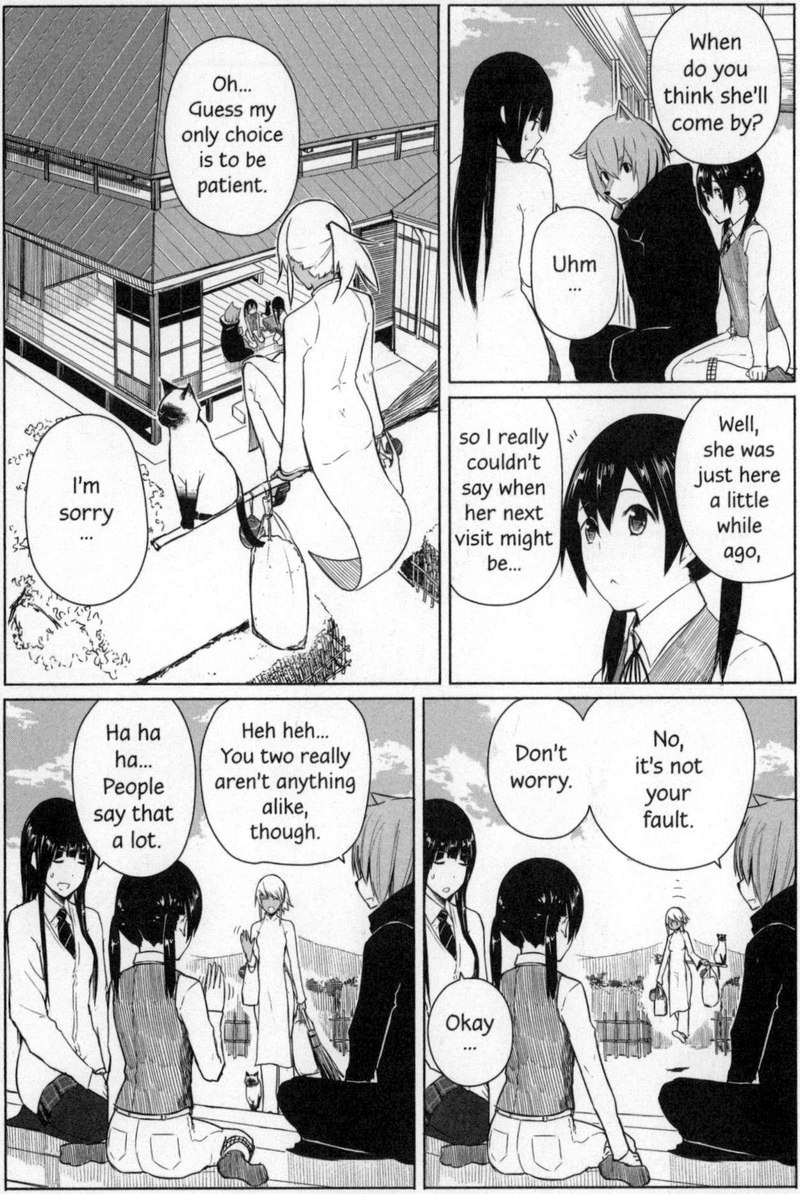
When do you think she'll come by?
Uhm ...
Well, she was just here a little while ago,
so I really couldn't say when her next visit might be...
Oh... Guess my only choice is to be patient.
I'm sorry ...
No, it's not your fault.
Don't worry.
Okay ...
Heh heh... You two really aren't anything alike, though.
Ha ha ha... People say that a lot.

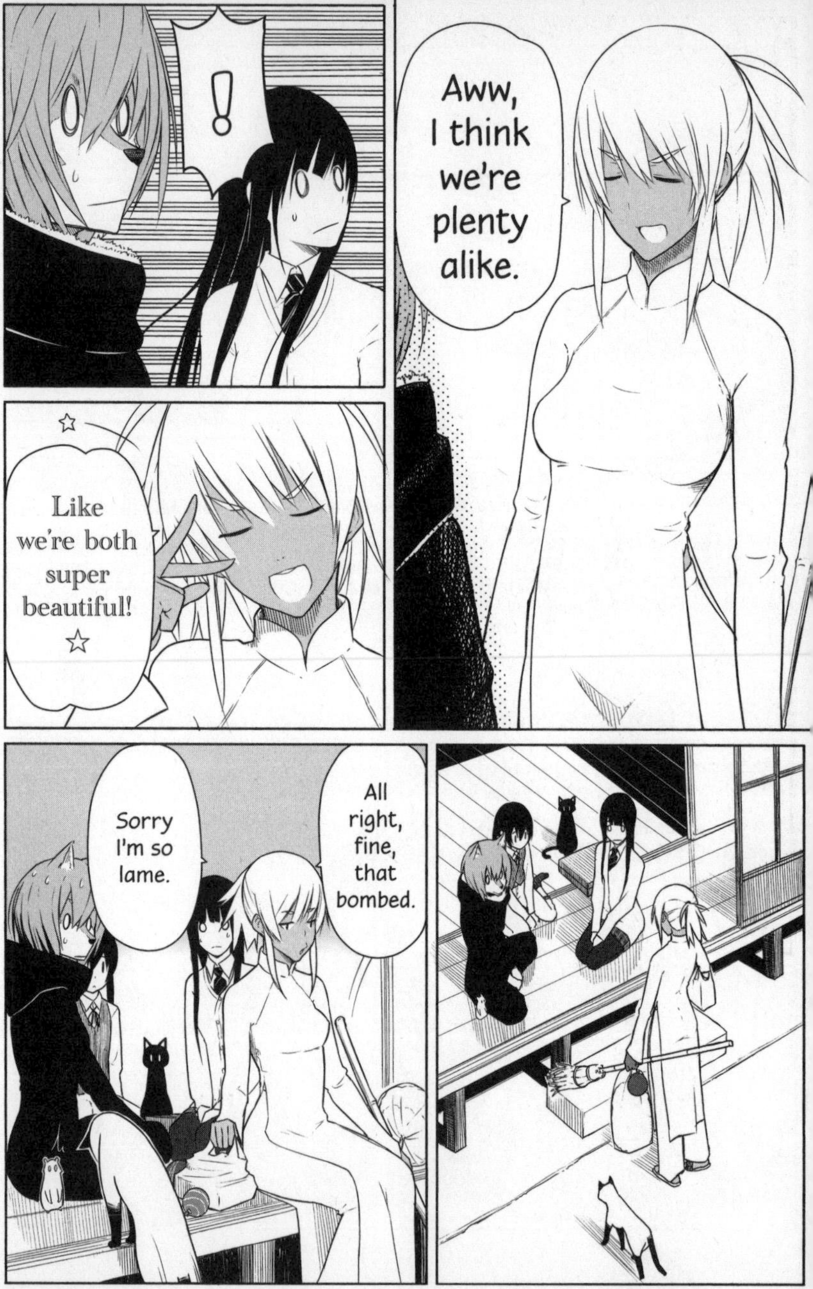
Aww, I think we're plenty alike.
!
☆ Like we're both super beautiful! ☆
All right, fine, that bombed.
Sorry I'm so lame.

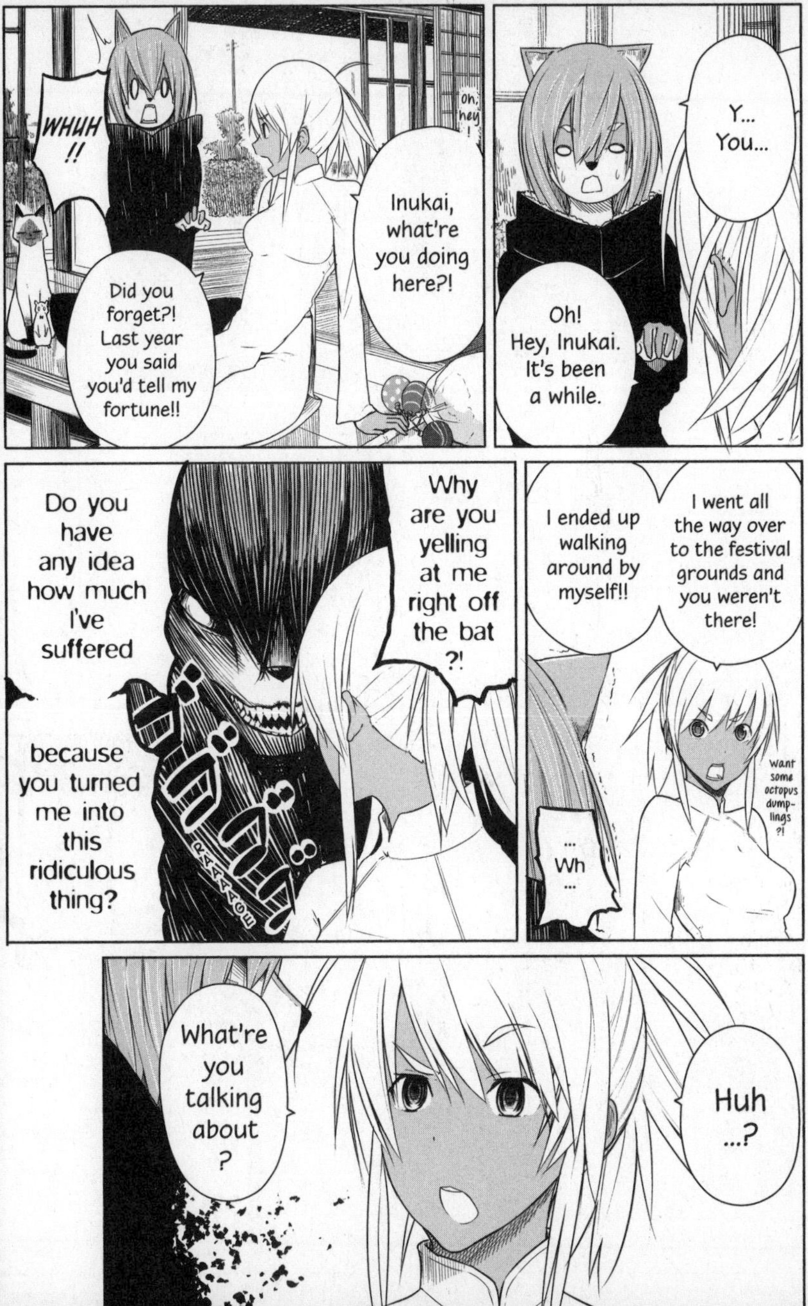
Y... You...
Oh! Hey, Inukai. It's been a while.
Oh, hey!
Inukai, what're you doing here?!
WHUH!!
Did you forget?! Last year you said you'd tell my fortune!!
I went all the way over to the festival grounds and you weren't there!
I ended up walking around by myself!!
Want some octopus dumplings?!
... Wh ...
Why are you yelling at me right off the bat?!
Do you have any idea how much I've suffered
because you turned me into this ridiculous thing?
Huh ...?
What're you talking about?

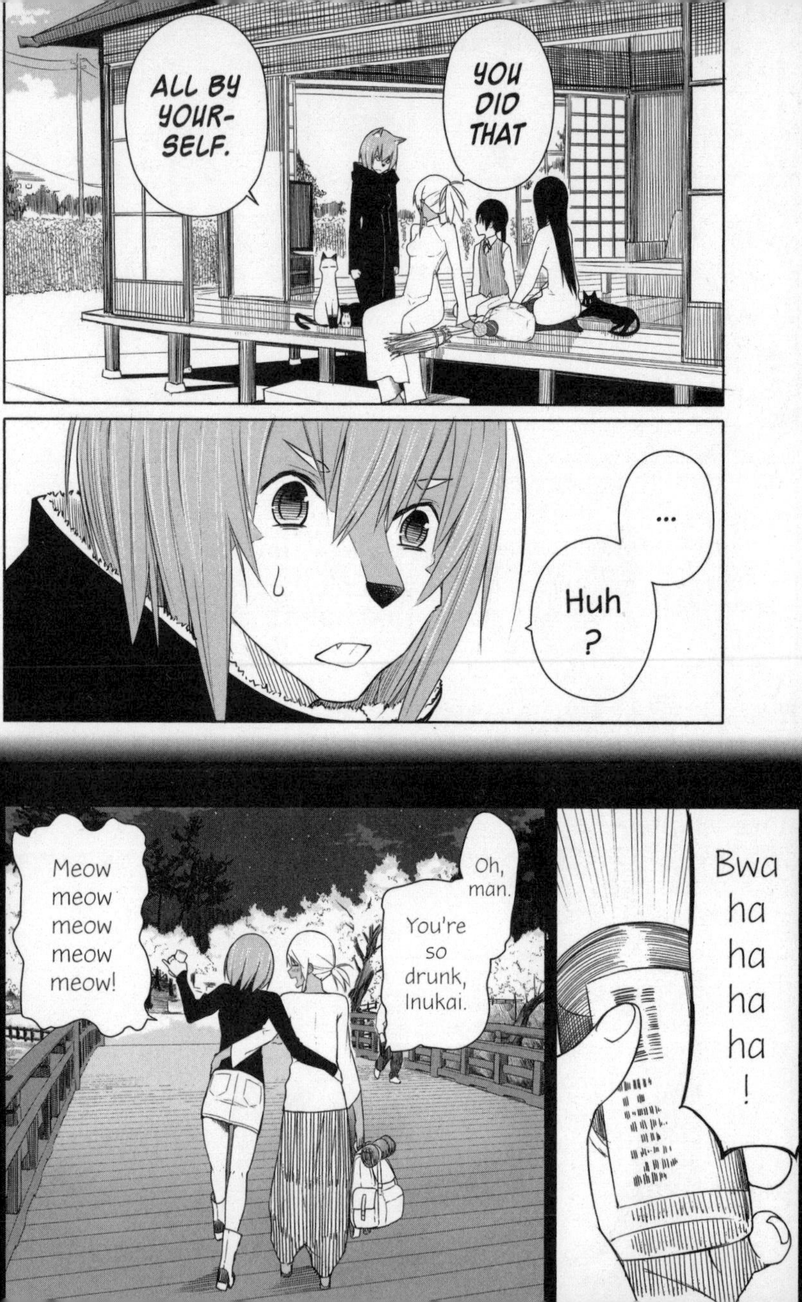
YOU DID THAT
ALL BY YOURSELF.
... Huh?
Bwa ha ha ha ha!
Oh, man.
You're so drunk, Inukai.
Meow meow meow meow meow!

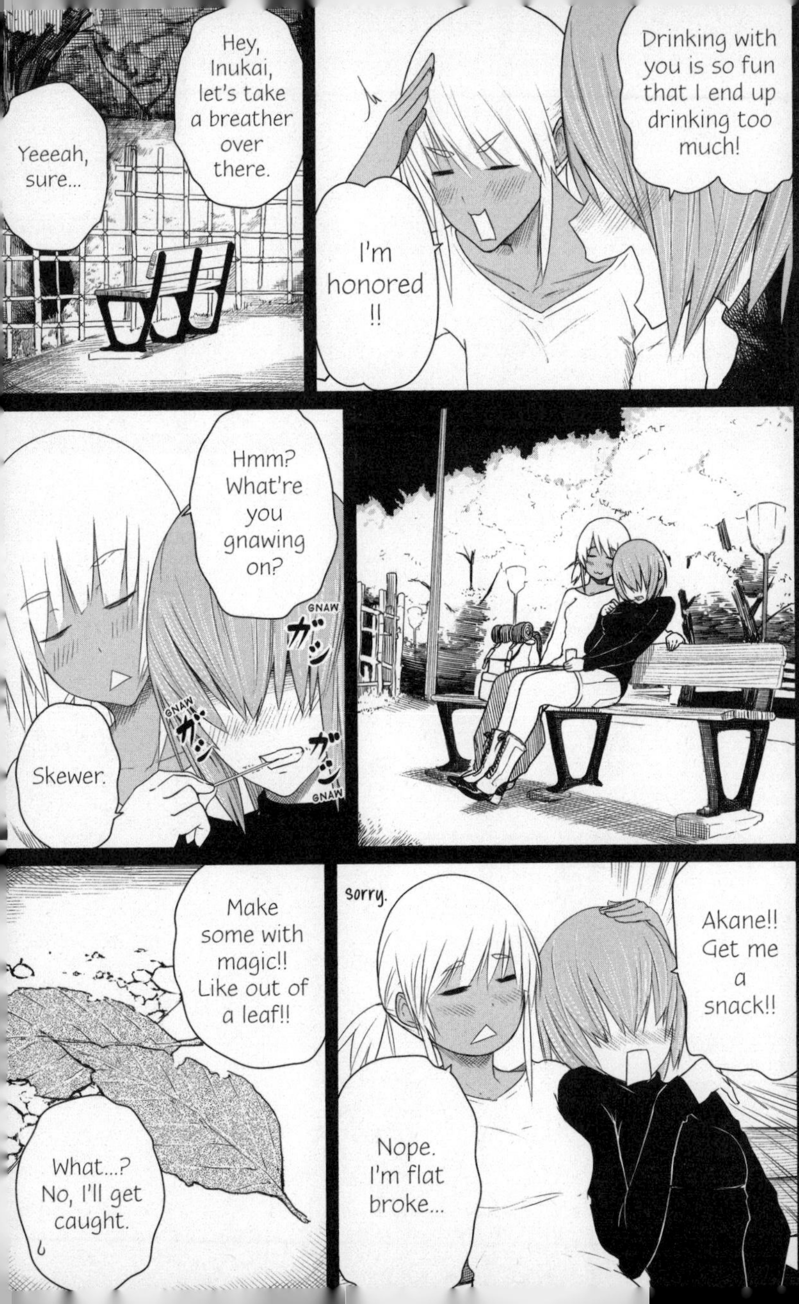
Drinking with you is so fun that I end up drinking too much!
I'm honored!!
Hey, Inukai, let's take a breather over there.
Yeeeah, sure...
Hmm? What're you gnawing on?
GNAW ガジ
GNAW ガジ
GNAW ガジ
Skewer.
Akane!! Get me a snack!!
sorry.
Nope. I'm flat broke...
Make some with magic!! Like out of a leaf!!
What...? No, I'll get caught.

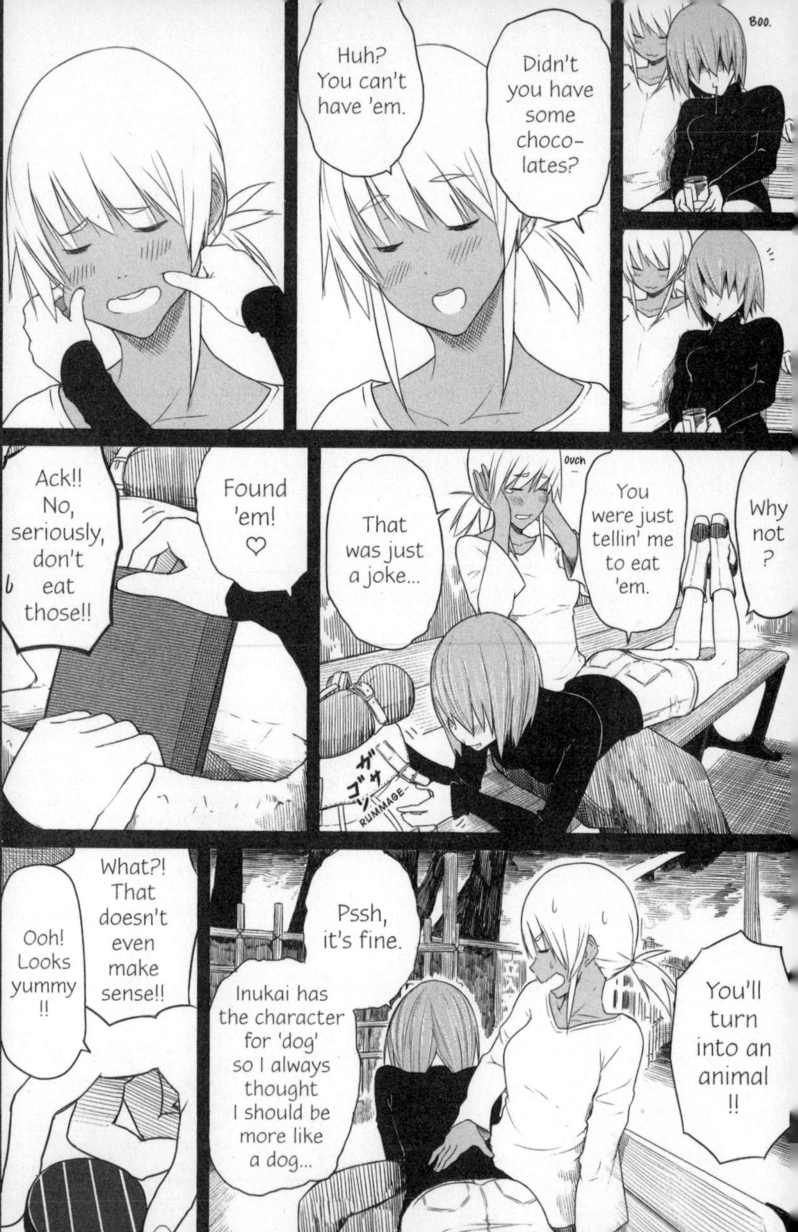
BOO.
Didn't you have some chocolates?
Huh? You can't have 'em.
Why not?
You were just tellin' me to eat 'em.
Ouch...
That was just a joke...
ガサ ゴソ
RUMMAGE
Found 'em! ♡
Ack!! No, seriously, don't eat those!!
You'll turn into an animal!!
Pssh, it's fine.
Inukai has the character for 'dog' so I always thought I should be more like a dog...
What?! That doesn't even make sense!!
Ooh! Looks yummy!!

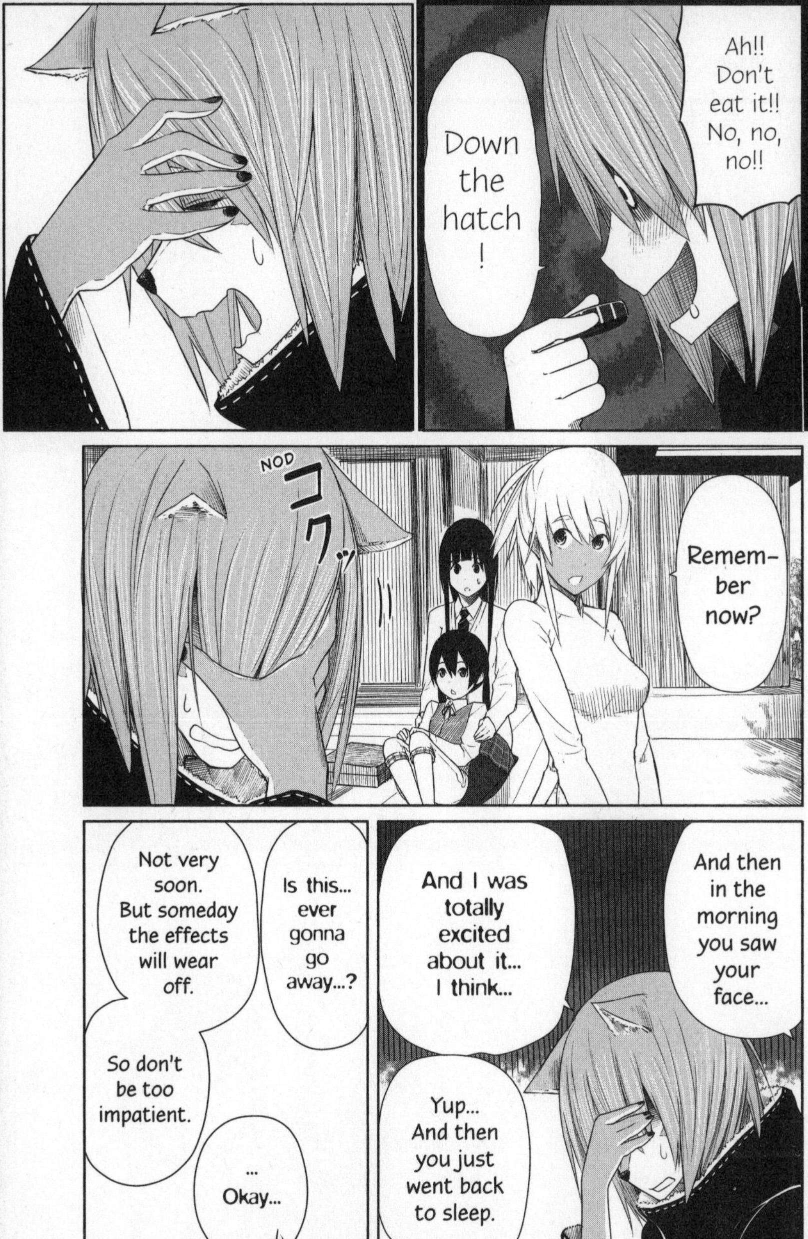
Ah!! Don't eat it!! No, no, no!!
Down the hatch!
Remember now?
NOD
コクッ
And then in the morning you saw your face...
And I was totally excited about it... I think...
Yup... And then you just went back to sleep.
Is this... ever gonna go away...?
Not very soon. But someday the effects will wear off.
So don't be too impatient.
... Okay...

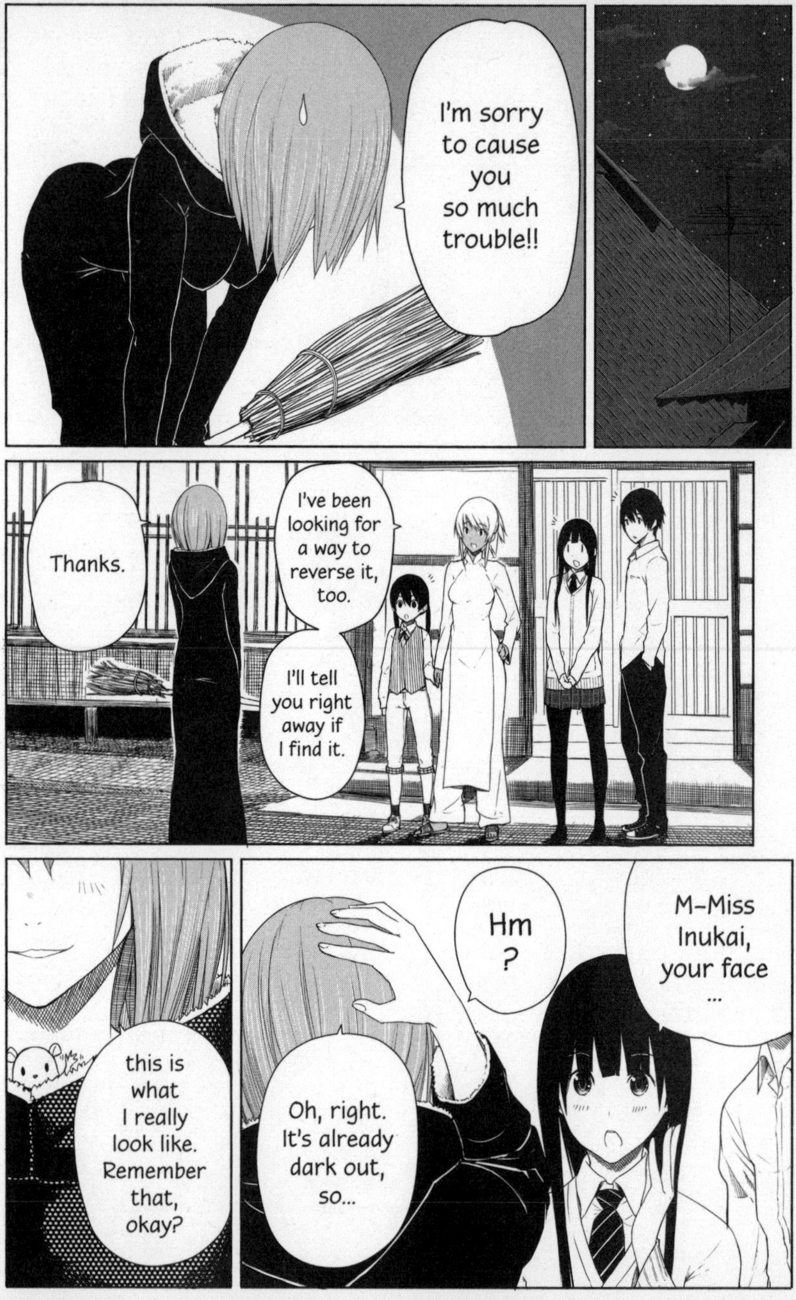
I'm sorry to cause you so much trouble!!
I've been looking for a way to reverse it, too.
I'll tell you right away if I find it.
Thanks.
M-Miss Inukai, your face ...
Hm ?
Oh, right. It's already dark out, so...
this is what I really look like. Remember that, okay?

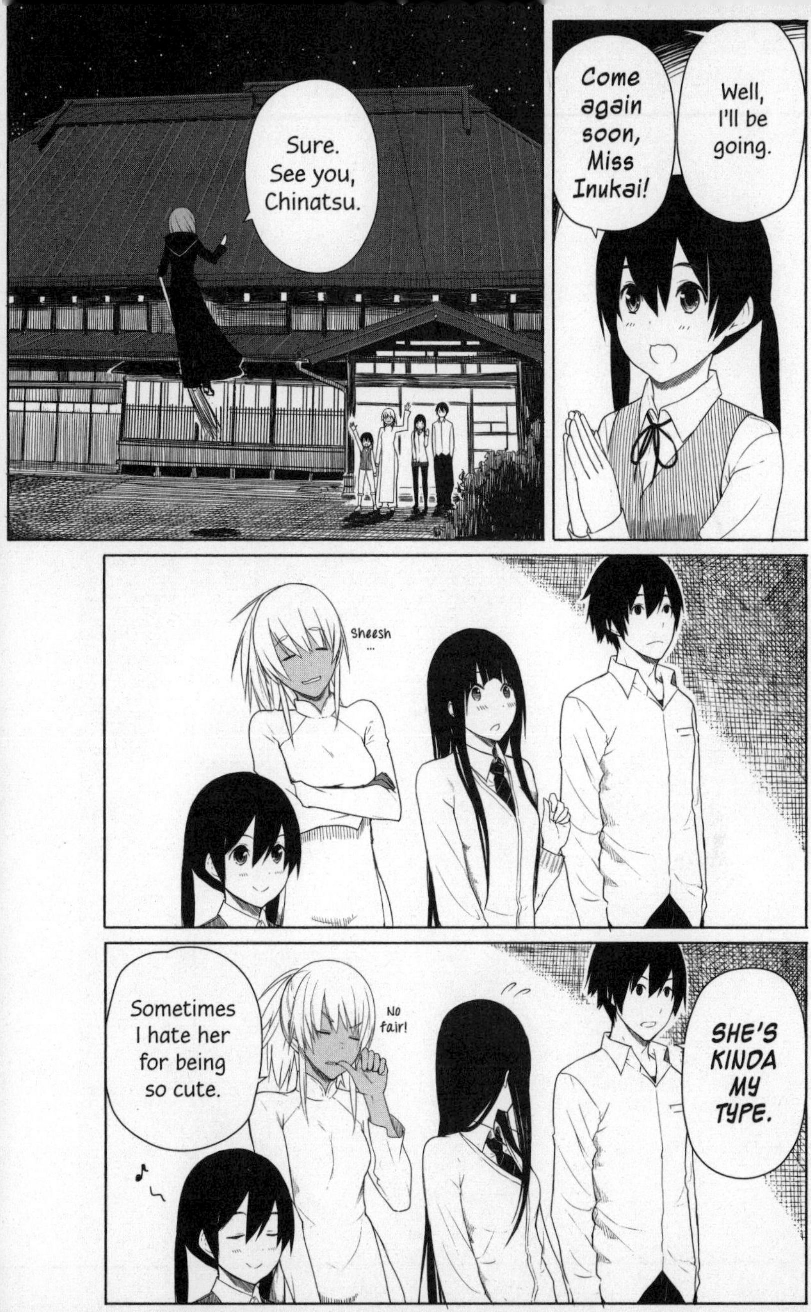
Well, I'll be going.
Come again soon, Miss Inukai!
Sure. See you, Chinatsu.
Sheesh...
SHE'S KINDA MY TYPE.
No fair!
Sometimes I hate her for being so cute.

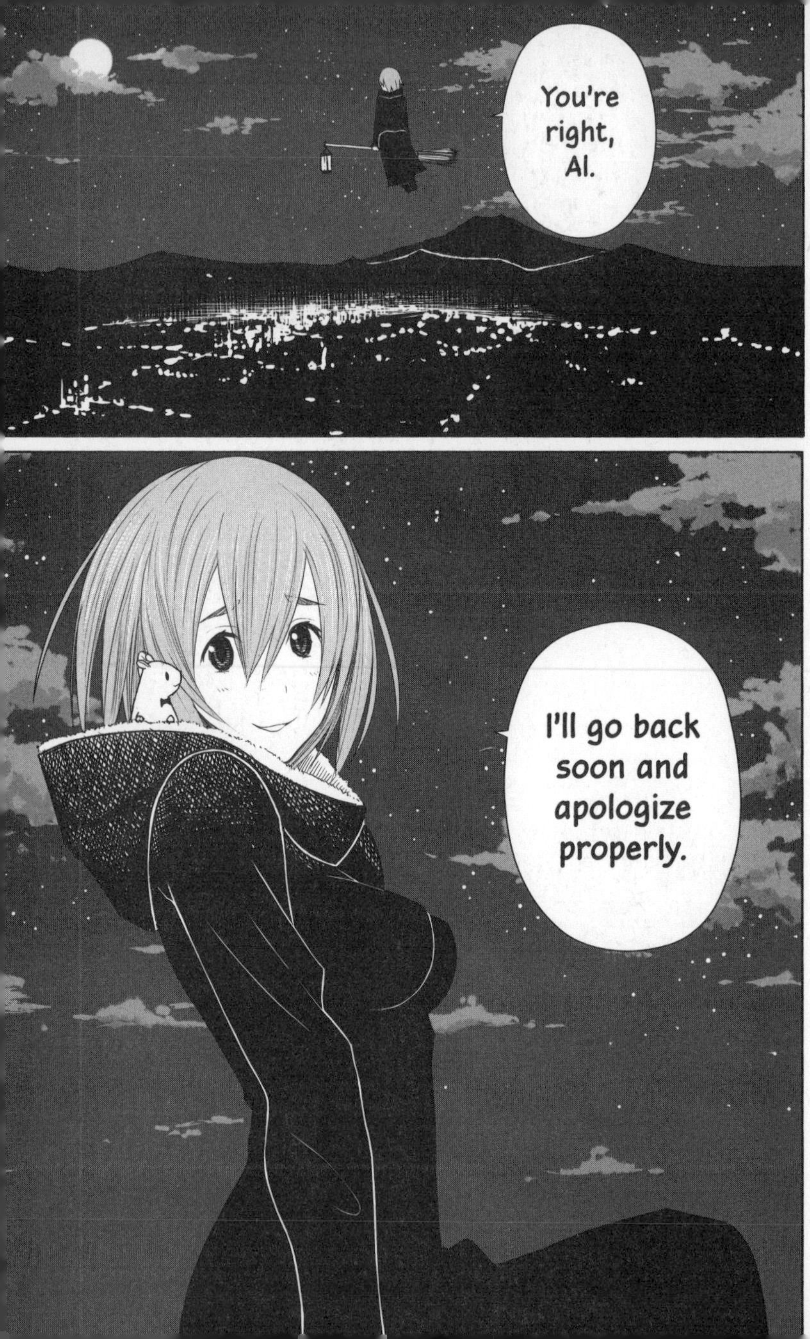
You're right, Al.
I'll go back soon and apologize properly.

Chapter 10
Chinatsu's Decision

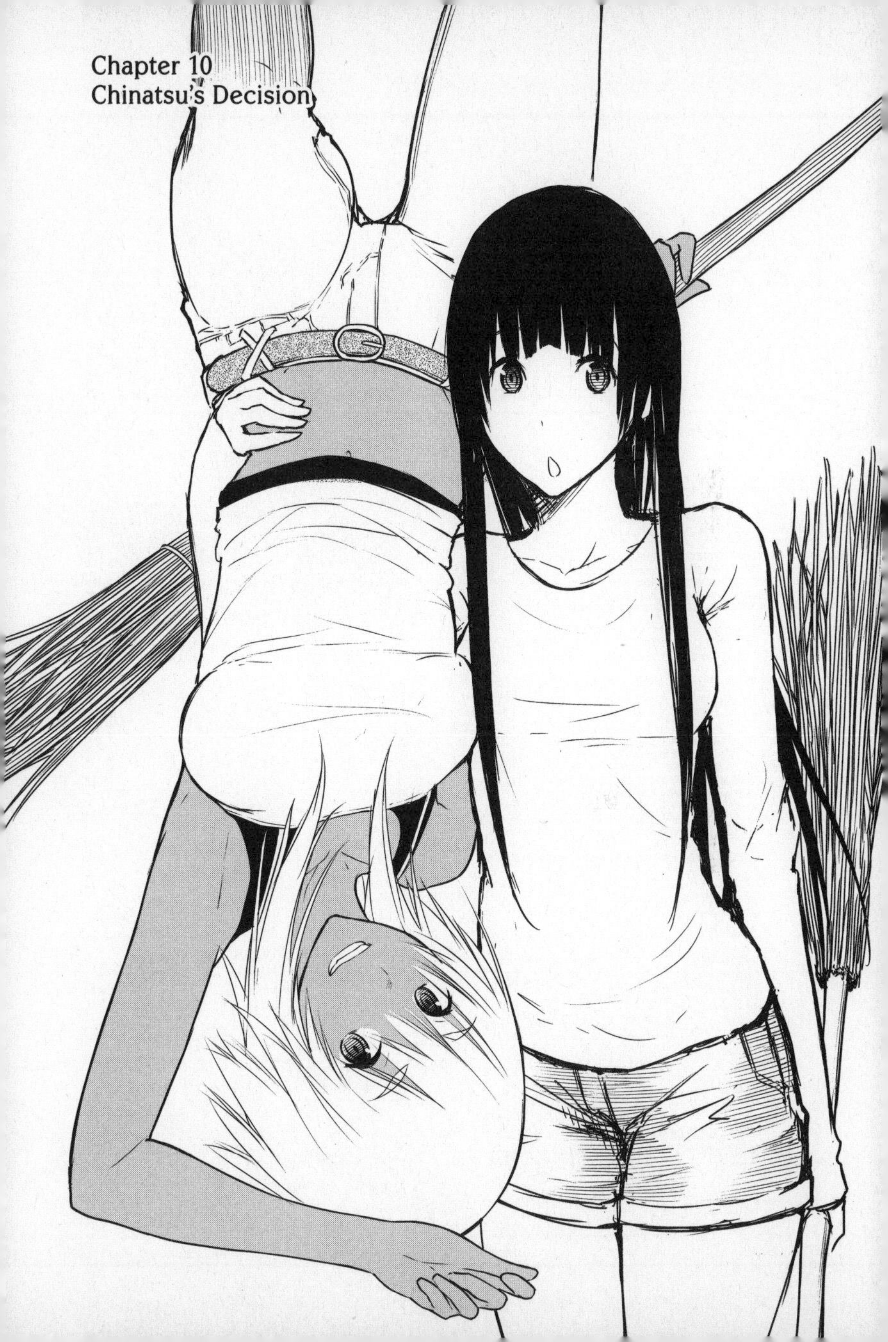

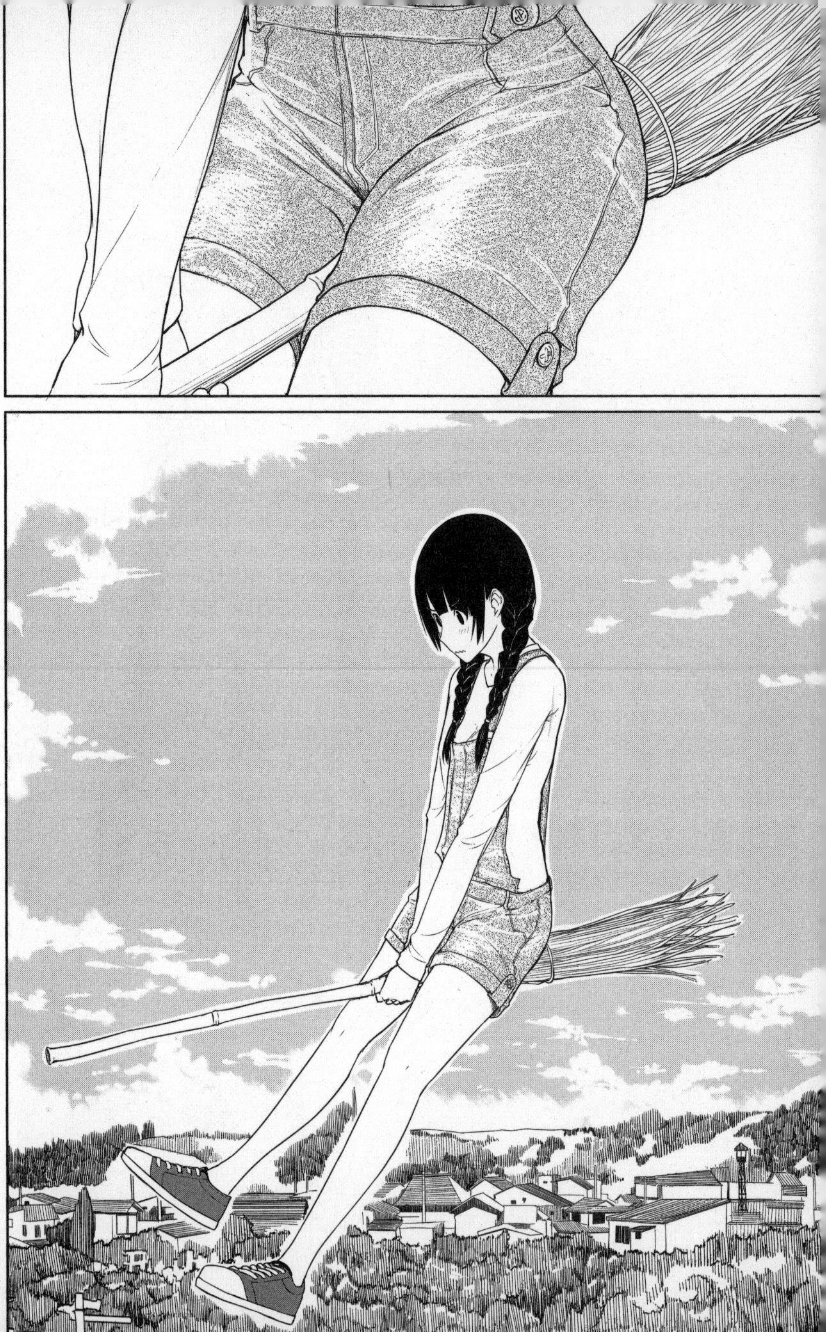

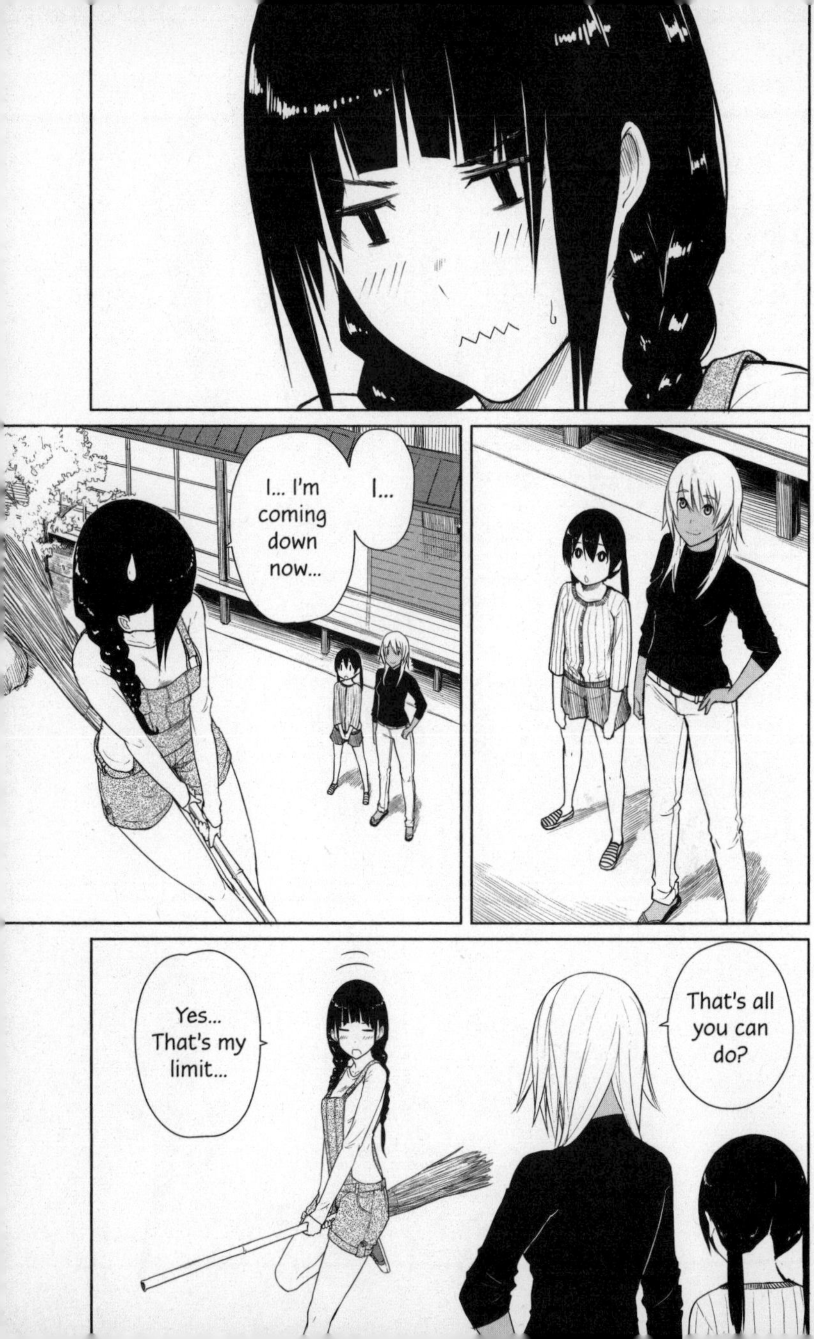
I...
I... I'm coming down now...
That's all you can do?
Yes... That's my limit...

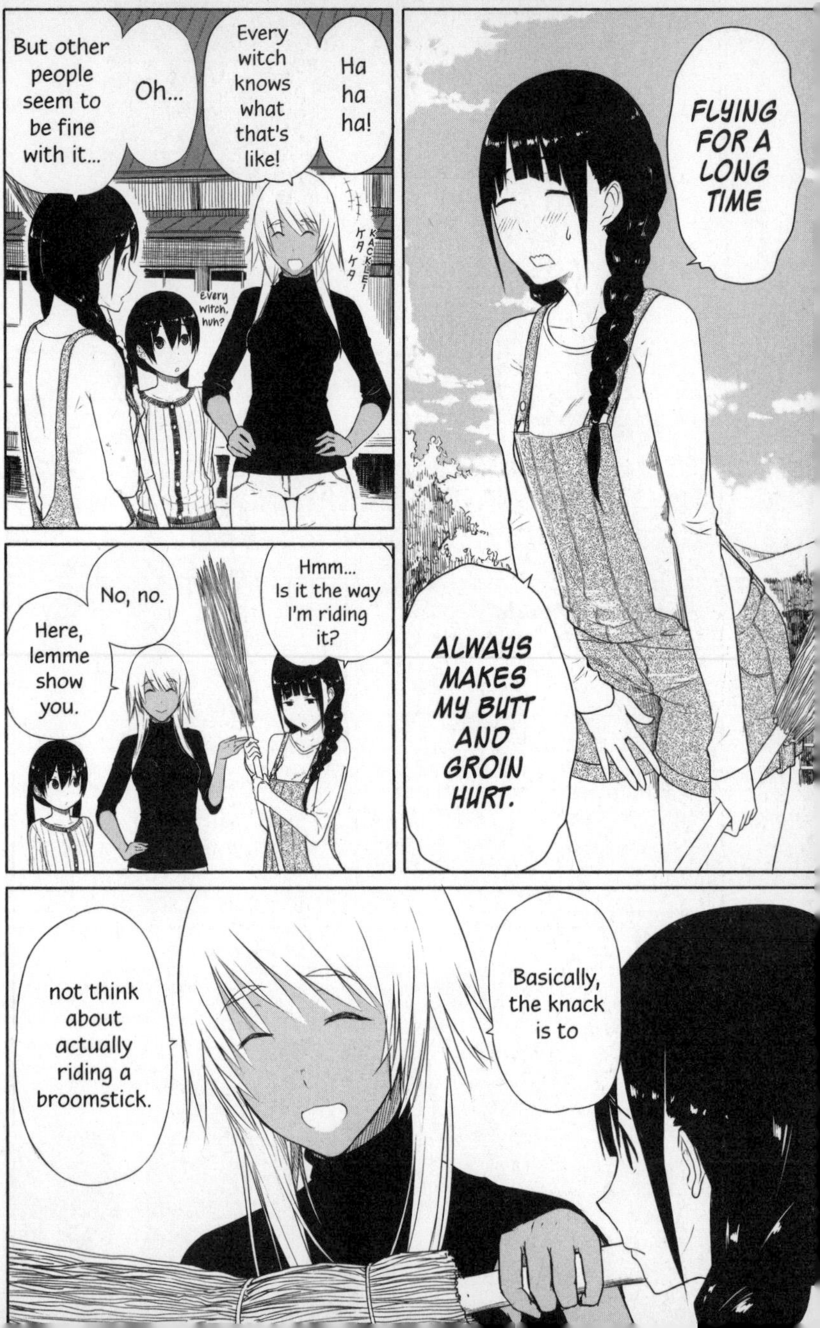
FLYING FOR A LONG TIME
ALWAYS MAKES MY BUTT AND GROIN HURT.
Ha ha ha!
Every witch knows what that's like!
KACKLE!
Oh...
But other people seem to be fine with it...
Every witch, huh?
Hmm... Is it the way I'm riding it?
No, no.
Here, lemme show you.
Basically, the knack is to
not think about actually riding a broomstick.

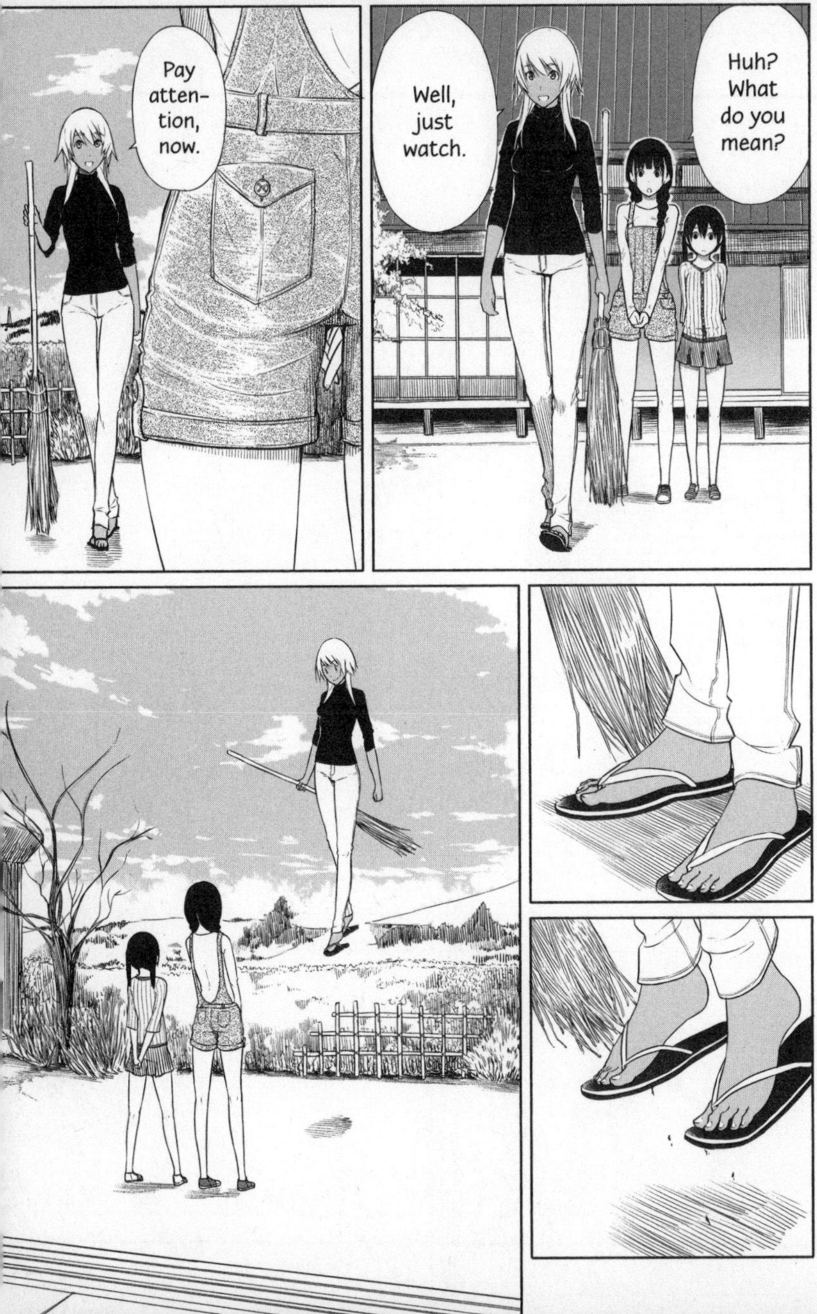
Huh? What do you mean?
Well, just watch.
Pay attention, now.

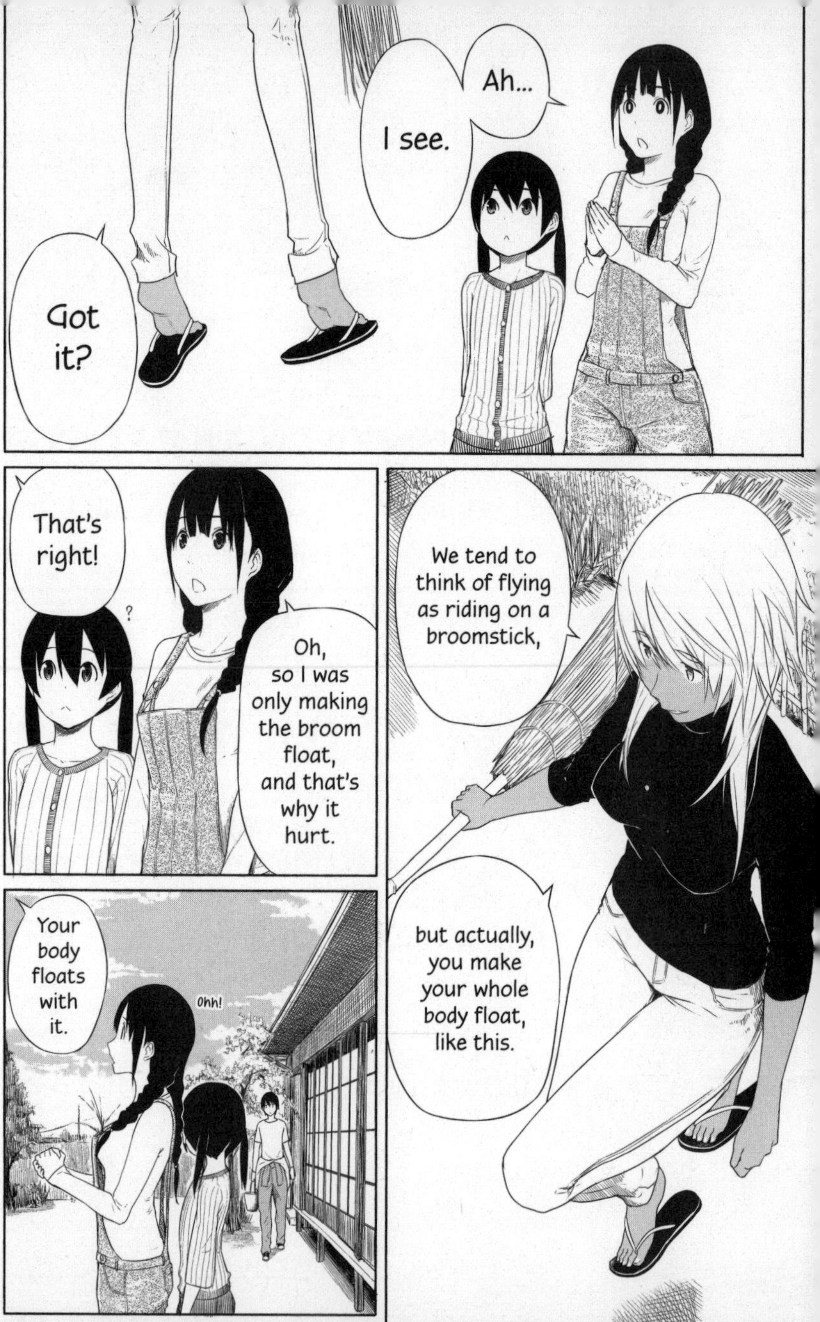

Ah...
I see.
Got it?
We tend to think of flying as riding on a broomstick,
but actually, you make your whole body float, like this.
Oh, so I was only making the broom float, and that's why it hurt.
?
That's right!
Your body floats with it.
Ohh!

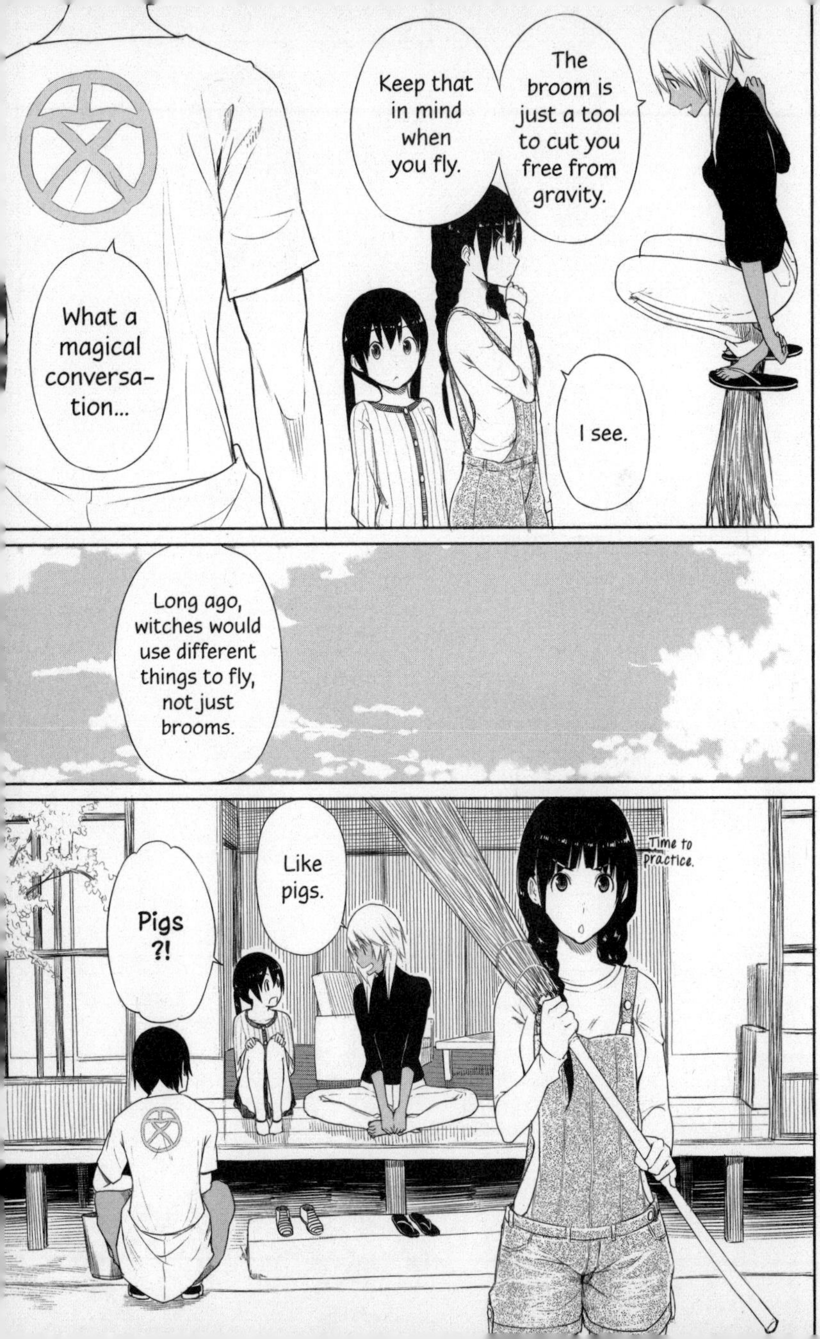
The broom is just a tool to cut you free from gravity.
Keep that in mind when you fly.
I see.
What a magical conversa-tion...
Long ago, witches would use different things to fly, not just brooms.
Time to practice.
Like pigs.
Pigs?!

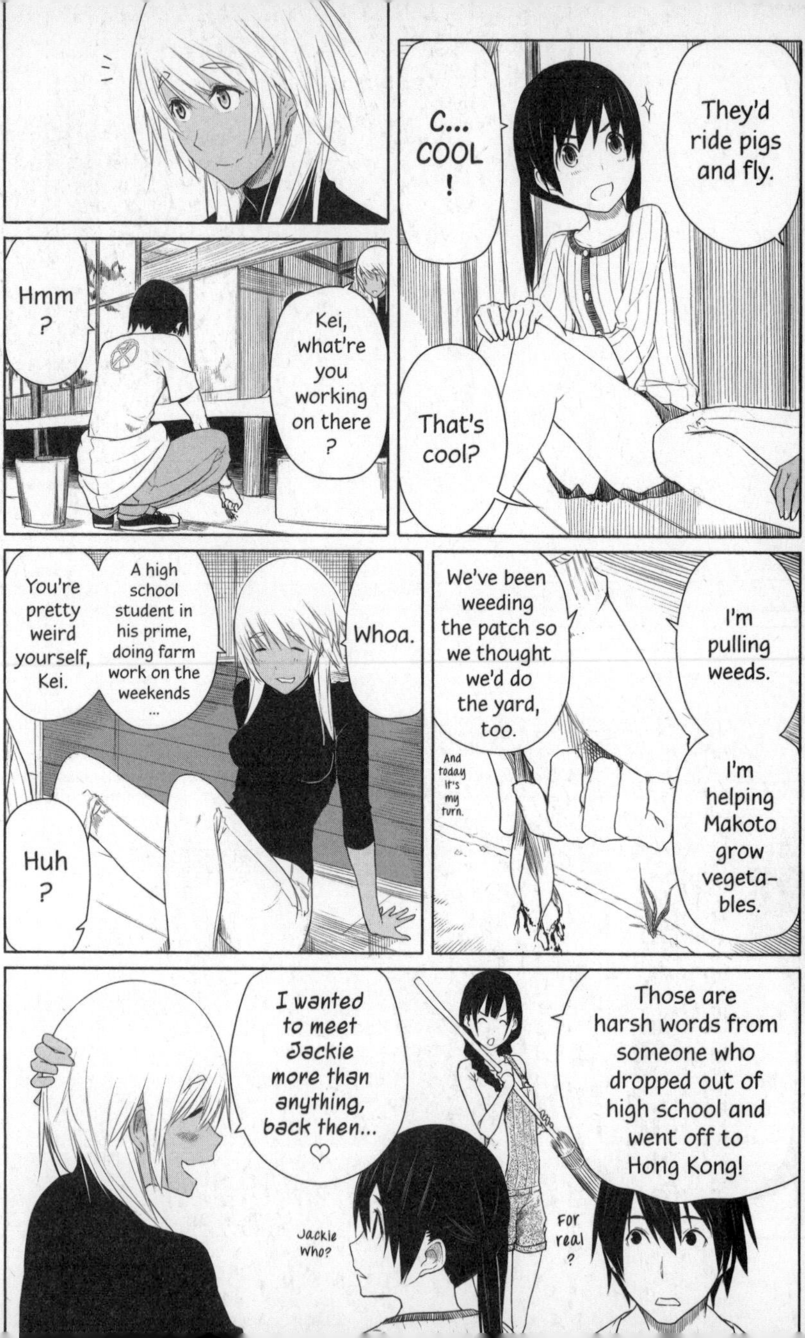
They'd ride pigs and fly.
C... COOL!
That's cool?
Kei, what're you working on there?
Hmm?
I'm pulling weeds.
I'm helping Makoto grow vegeta-bles.
We've been weeding the patch so we thought we'd do the yard, too.
And today it's my turn.
Whoa.
A high school student in his prime, doing farm work on the weekends...
You're pretty weird yourself, Kei.
Huh?
Those are harsh words from someone who dropped out of high school and went off to Hong Kong!
For real?
I wanted to meet Jackie more than anything, back then... ♡
Jackie who?

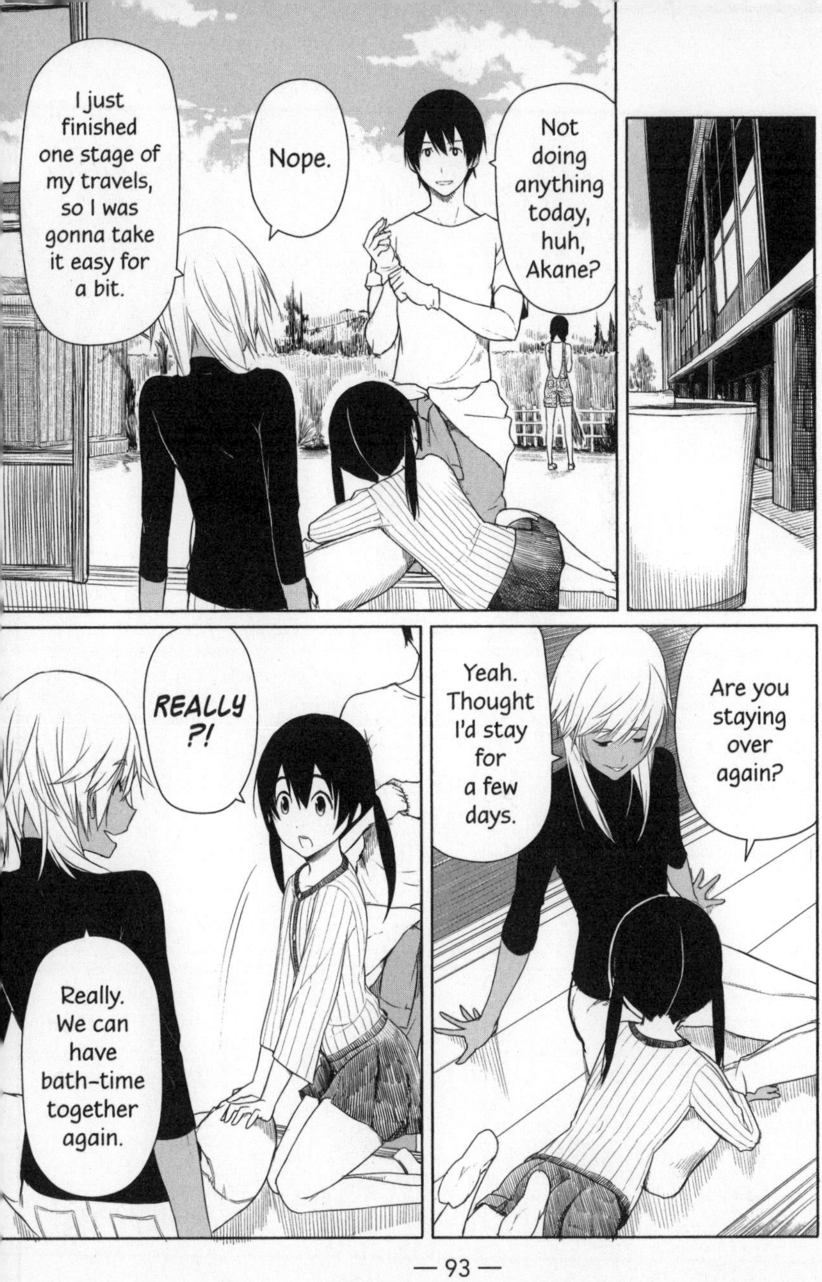
Not doing anything today, huh, Akane?
Nope.
I just finished one stage of my travels, so I was gonna take it easy for a bit.
Are you staying over again?
Yeah. Thought I'd stay for a few days.
REALLY?!
Really. We can have bath-time together again.

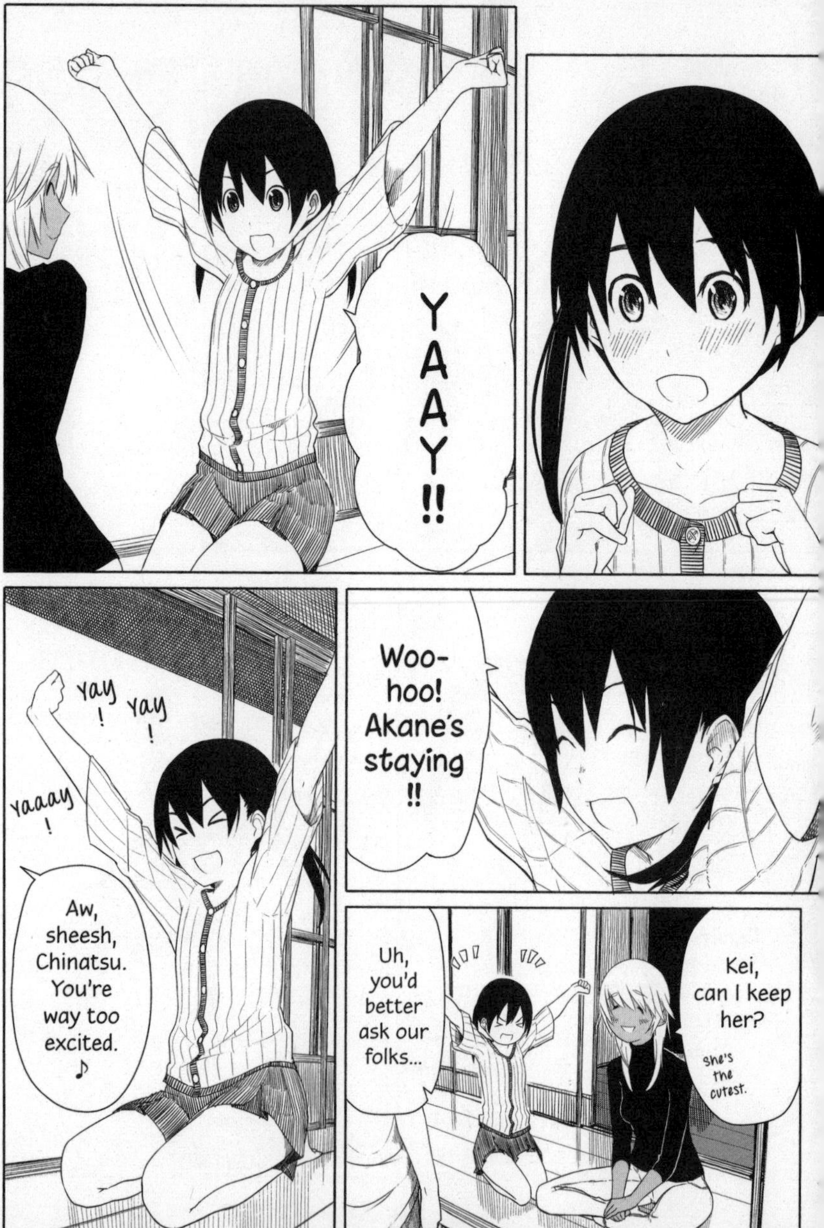
YAAY!!
Woo-hoo! Akane's staying!!
Kei, can I keep her?
She's the cutest.
Uh, you'd better ask our folks...
Yay!
Yay!
Yaaay!
Aw, sheesh, Chinatsu. You're way too excited. ♪

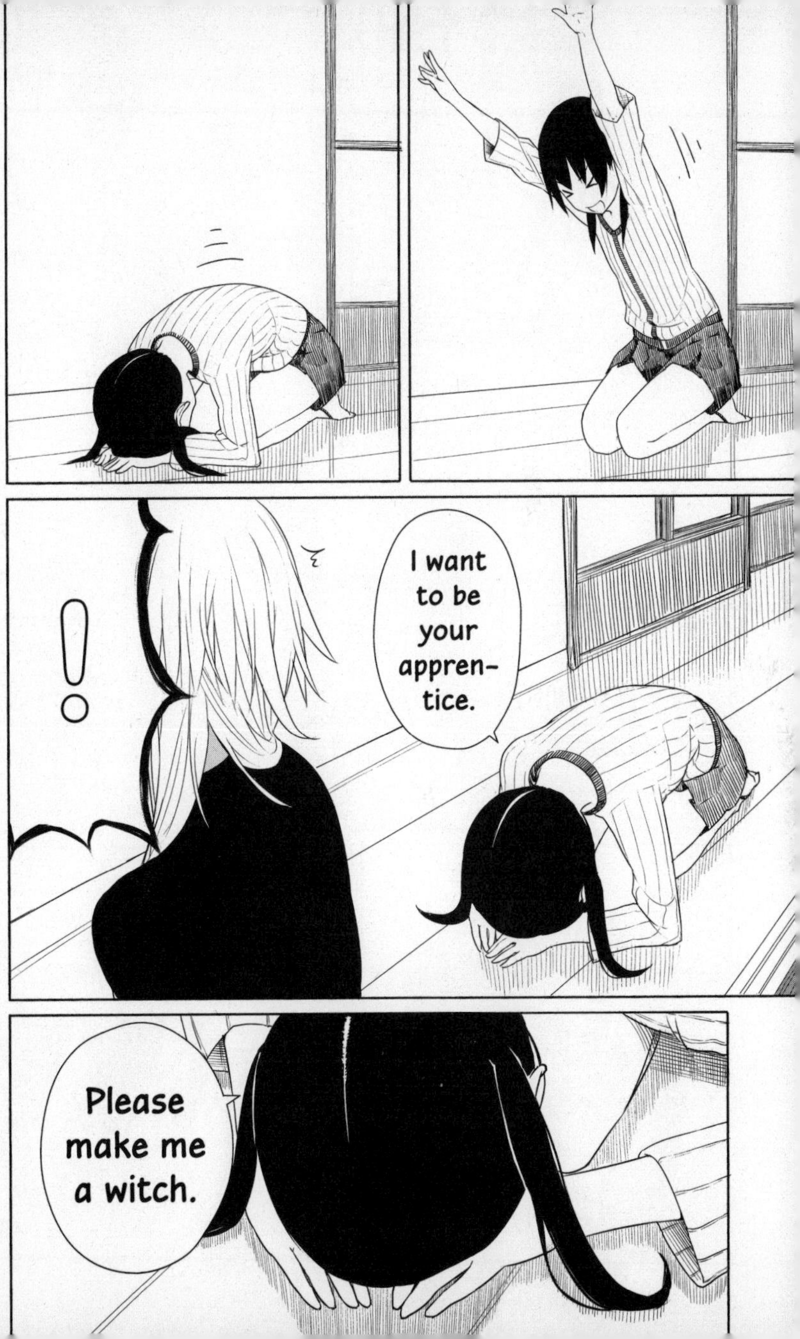
I want to be your apprentice.
!
Please make me a witch.

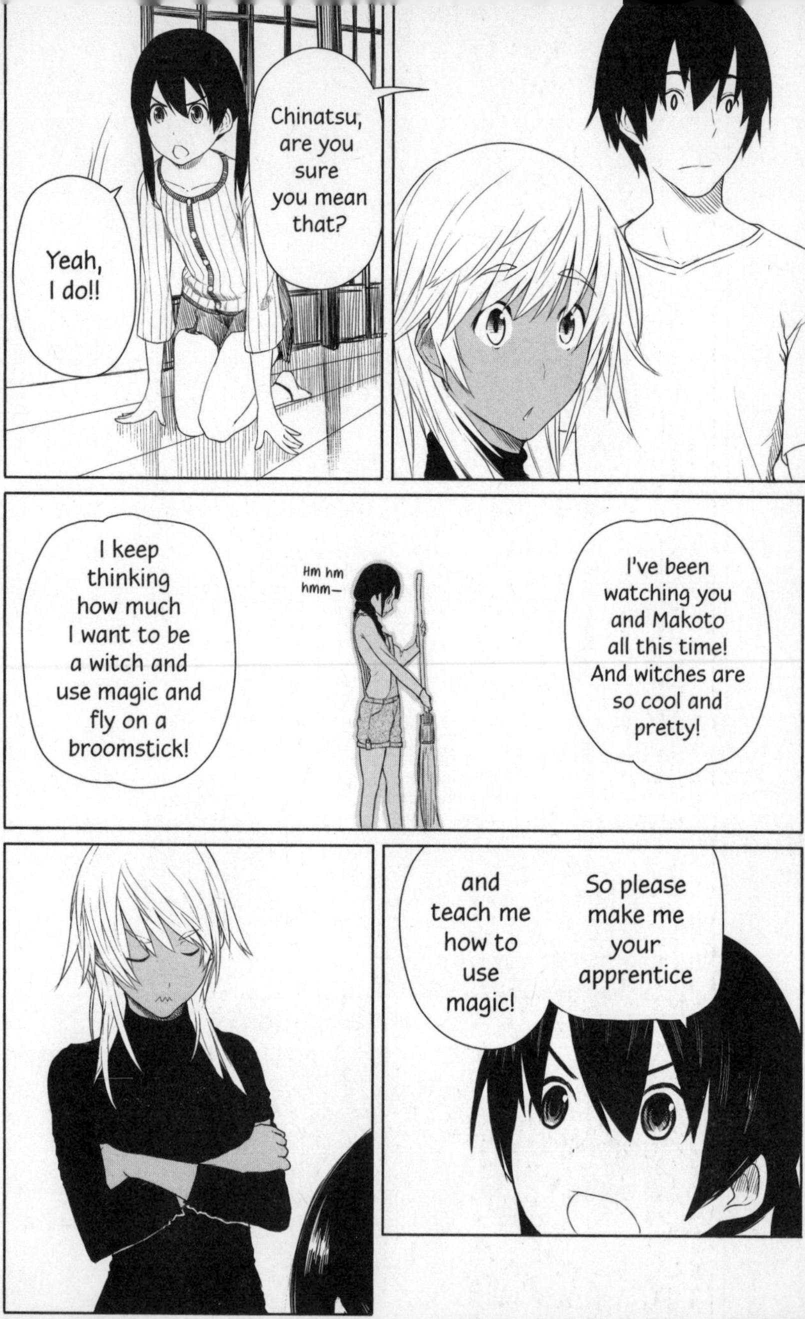
Chinatsu, are you sure you mean that?
Yeah, I do!!
I've been watching you and Makoto all this time! And witches are so cool and pretty!
Hm hm hmm–
I keep thinking how much I want to be a witch and use magic and fly on a broomstick!
So please make me your apprentice
and teach me how to use magic!

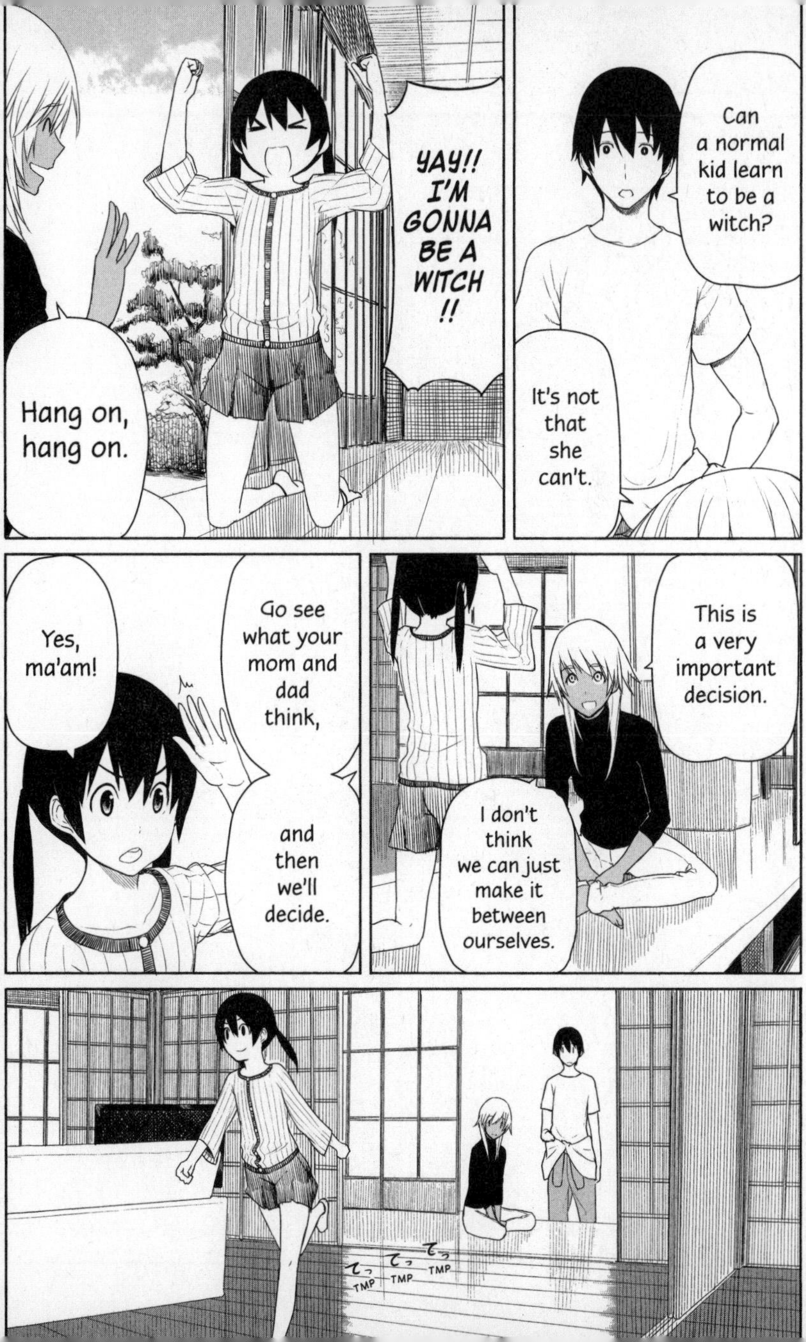
Can a normal kid learn to be a witch?
It's not that she can't.
YAY!! I'M GONNA BE A WITCH !!
Hang on, hang on.
This is a very important decision.
I don't think we can just make it between ourselves.
Go see what your mom and dad think,
and then we'll decide.
Yes, ma'am!
てっ TMP
てっ TMP
てっ TMP

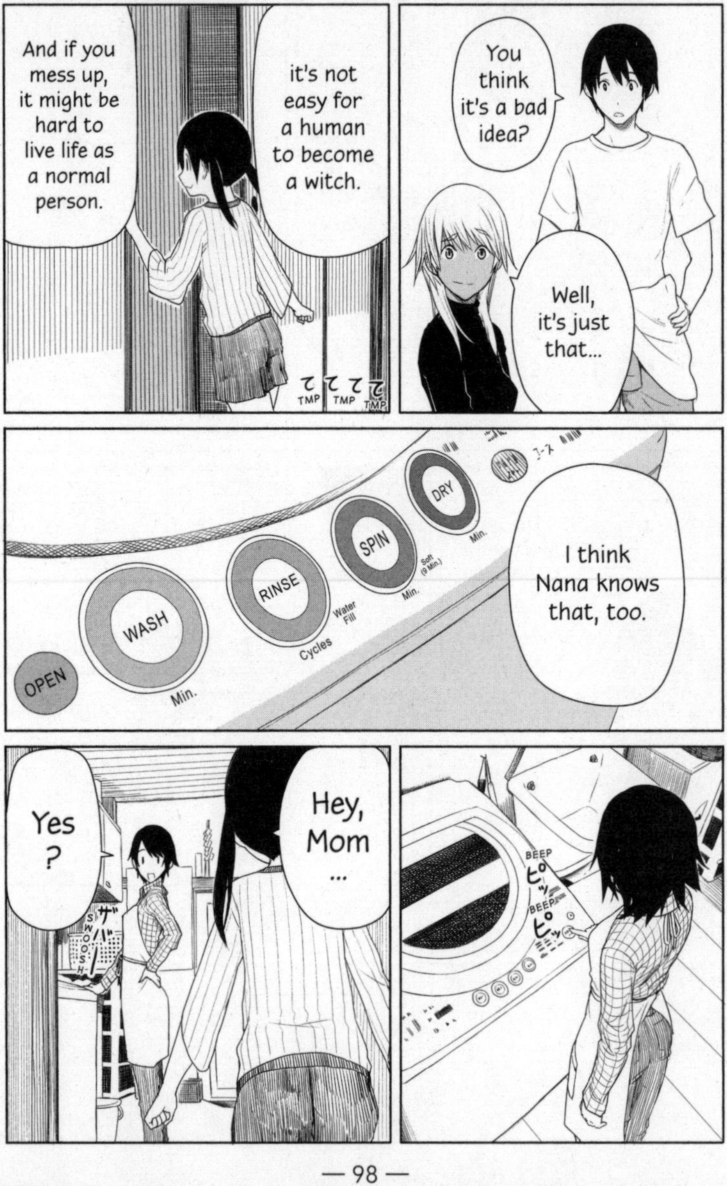
You think it's a bad idea?
Well, it's just that...
it's not easy for a human to become a witch.
And if you mess up, it might be hard to live life as a normal person.
てててて
TMP TMP TMP
I think Nana knows that, too.
DRY
Min.
SPIN
Soft (9 Min.)
Min.
RINSE
Water Fill
Cycles
WASH
Min.
OPEN
BEEP
ピッ
BEEP
ピッ
Hey, Mom ...
Yes ?
ザバー
SWOOSH

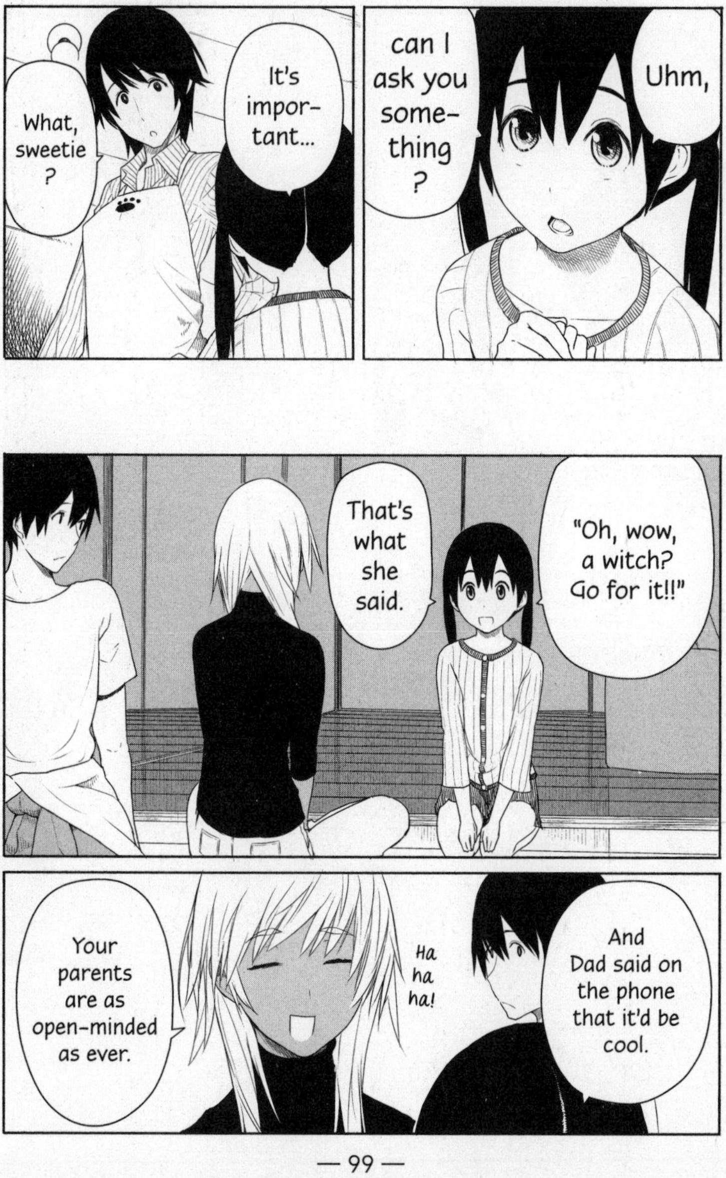
Uhm,
can I ask you some-thing?
It's impor-tant...
What, sweetie?
"Oh, wow, a witch? Go for it!!"
That's what she said.
And Dad said on the phone that it'd be cool.
Ha ha ha!
Your parents are as open-minded as ever.

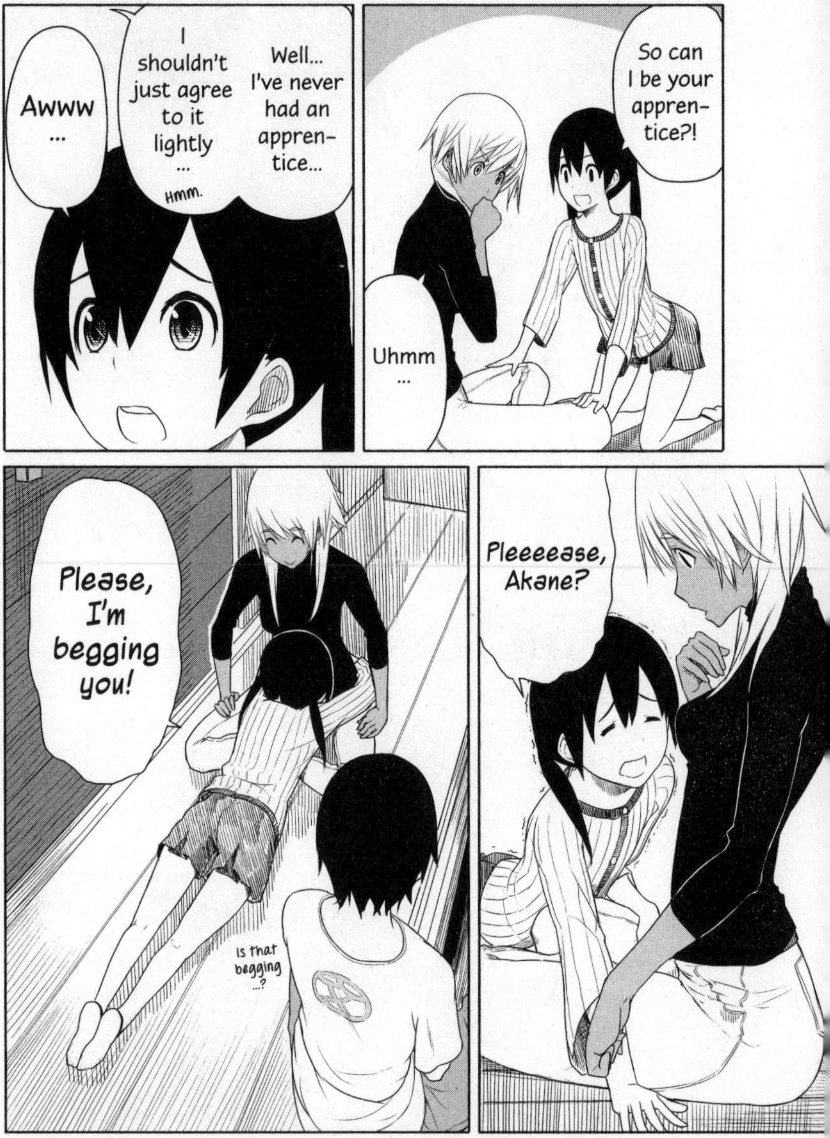
So can I be your apprentice?!
Uhmm ...
Well... I've never had an apprentice...
I shouldn't just agree to it lightly ...
Hmm.
Awww ...
Pleeeease, Akane?
Please, I'm begging you!
Is that begging ...?

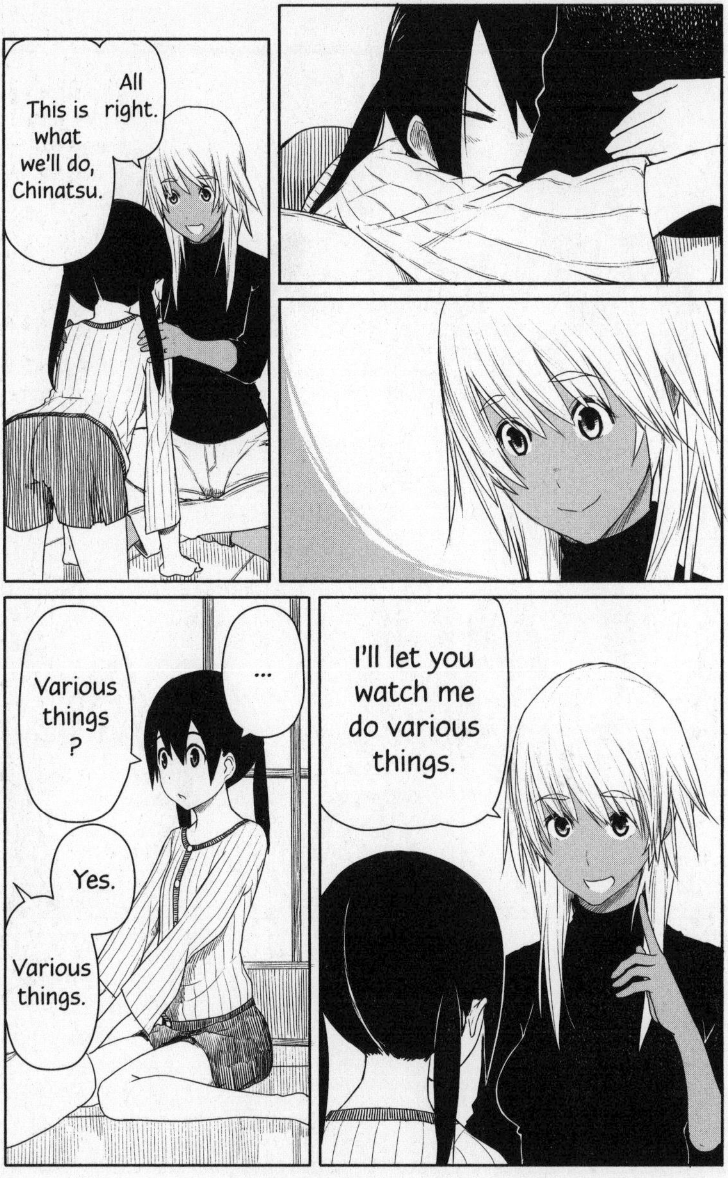
All right. This is what we'll do, Chinatsu.
I'll let you watch me do various things.
...
Various things?
Yes.
Various things.

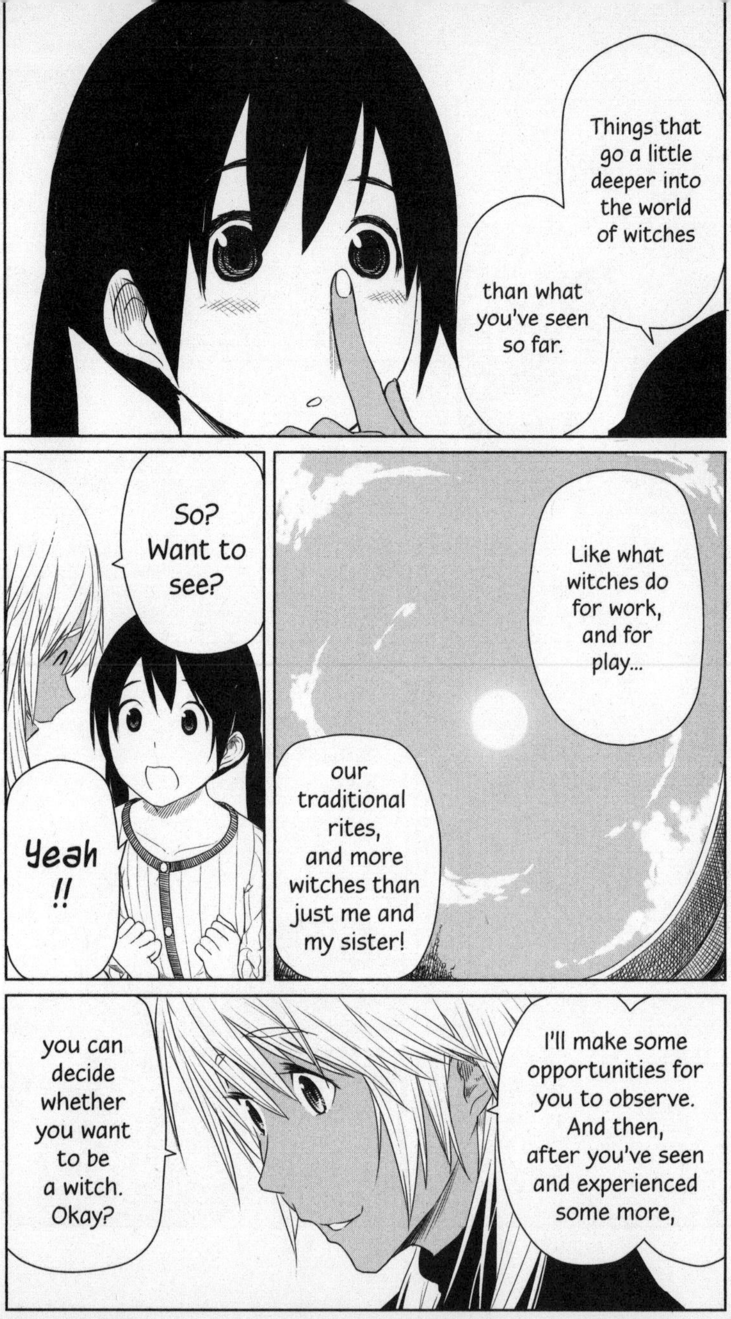
Things that go a little deeper into the world of witches
than what you've seen so far.
Like what witches do for work, and for play...
our traditional rites, and more witches than just me and my sister!
So? Want to see?
Yeah !!
I'll make some opportunities for you to observe. And then, after you've seen and experienced some more,
you can decide whether you want to be a witch. Okay?

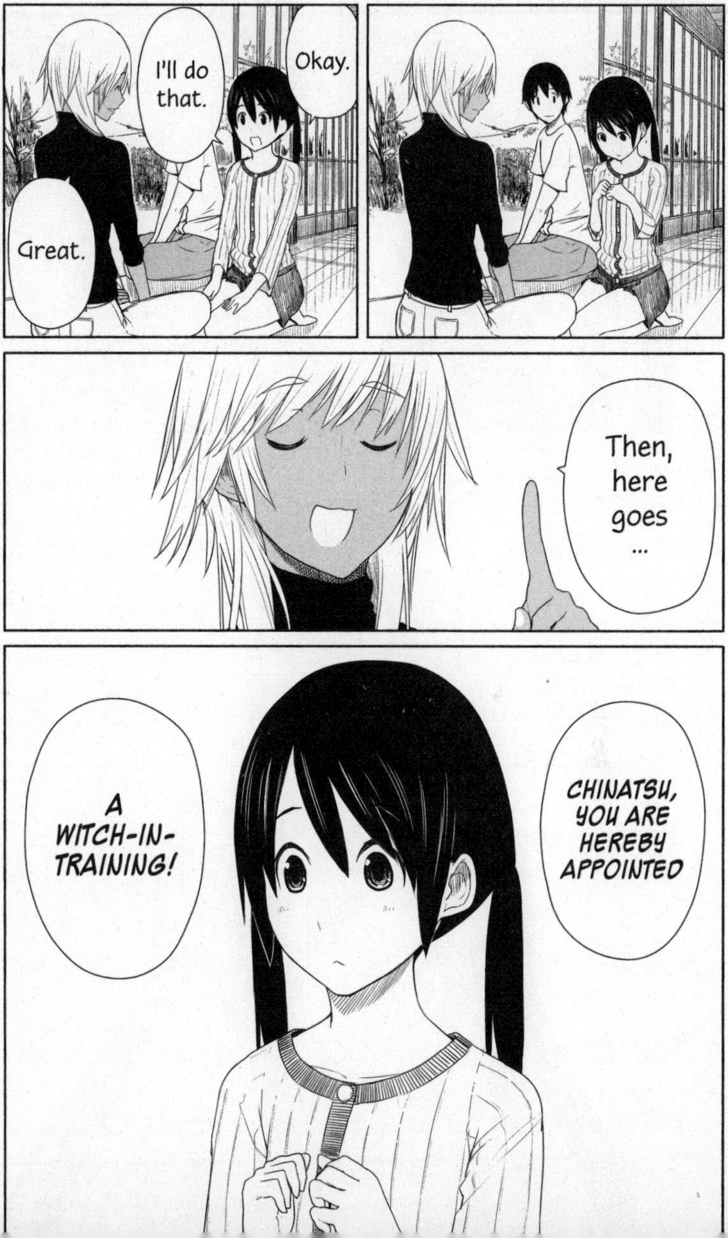
Okay.
I'll do that.
Great.
Then, here goes ...
CHINATSU, YOU ARE HEREBY APPOINTED
A WITCH-IN-TRAINING!

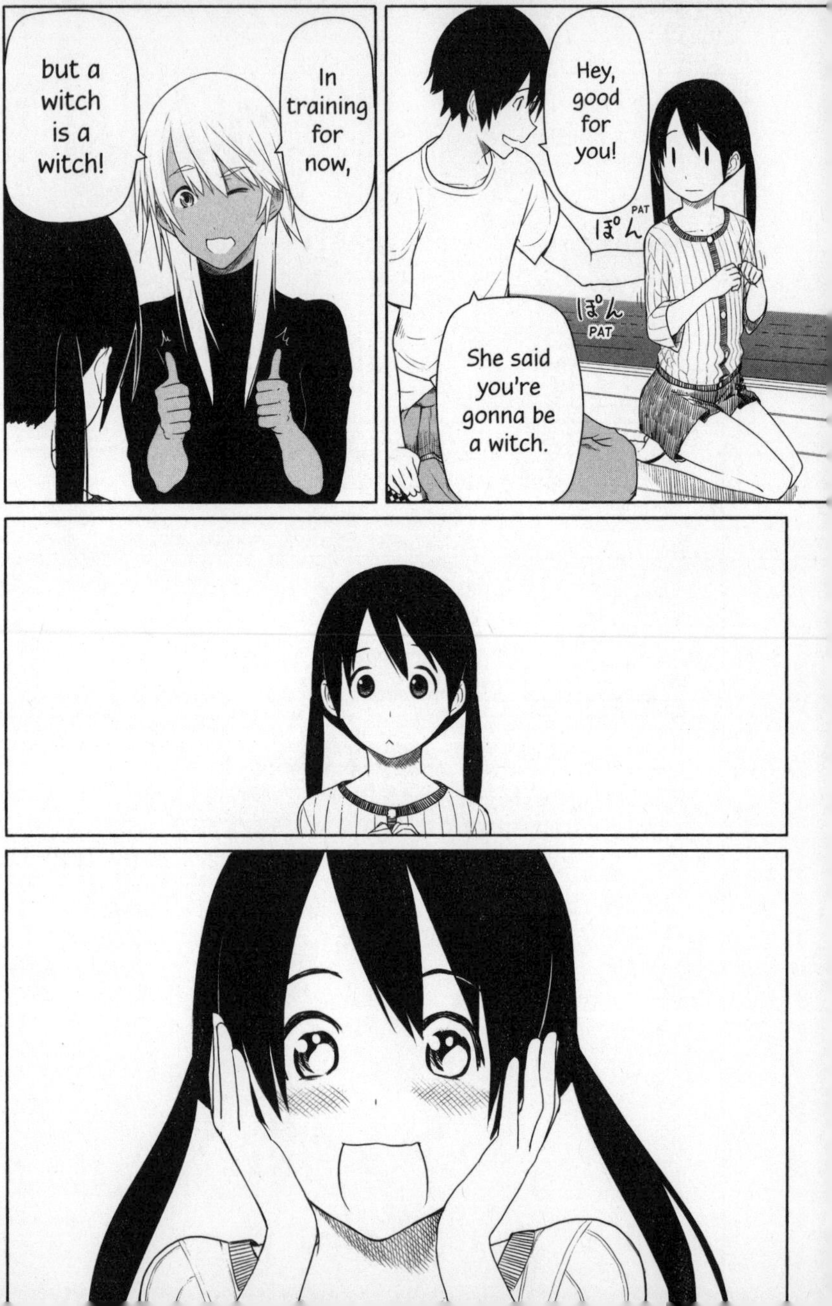
Hey, good for you!
ぽん PAT
ぽん PAT
She said you're gonna be a witch.
In training for now,
but a witch is a witch!

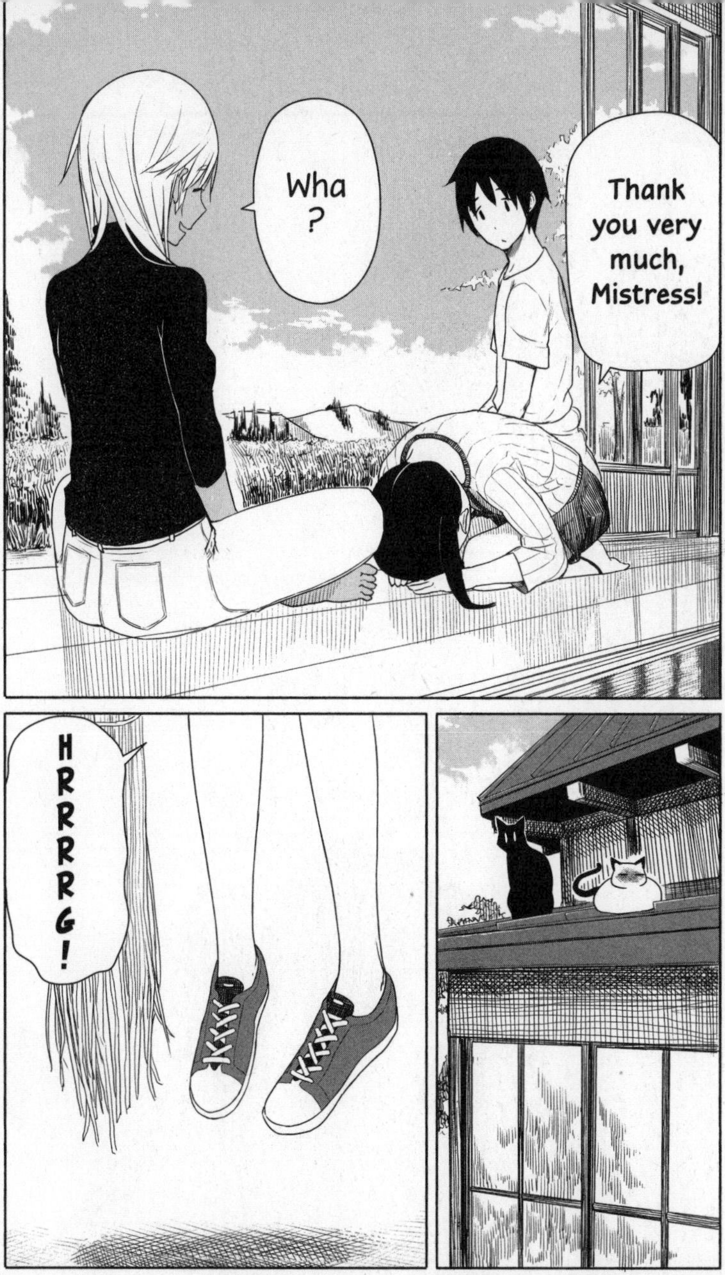
Thank you very much, Mistress!
Wha ?
HRRRRG!

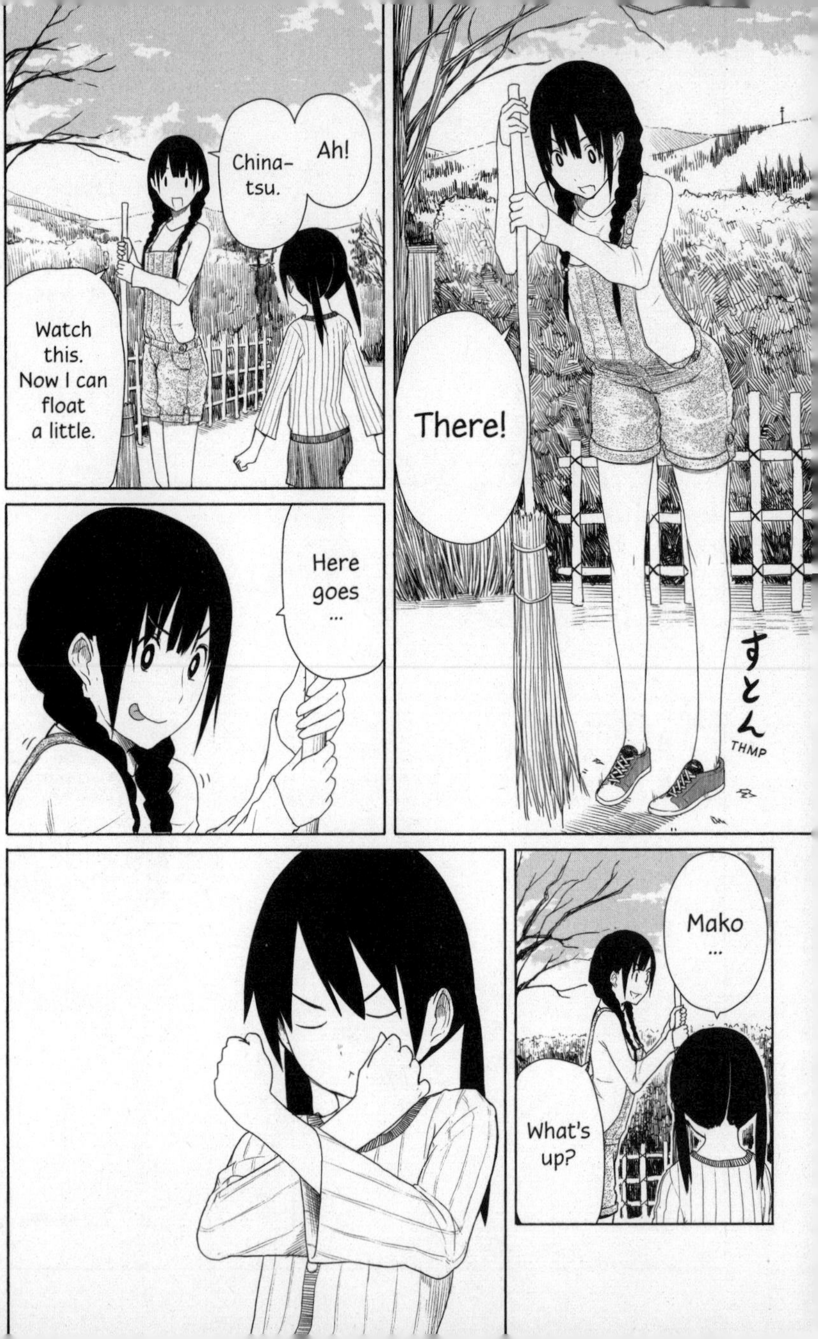
Ah!
China-tsu.
Watch this. Now I can float a little.
Here goes ...
There!
すとん
THMP
Mako ...
What's up?

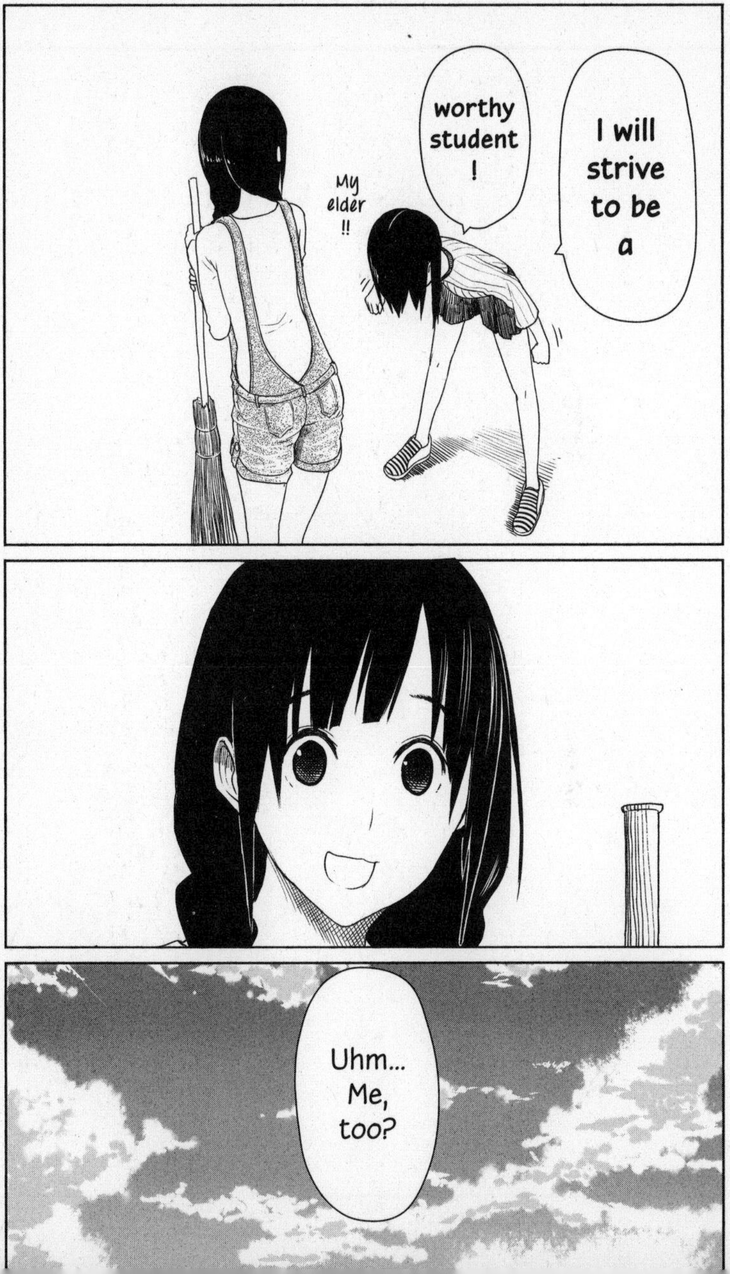
I will strive to be a
worthy student !
My elder !!
Uhm... Me, too?

Chapter 11
Uncanny Candy

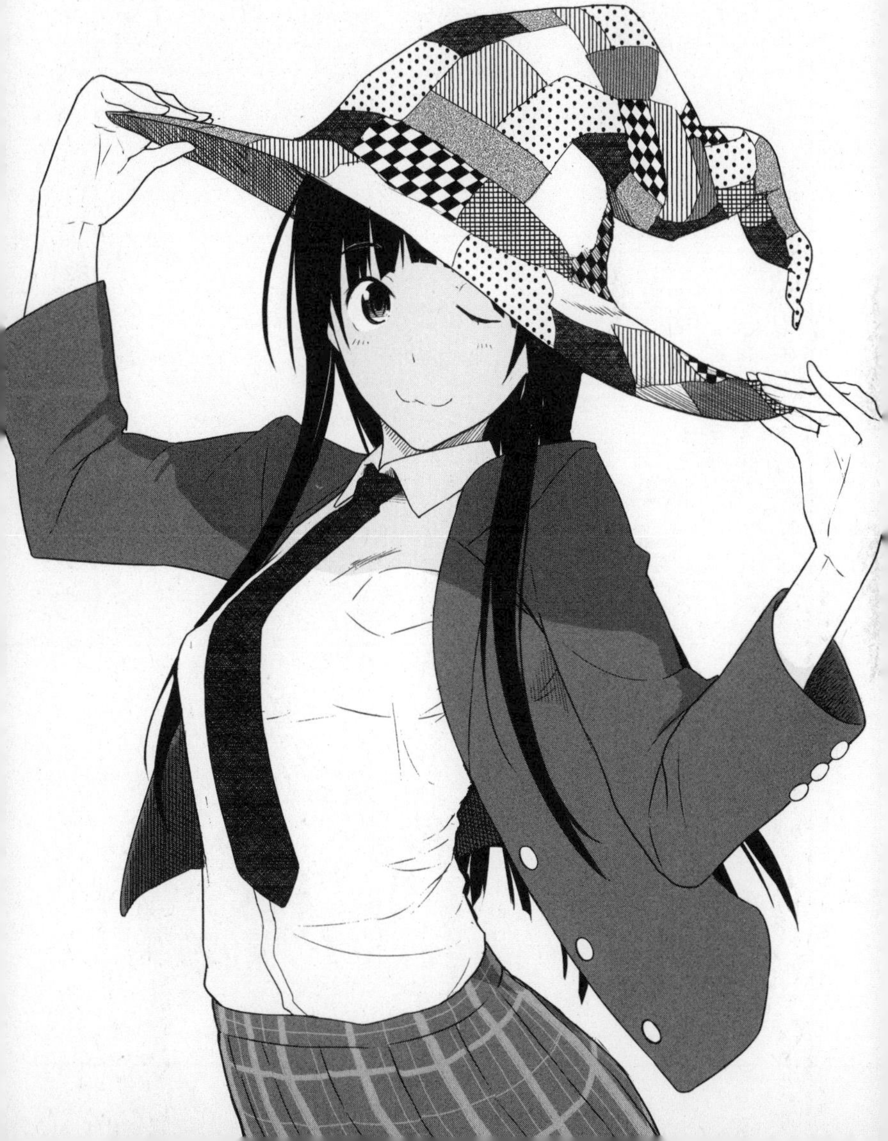

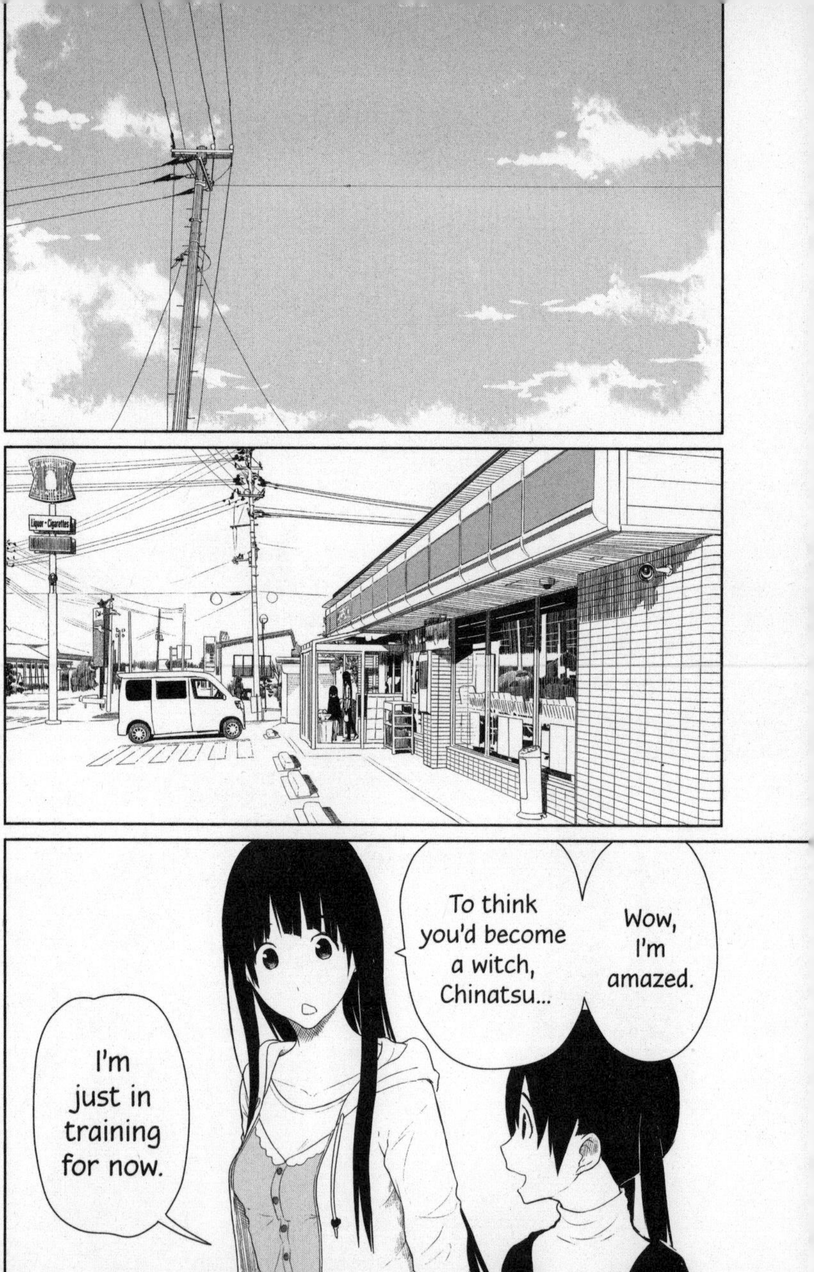
Liquor • Cigarettes
Wow, I'm amazed.
To think you'd become a witch, Chinatsu...
I'm just in training for now.

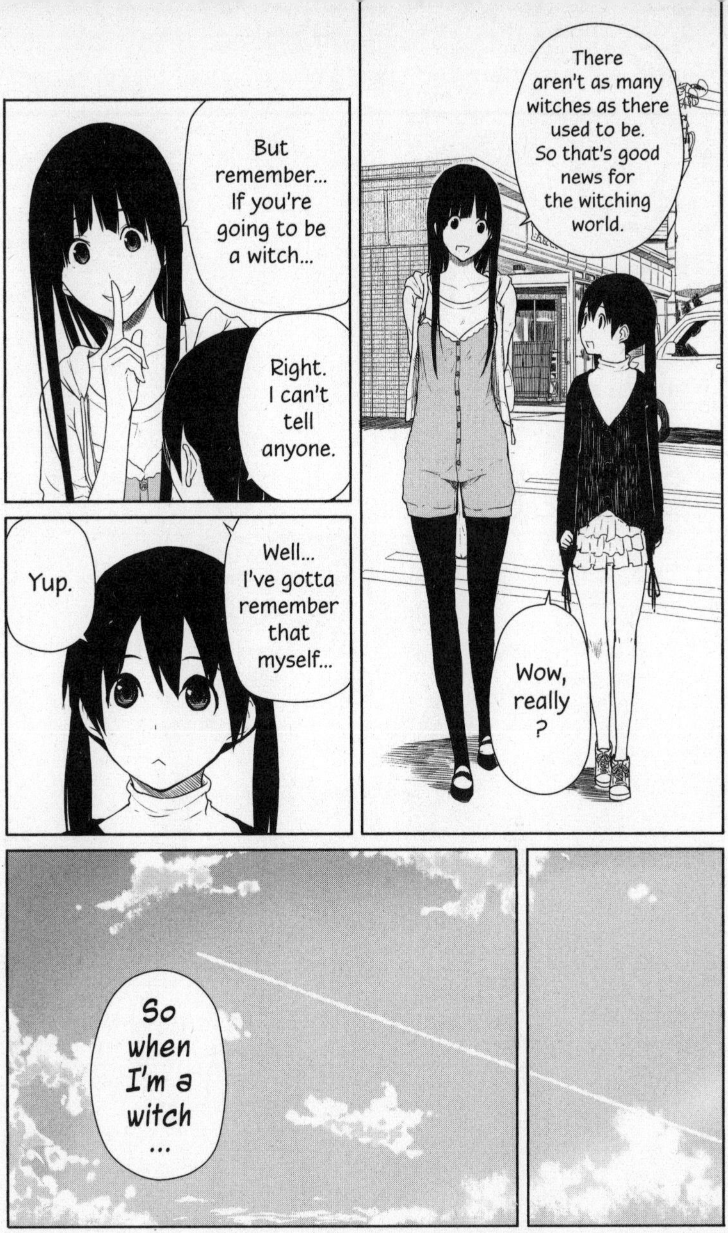
There aren't as many witches as there used to be. So that's good news for the witching world.
Wow, really ?
But remember... If you're going to be a witch...
Right. I can't tell anyone.
Well... I've gotta remember that myself...
Yup.
So when I'm a witch ...

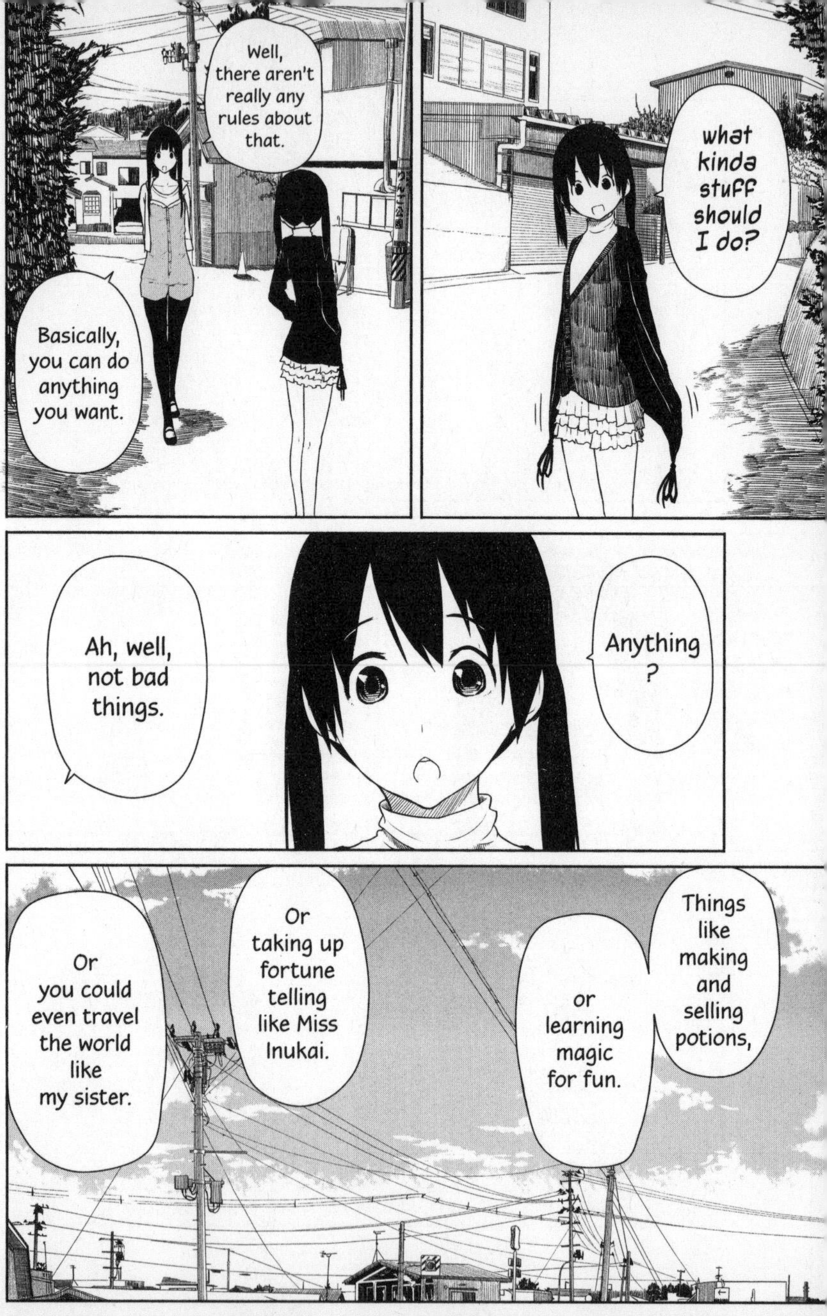
what kinda stuff should I do?
Well, there aren't really any rules about that.
Basically, you can do anything you want.
Anything?
Ah, well, not bad things.
Things like making and selling potions,
or learning magic for fun.
Or taking up fortune telling like Miss Inukai.
Or you could even travel the world like my sister.

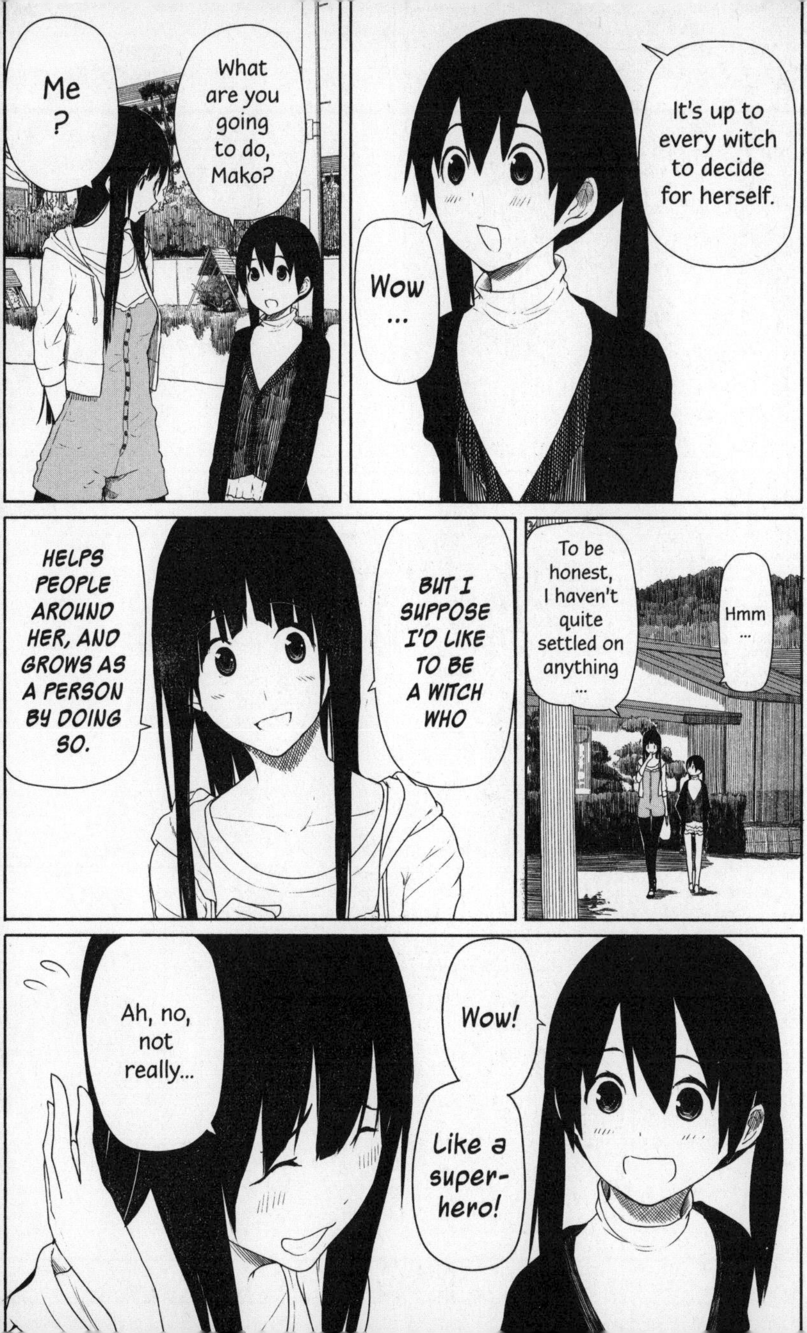
It's up to every witch to decide for herself.
Wow ...
What are you going to do, Mako?
Me ?
Hmm ...
To be honest, I haven't quite settled on anything ...
BUT I SUPPOSE I'D LIKE TO BE A WITCH WHO
HELPS PEOPLE AROUND HER, AND GROWS AS A PERSON BY DOING SO.
Wow!
Like a super-hero!
Ah, no, not really...

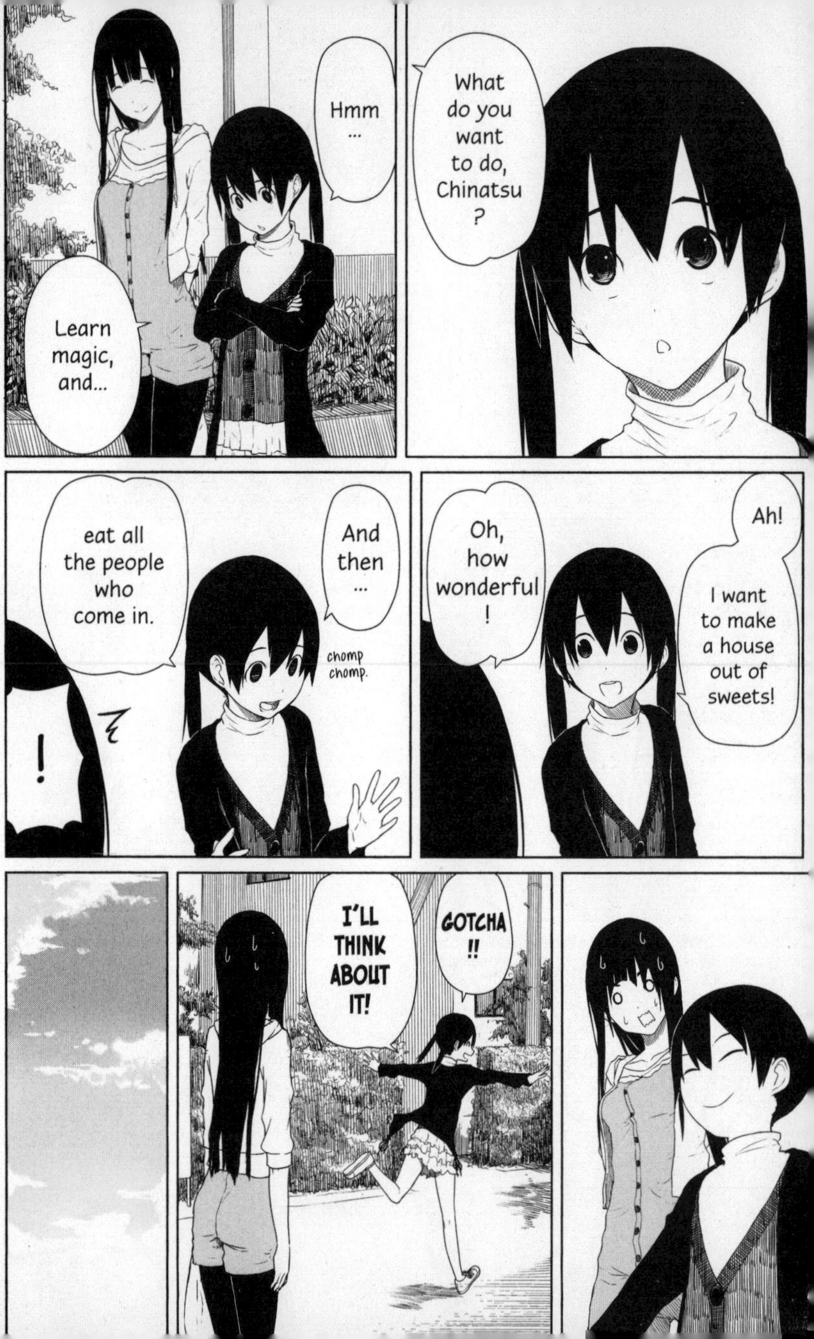
What do you want to do, Chinatsu?
Hmm ...
Learn magic, and...
Ah!
I want to make a house out of sweets!
Oh, how wonderful!
And then ...
chomp chomp.
eat all the people who come in.
GOTCHA!!
I'LL THINK ABOUT IT!

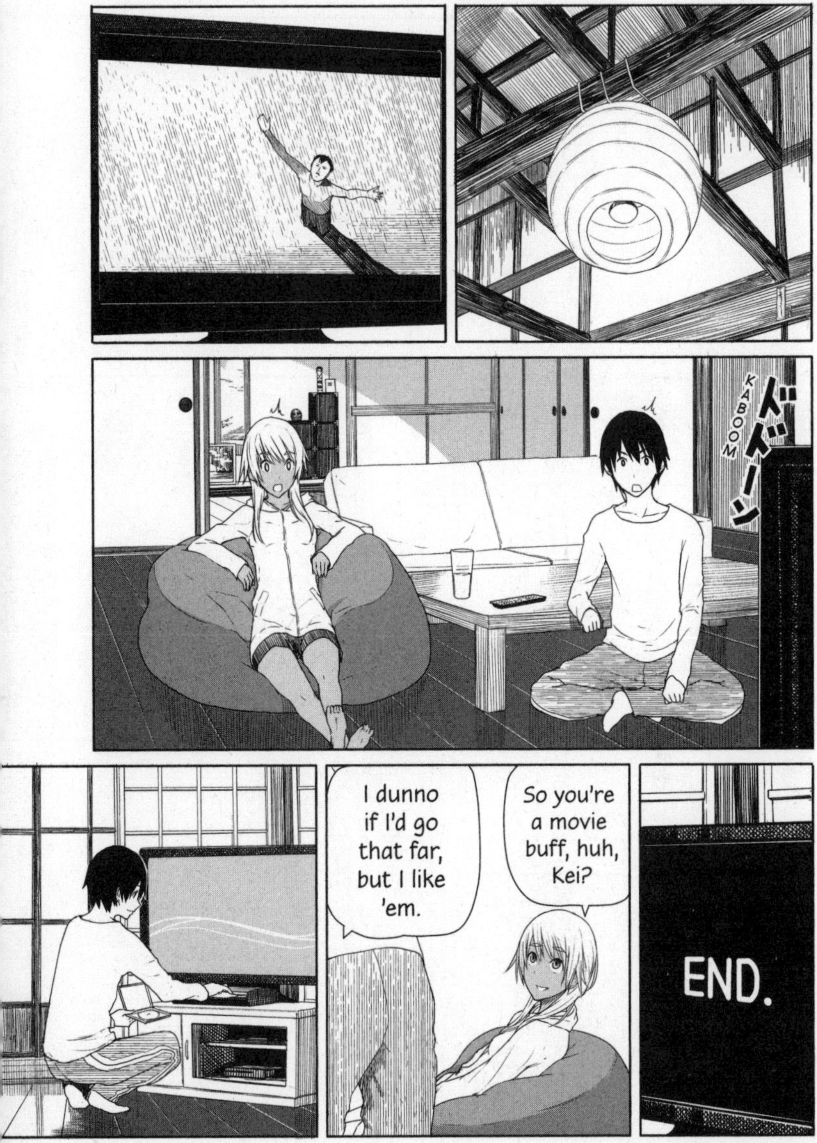
ドドーン
KABOOM
END.
So you're a movie buff, huh, Kei?
I dunno if I'd go that far, but I like 'em.

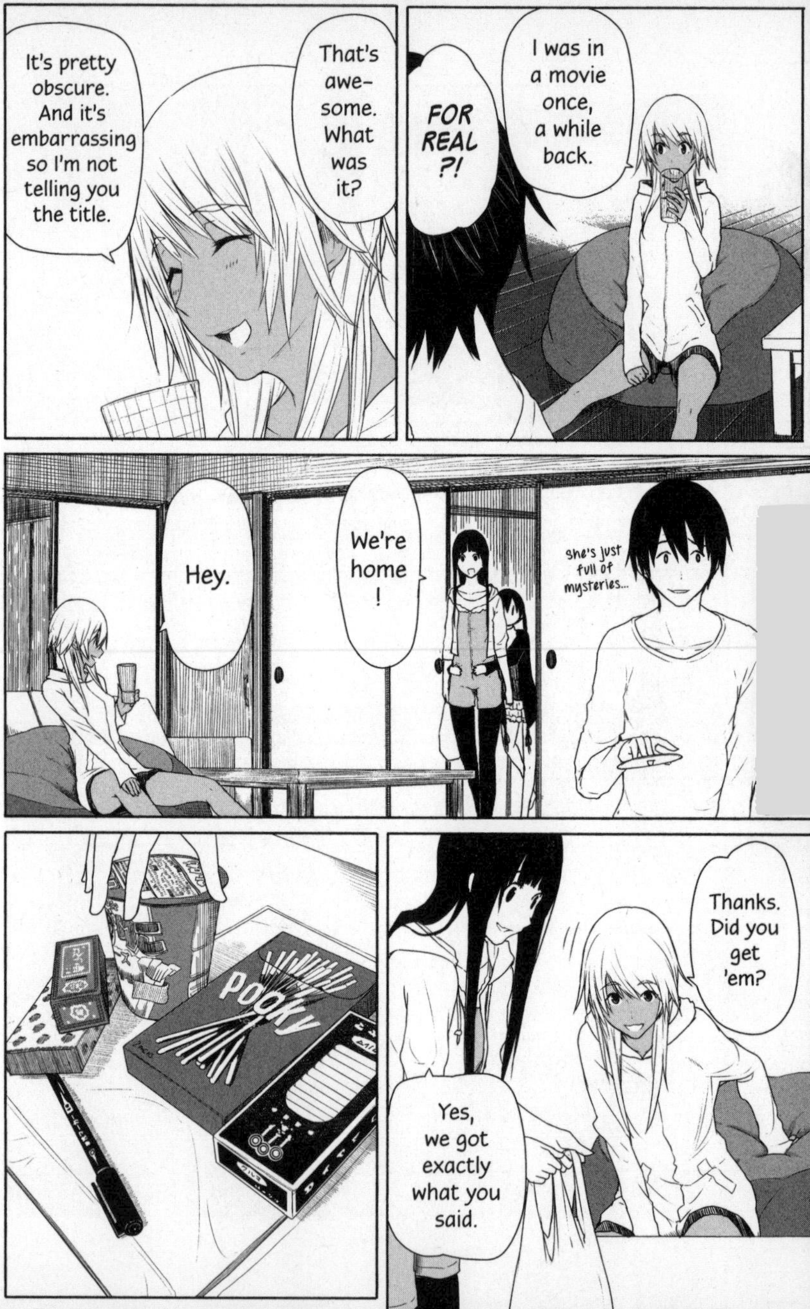
I was in a movie once, a while back.
FOR REAL?!
That's awe-some. What was it?
It's pretty obscure. And it's embarrassing so I'm not telling you the title.
she's just full of mysteries...
We're home!
Hey.
Thanks. Did you get 'em?
Yes, we got exactly what you said.
POOKY

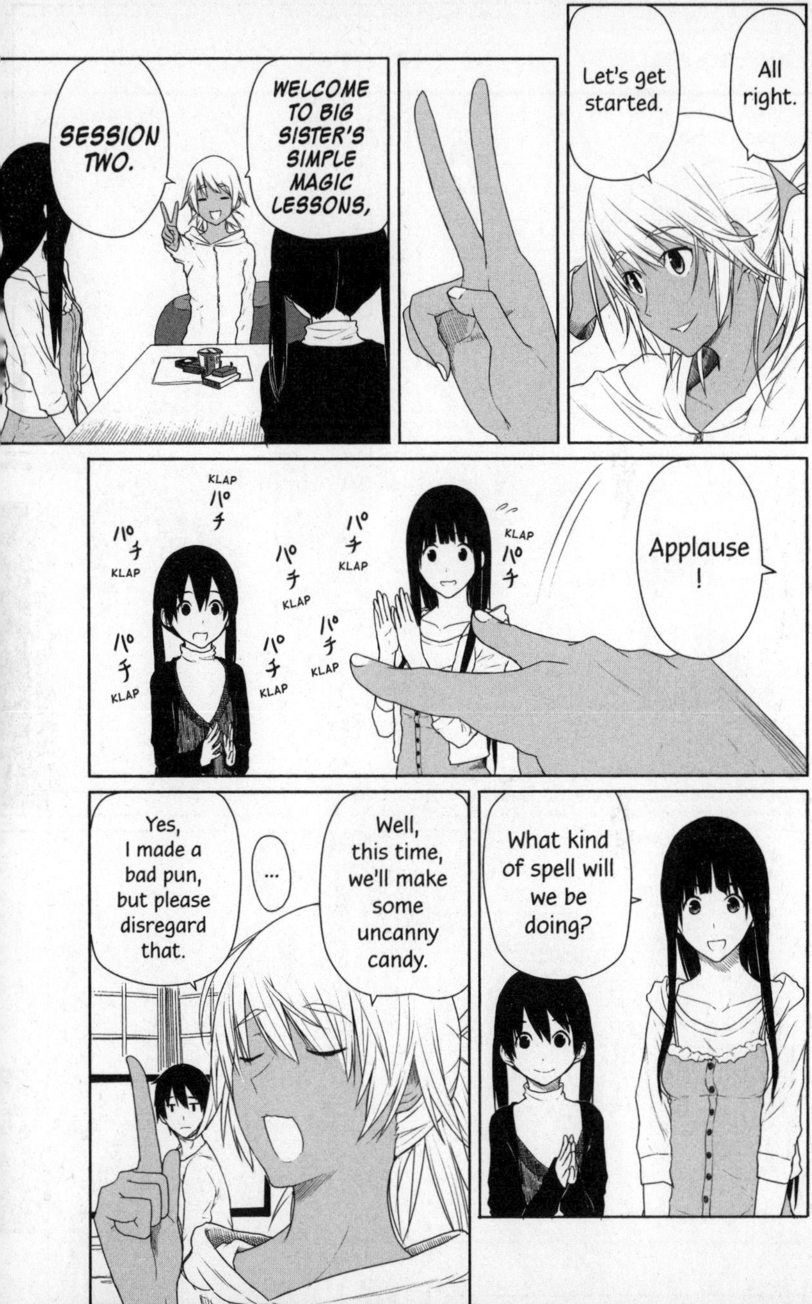
All right.
Let's get started.
WELCOME TO BIG SISTER'S SIMPLE MAGIC LESSONS,
SESSION TWO.
Applause!
KLAP パチ
パチ KLAP
パチ KLAP
パチ KLAP
KLAP パチ
パチ KLAP
パチ KLAP
パチ KLAP
What kind of spell will we be doing?
Well, this time, we'll make some uncanny candy.
...
Yes, I made a bad pun, but please disregard that.

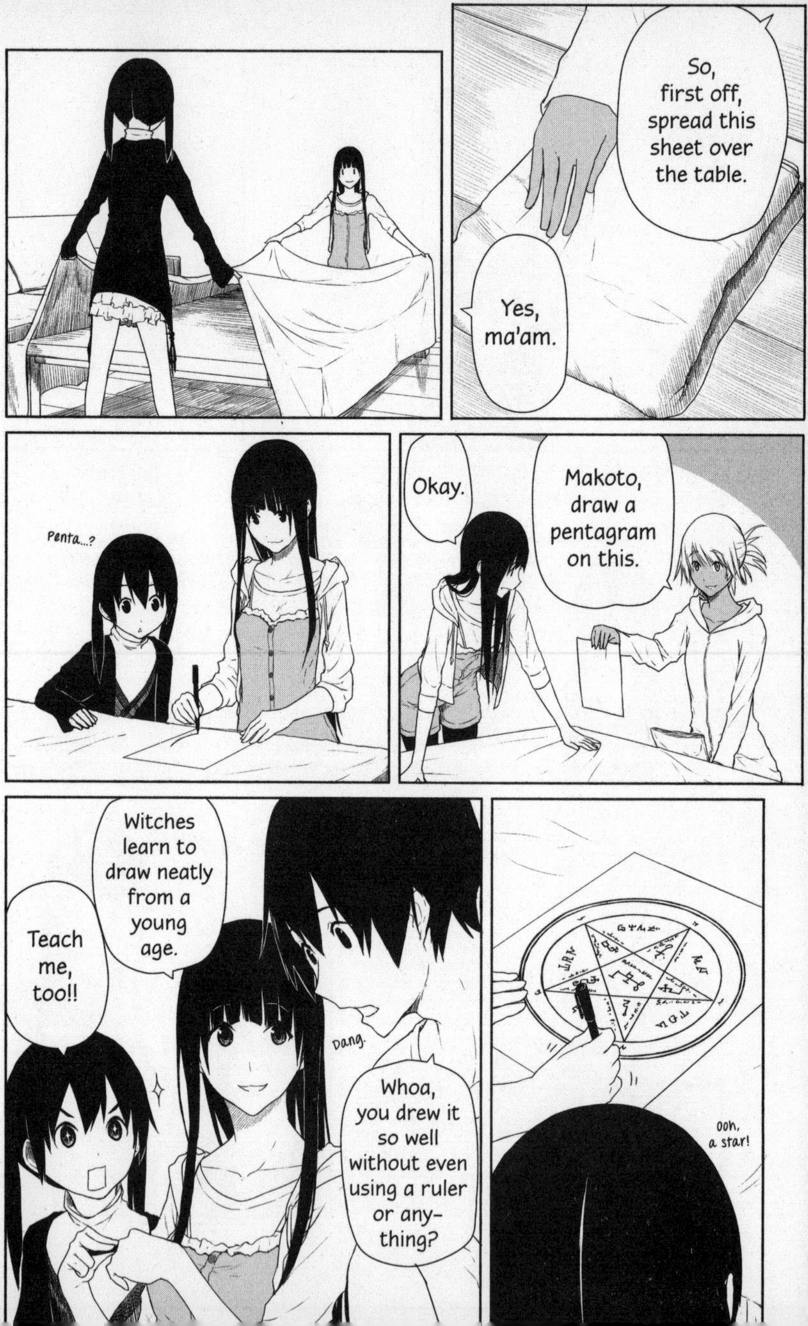
So, first off, spread this sheet over the table.
Yes, ma'am.
Makoto, draw a pentagram on this.
Okay.
Penta...?
Ooh, a star!
Whoa, you drew it so well without even using a ruler or any-thing?
Dang.
Witches learn to draw neatly from a young age.
Teach me, too!!

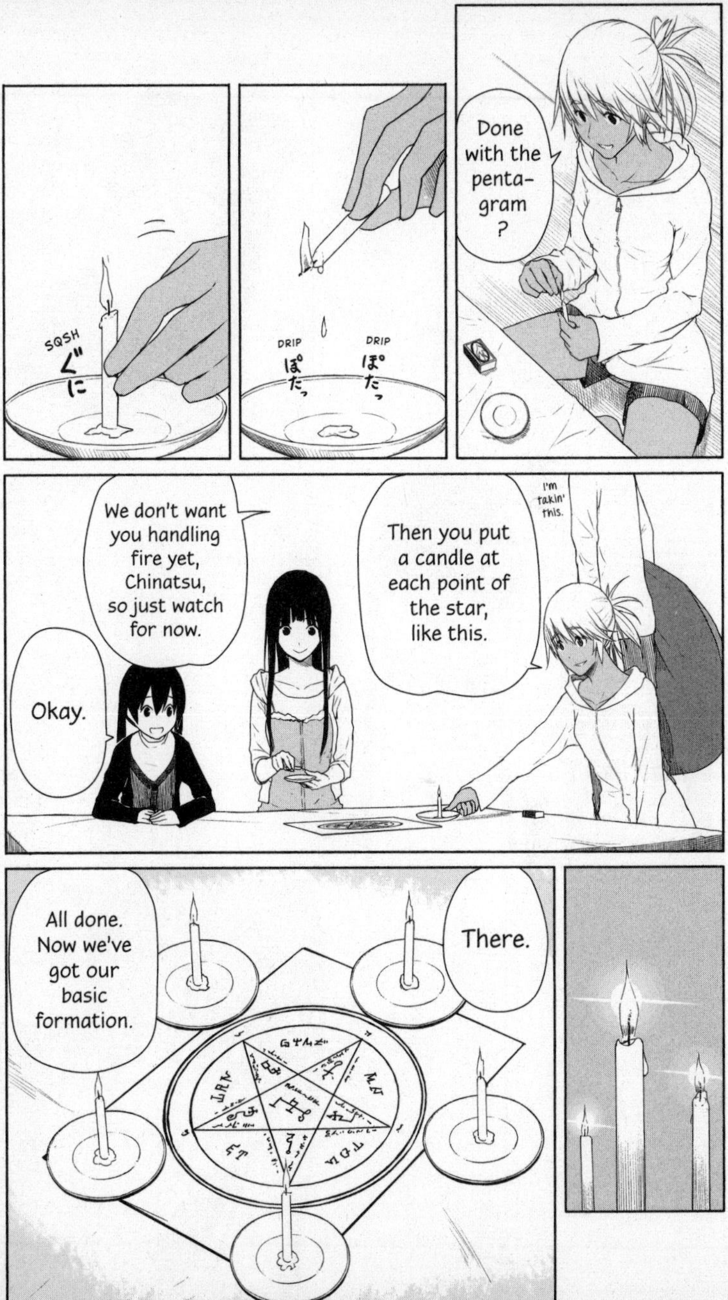

Done with the penta-gram?
DRIP
ぽたっ
DRIP
ぽたっ
SQSH
ぐに
I'm takin' this.
Then you put a candle at each point of the star, like this.
We don't want you handling fire yet, Chinatsu, so just watch for now.
Okay.
There.
All done. Now we've got our basic formation.

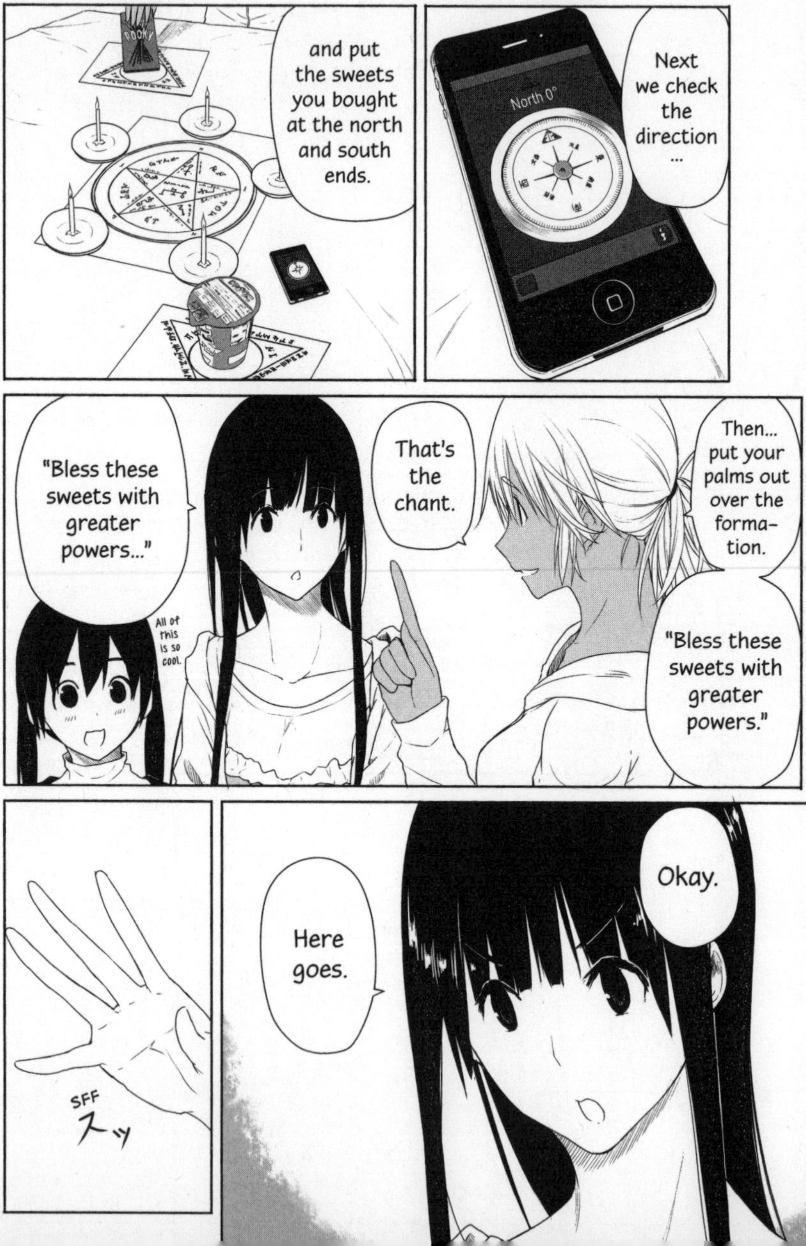
Next we check the direction ...
North 0°
and put the sweets you bought at the north and south ends.
Then... put your palms out over the formation.
"Bless these sweets with greater powers."
That's the chant.
"Bless these sweets with greater powers..."
All of this is so cool.
Okay.
Here goes.
SFF
スッ

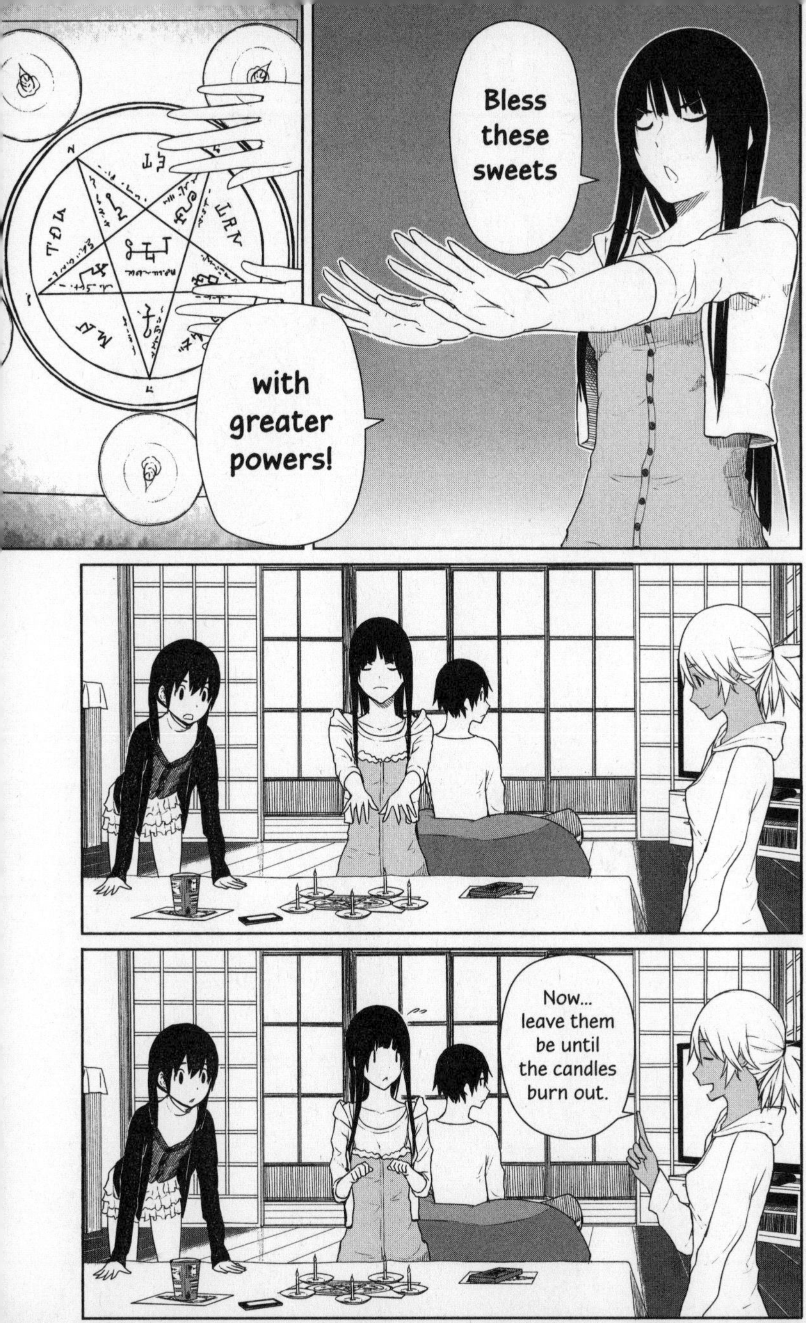
Bless these sweets
with greater powers!
Now... leave them be until the candles burn out.

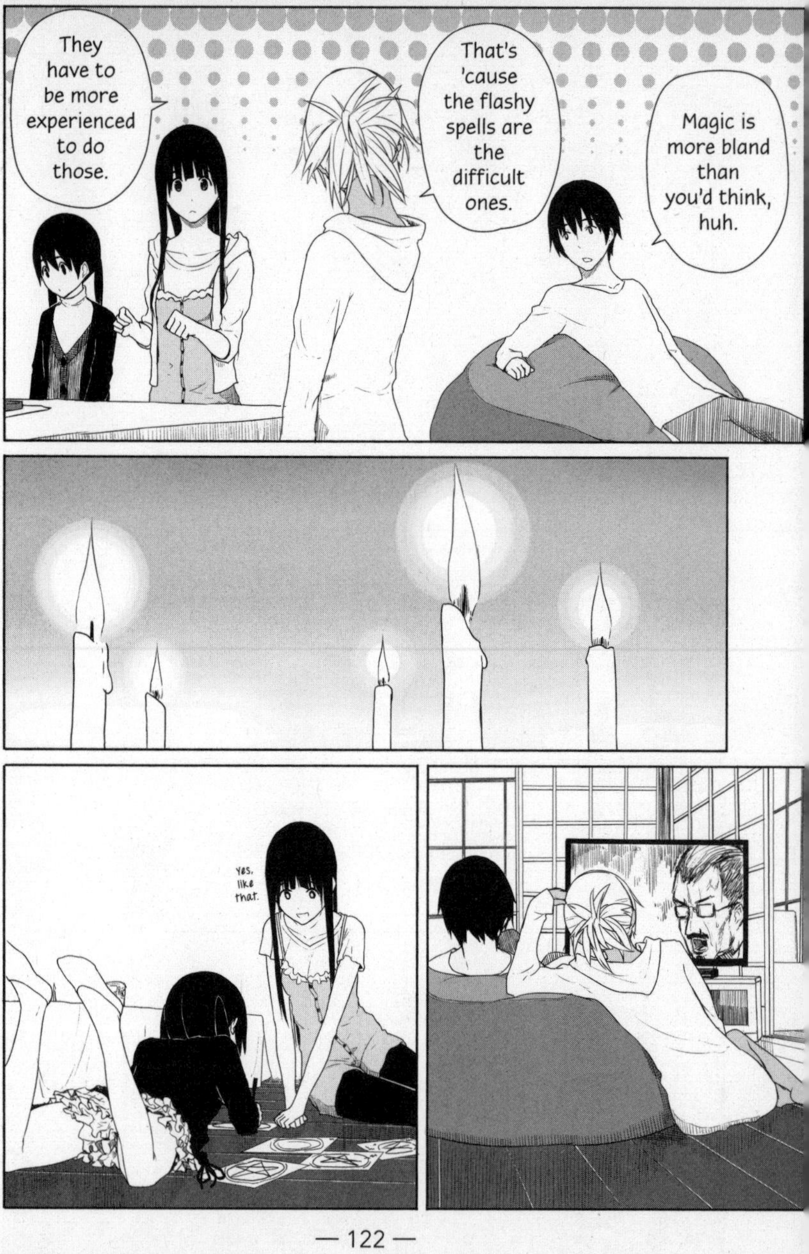
Magic is more bland than you'd think, huh.
That's 'cause the flashy spells are the difficult ones.
They have to be more experienced to do those.
Yes, like that.

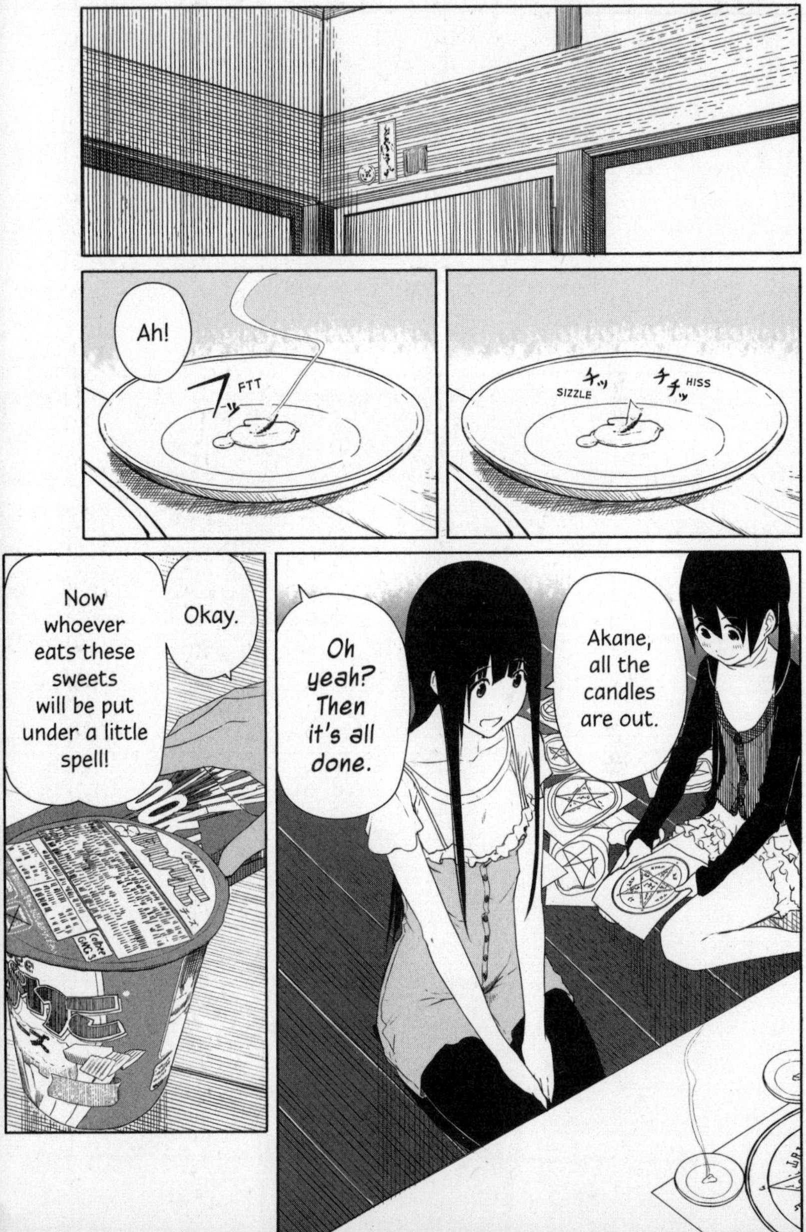

チッ SIZZLE
チチッ HISS
Ah!
FTT
Akane, all the candles are out.
Oh yeah? Then it's all done.
Okay.
Now whoever eats these sweets will be put under a little spell!

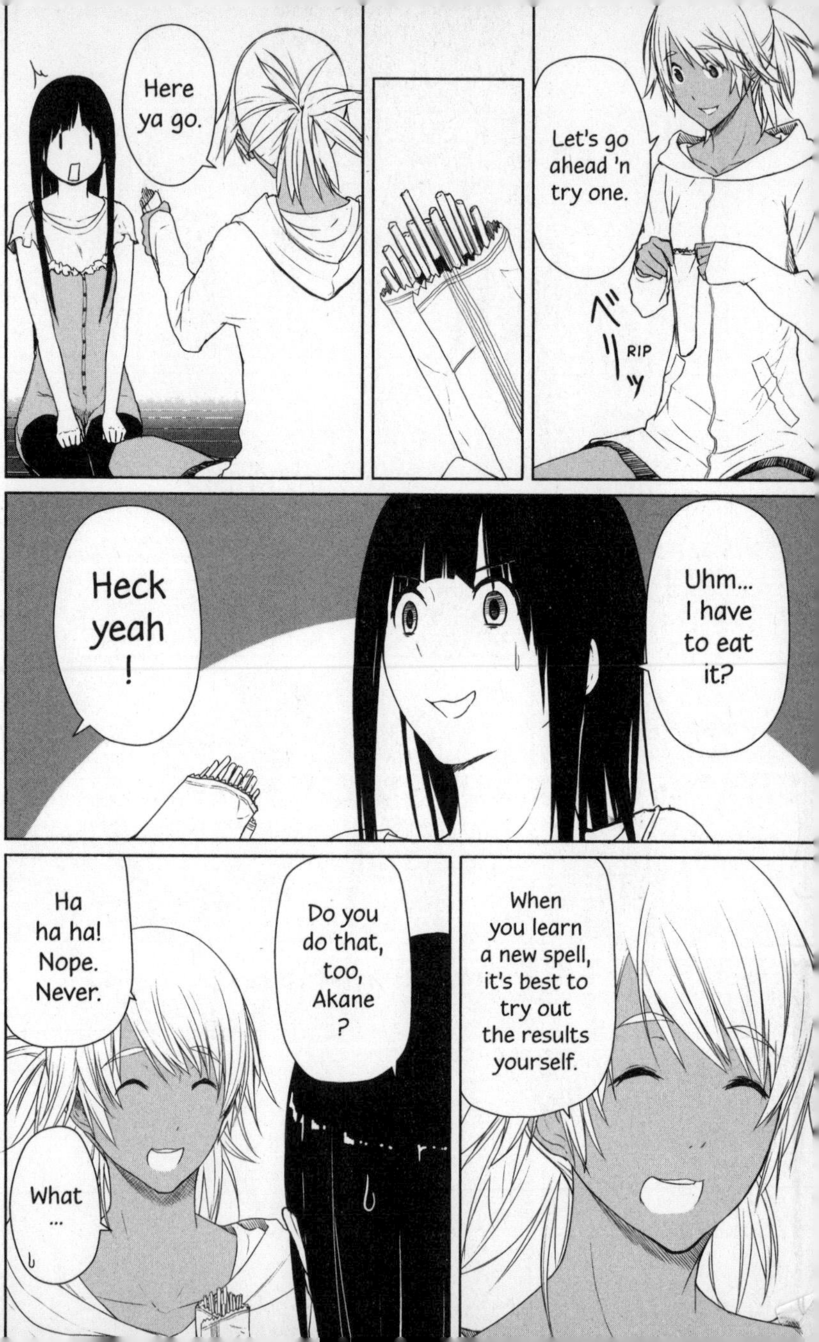
Let's go ahead 'n try one.
ベリッ
RIP
Here ya go.
Uhm... I have to eat it?
Heck yeah!
When you learn a new spell, it's best to try out the results yourself.
Do you do that, too, Akane?
Ha ha ha! Nope. Never.
What ...

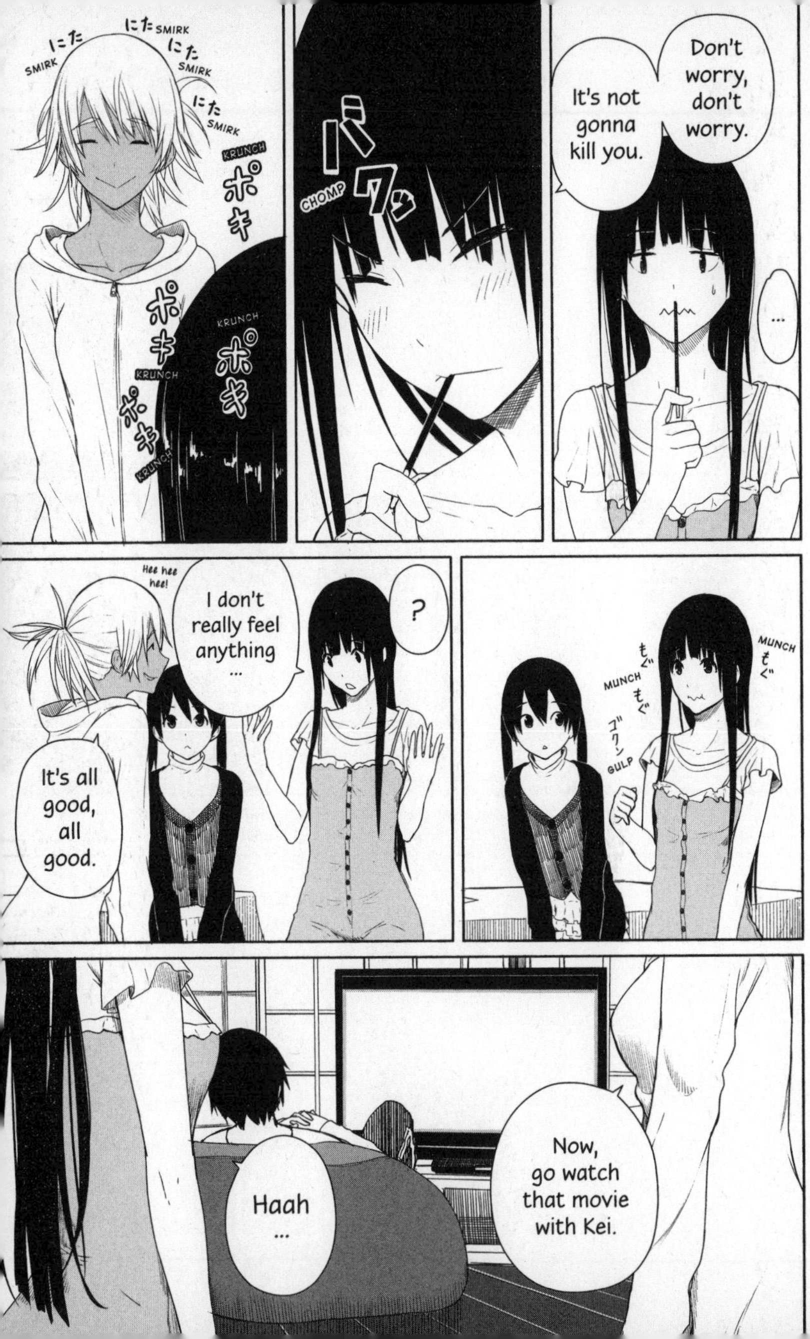
Don't worry, don't worry.
It's not gonna kill you.
...
パクッ
CHOMP
にた SMIRK
にた SMIRK
にた SMIRK
にた SMIRK
ポキ KRUNCH
ポキ KRUNCH
ポキ KRUNCH
ポキ KRUNCH
もぐ MUNCH
もぐ MUNCH
ゴクン GULP
?
I don't really feel anything ...
Hee hee hee!
It's all good, all good.
Now, go watch that movie with Kei.
Haah ...

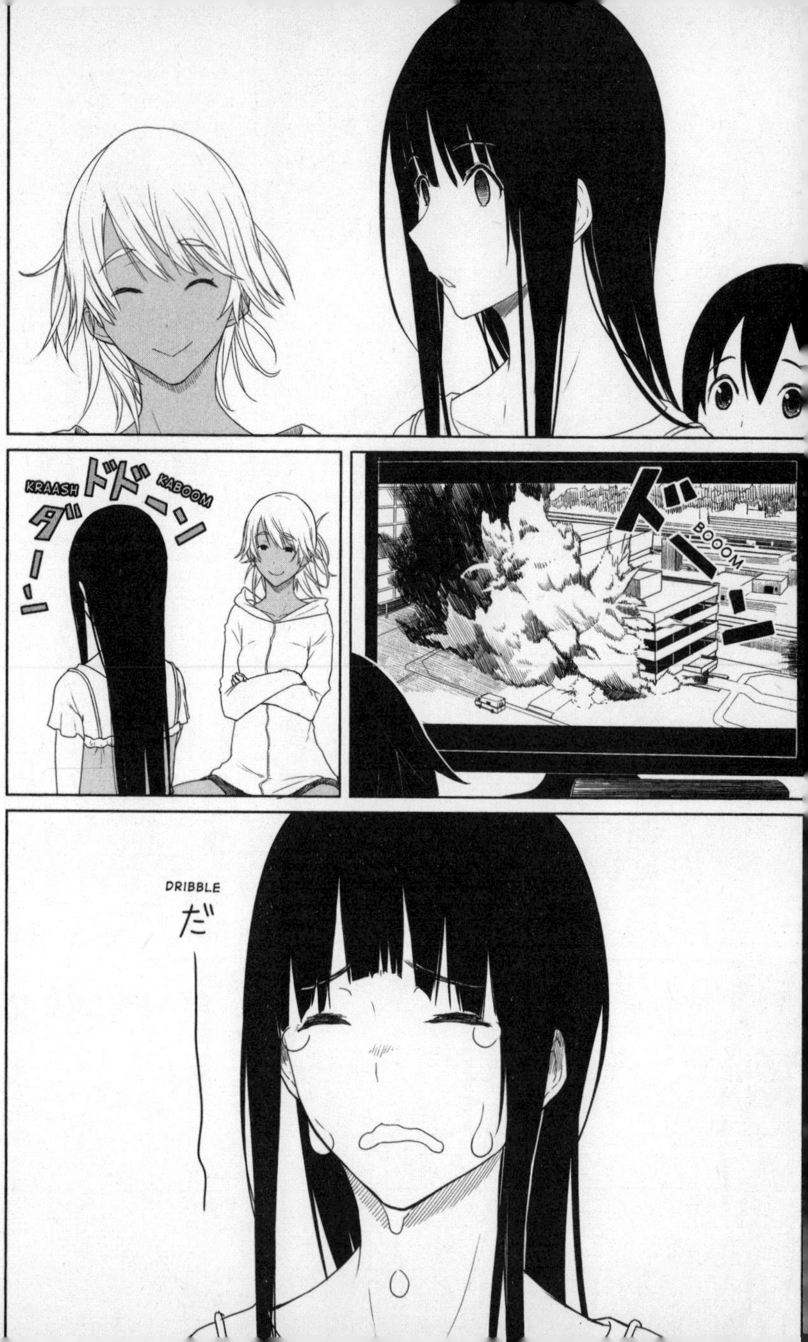
BOOOM
ドドーン
KABOOM
ダーー
KRAASH
DRIBBLE
だ

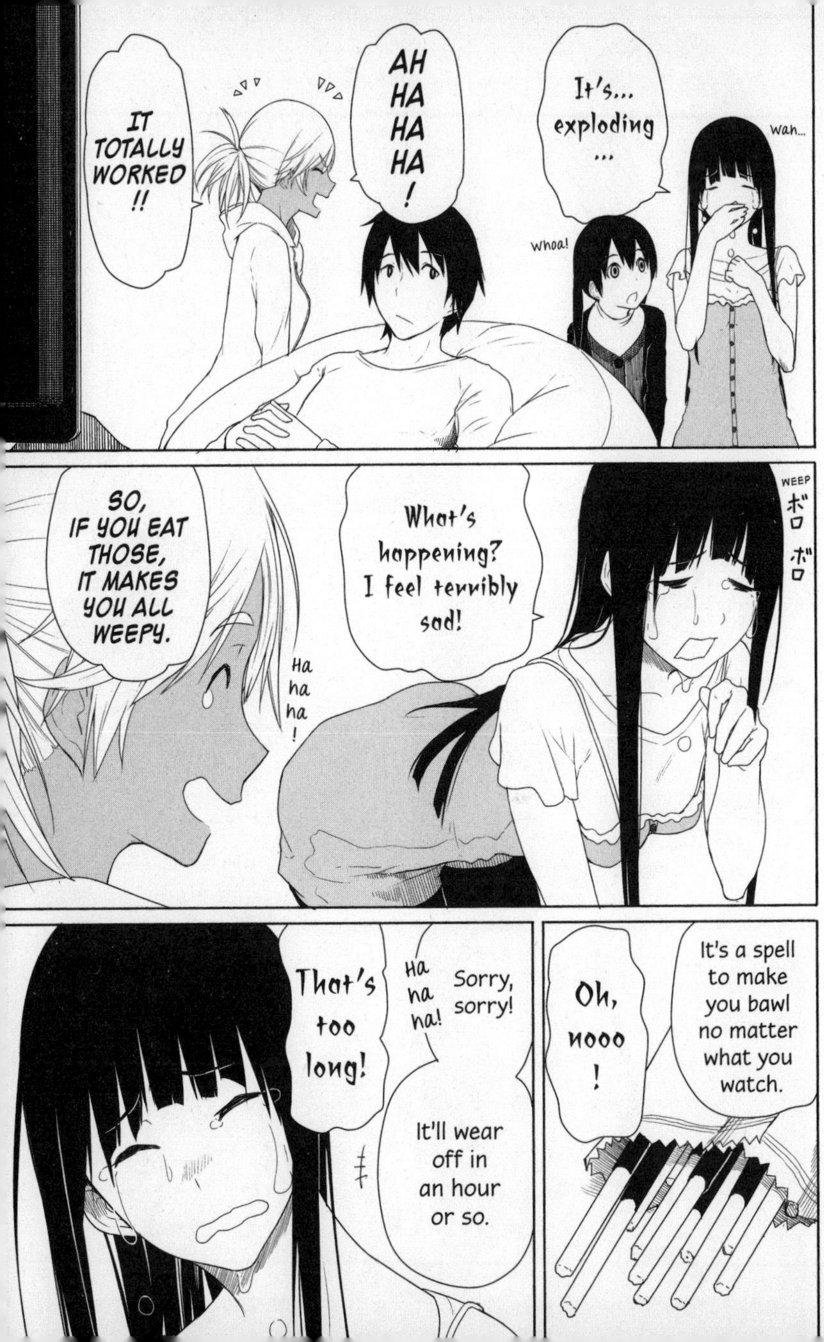
wah...
It's... exploding ...
Whoa!
AH HA HA HA!
IT TOTALLY WORKED!!
WEEP
ボロ ボロ
What's happening? I feel terribly sad!
Ha ha ha!
SO, IF YOU EAT THOSE, IT MAKES YOU ALL WEEPY.
It's a spell to make you bawl no matter what you watch.
Oh, nooo!
Sorry, sorry!
Ha ha ha!
That's too long!
It'll wear off in an hour or so.

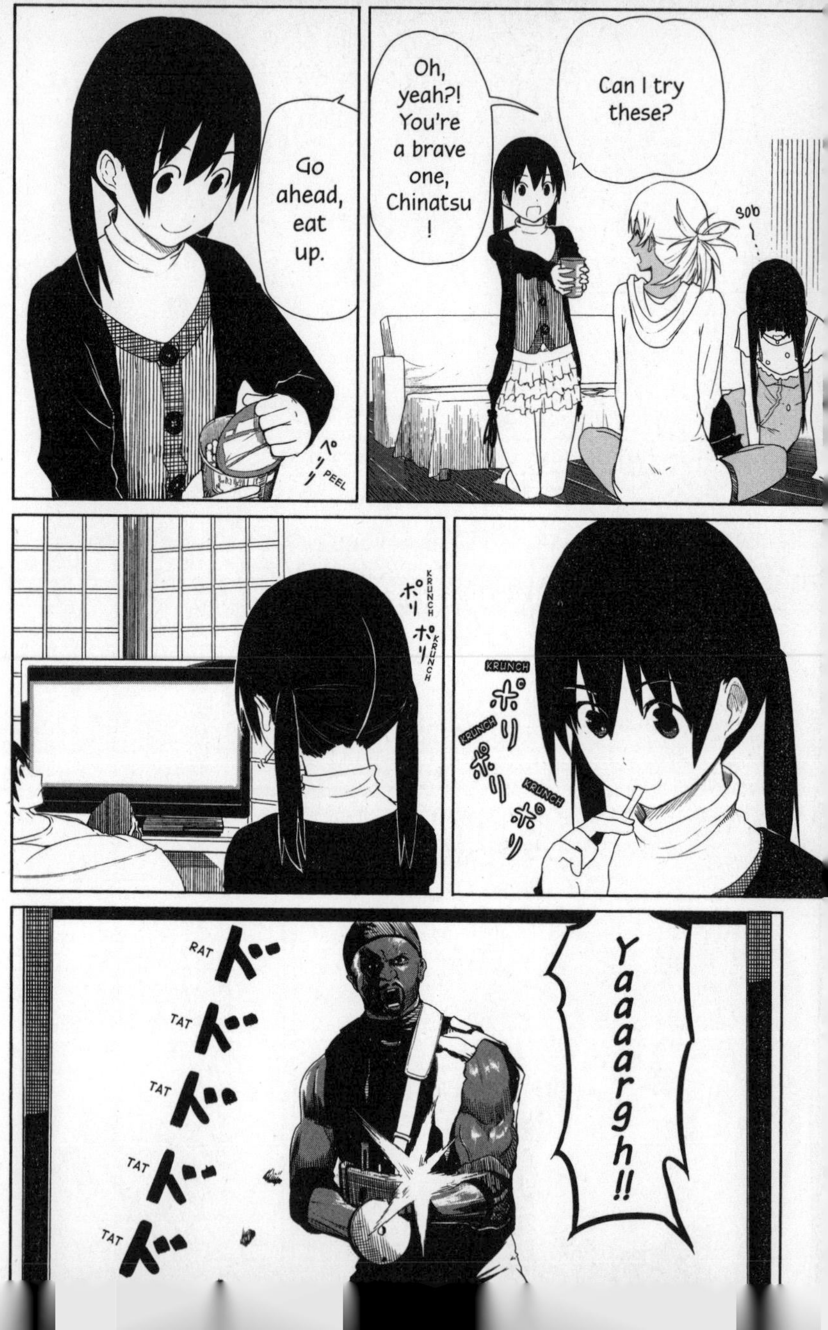
Can I try these?
Oh, yeah?! You're a brave one, Chinatsu!
sob...
Go ahead, eat up.
ペリ
PEEL
KRUNCH
ポリ
KRUNCH
ポリ
KRUNCH
ポ
KRUNCH
ポリ
KRUNCH
ポリ
KRUNCH
Yaaaargh!!
RAT
ド
TAT
ド
TAT
ド
TAT
ド
TAT
ド

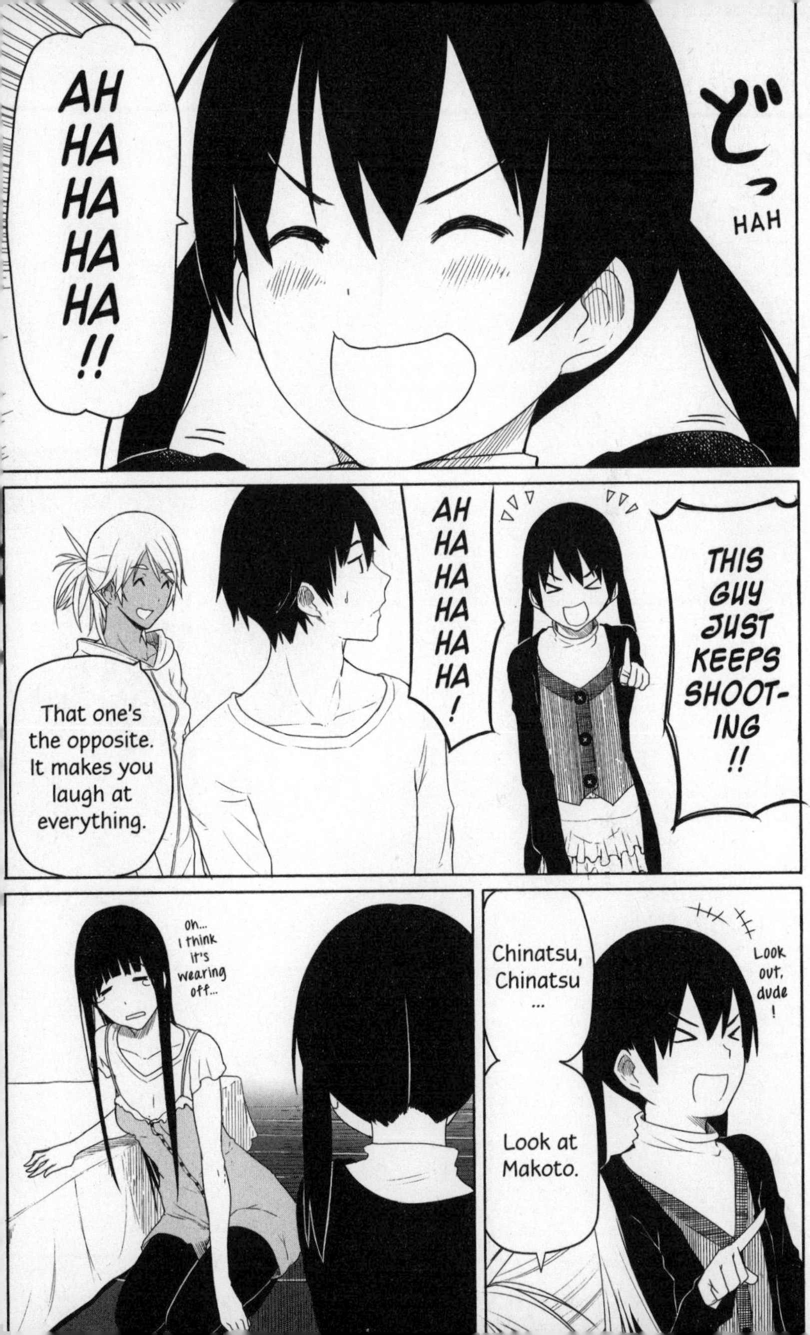
どっ
HAH
AH HA HA HA HA HA!!
THIS GUY JUST KEEPS SHOOTING!!
AH HA HA HA HA HA HA!
That one's the opposite. It makes you laugh at everything.
Look out, dude!
Chinatsu, Chinatsu...
Look at Makoto.
Oh... I think it's wearing off...

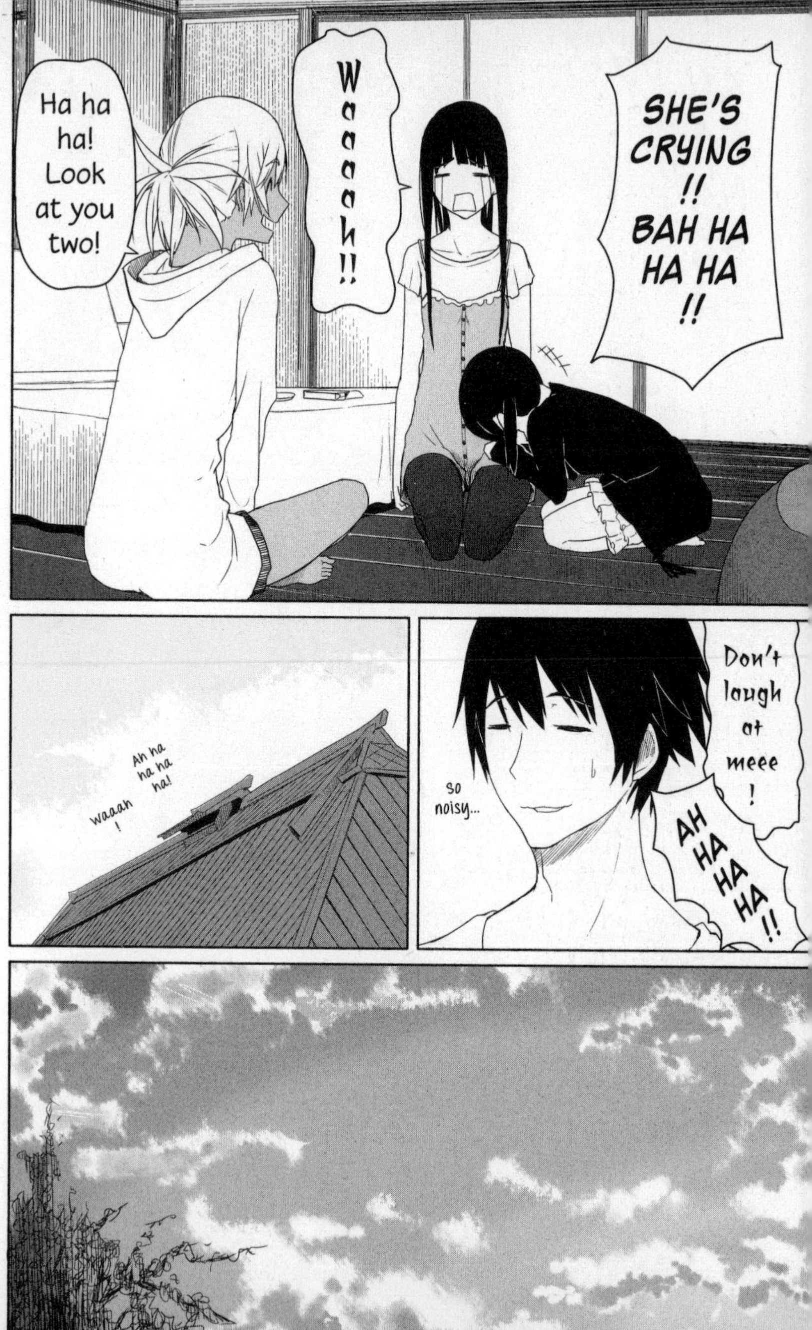
SHE'S CRYING!! BAH HA HA HA!!
Waaaah!!
Ha ha ha! Look at you two!
Don't laugh at meee!
AH HA HA HA!!
so noisy...
Ah ha ha ha ha!
waaah!

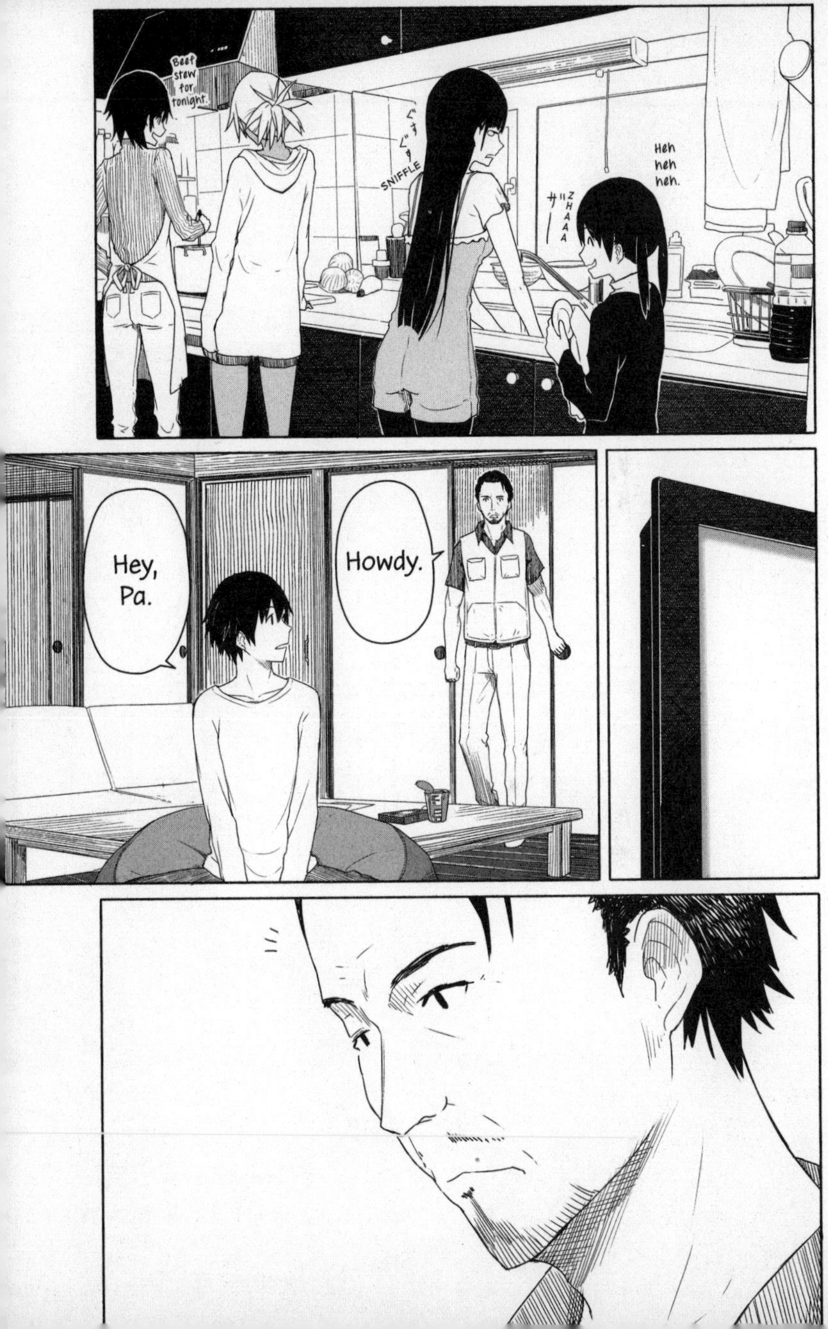
Heh heh heh.
ザー
ZHAAA
ぐすぐす
SNIFFLE
Beef stew for tonight.
Howdy.
Hey, Pa.

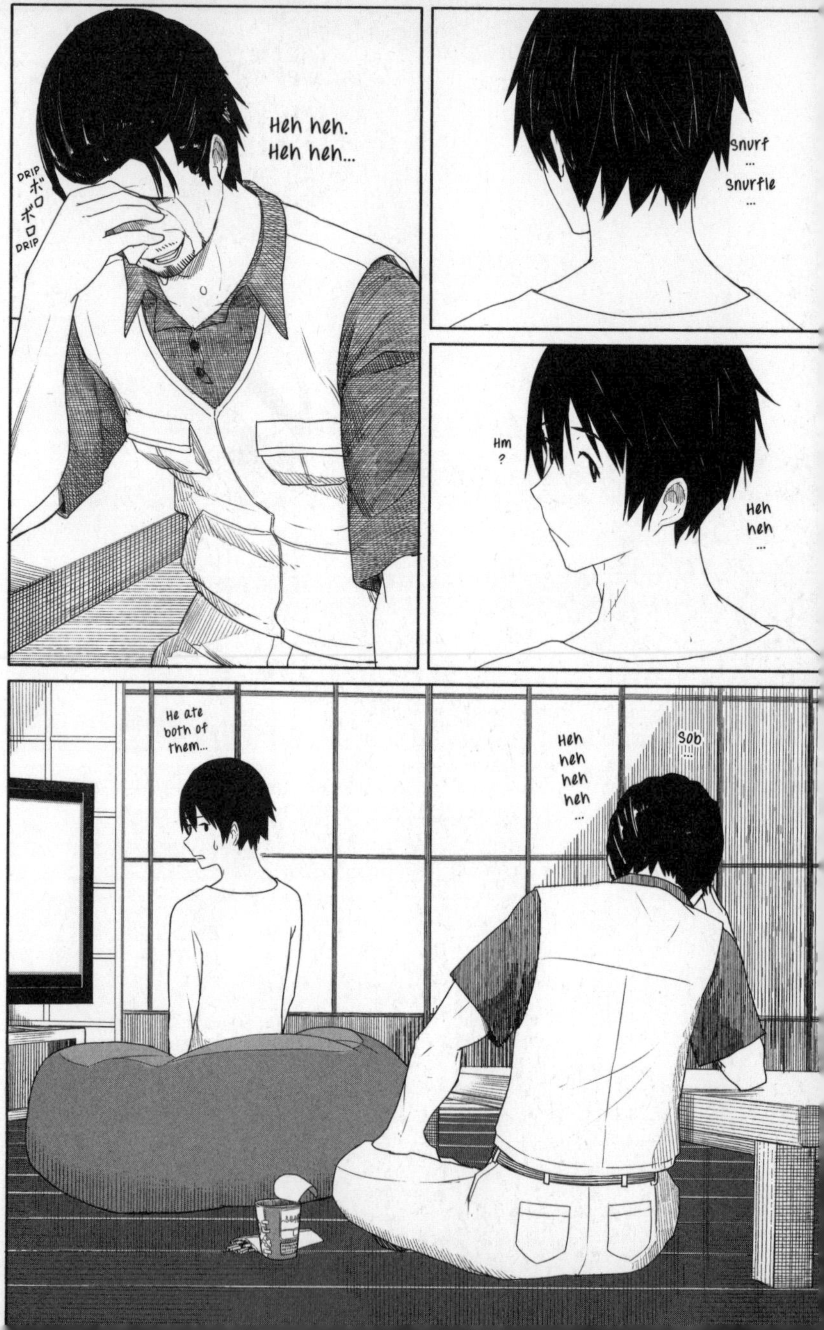
Snurf ... Snurfle ...
Hm ?
Heh heh ...
Heh heh. Heh heh...
DRIP ボロボロ DRIP
Sob ...
Heh heh heh heh ...
He ate both of them...

Chapter 12
The Mountains in Spring

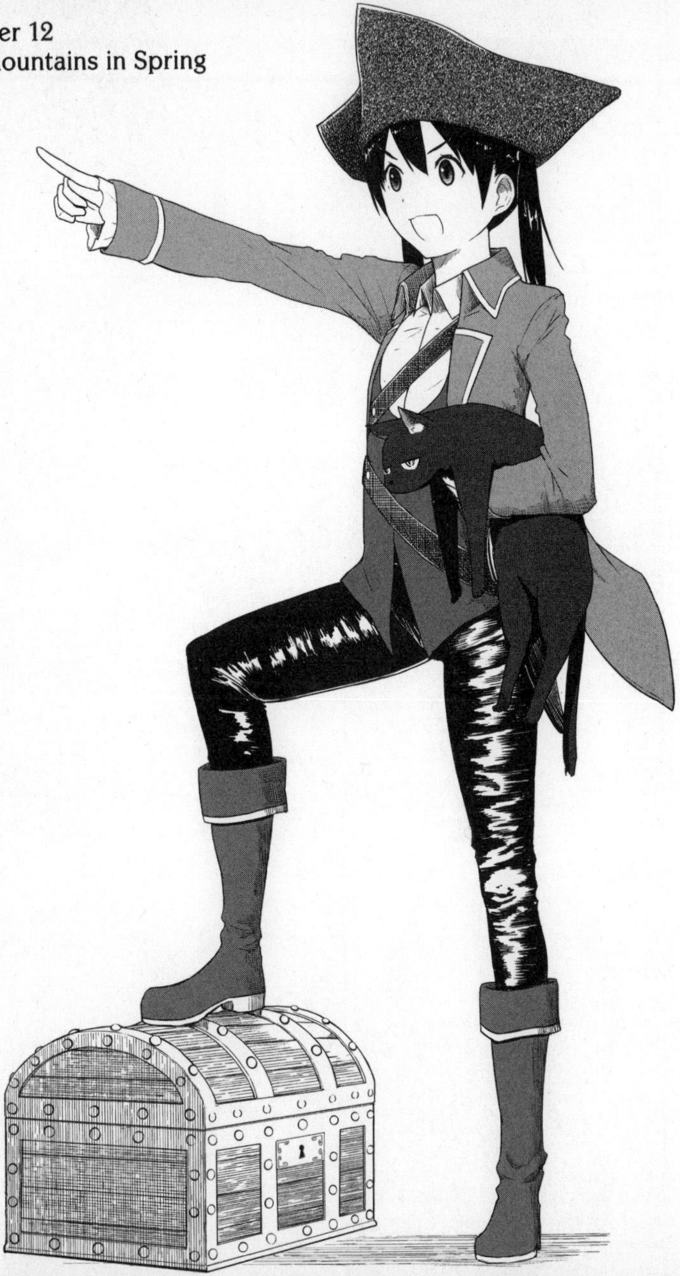

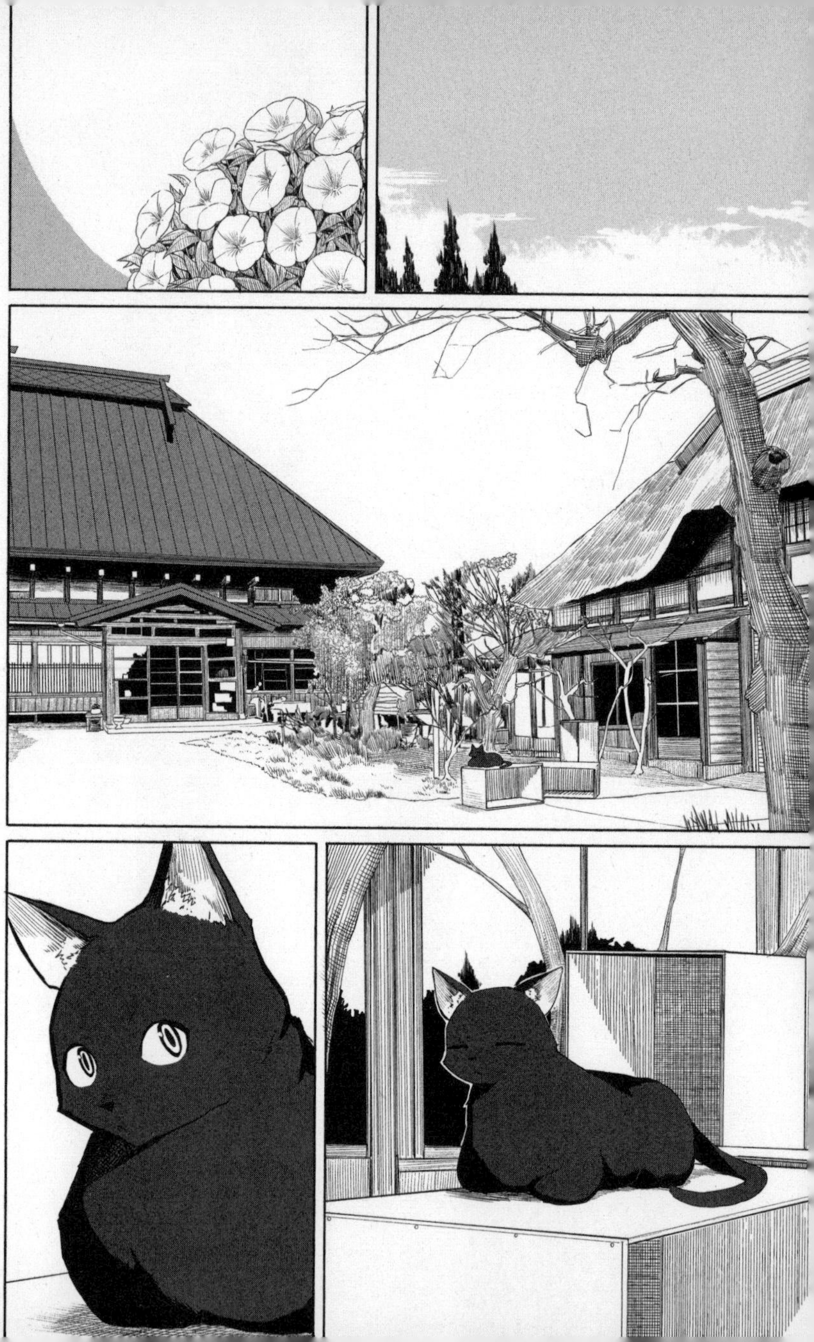

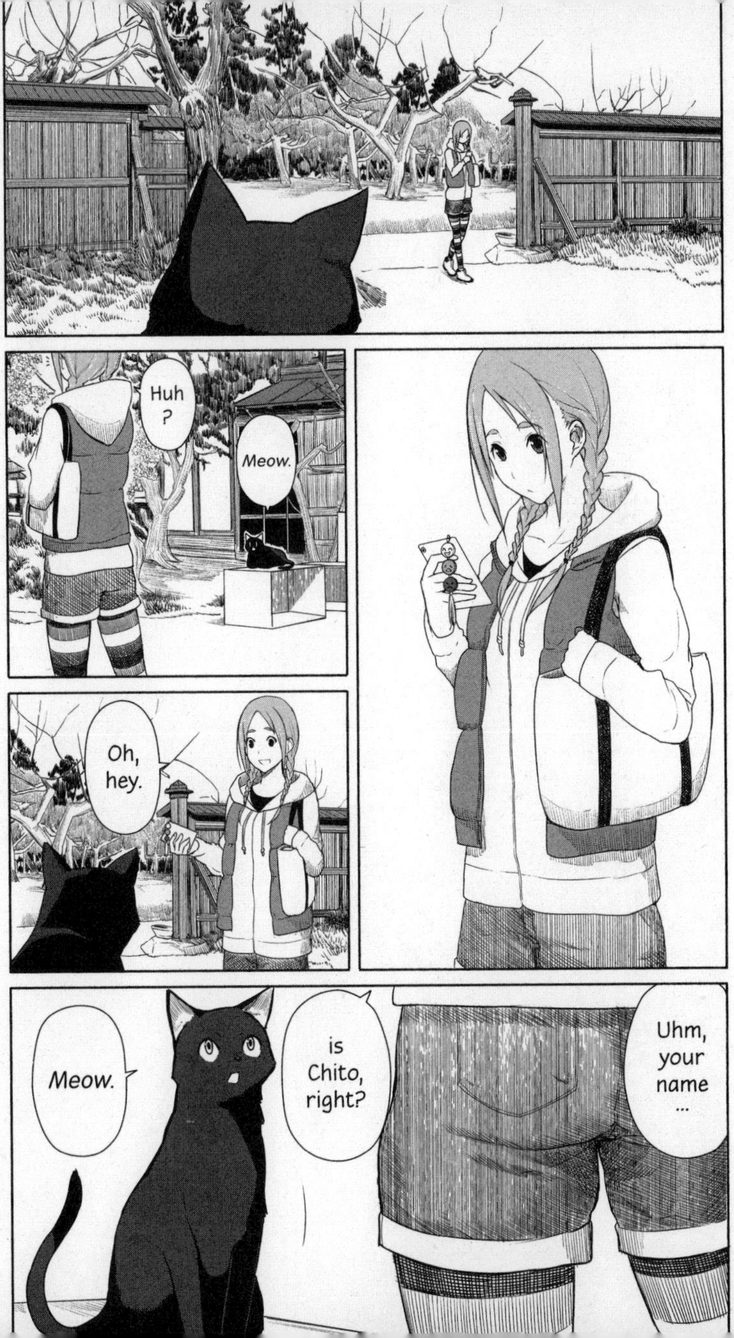
Meow.
Huh?
Oh, hey.
Uhm, your name ...
is Chito, right?
Meow.

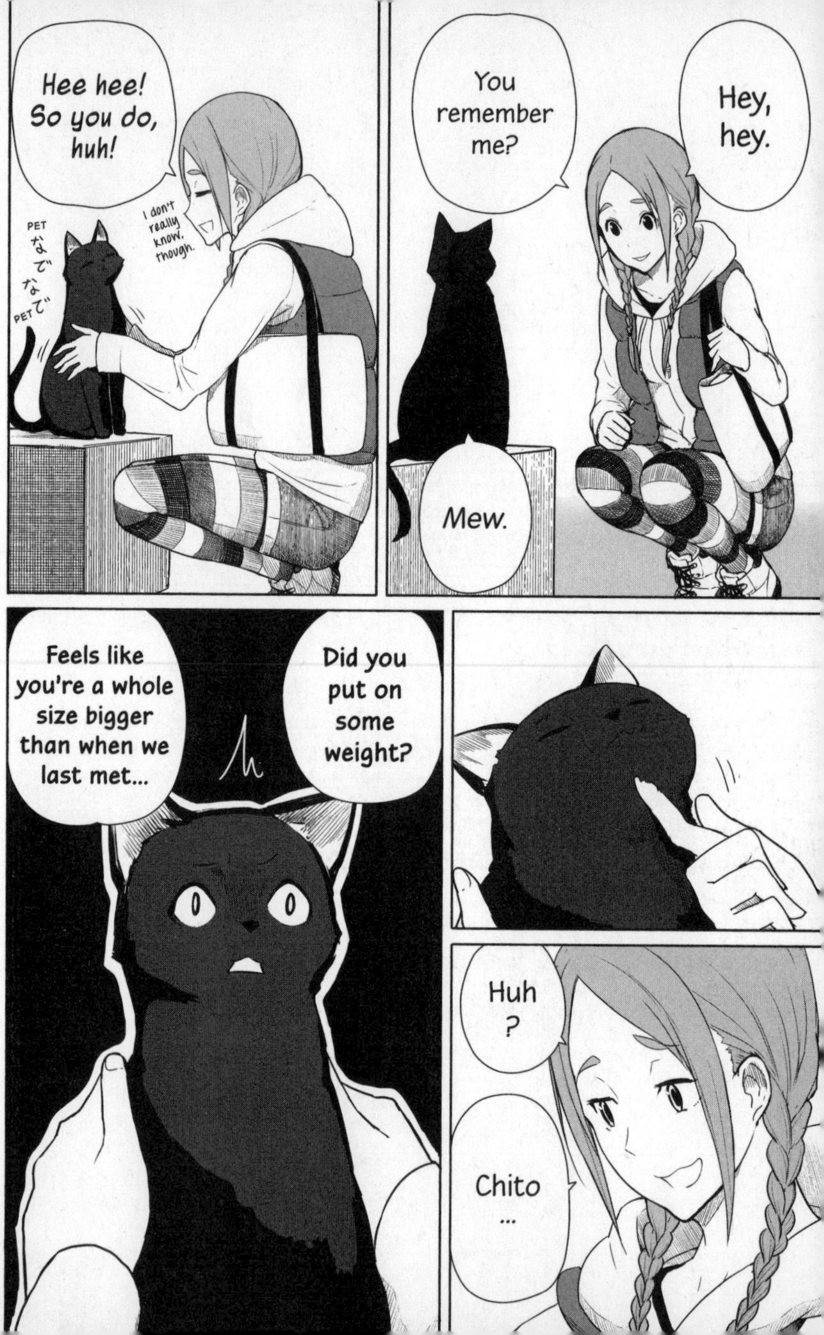
Hey, hey.
You remember me?
Mew.
Hee hee! So you do, huh!
I don't really know, though.
PET なで なで PET
Huh ?
Chito ...
Did you put on some weight?
Feels like you're a whole size bigger than when we last met...

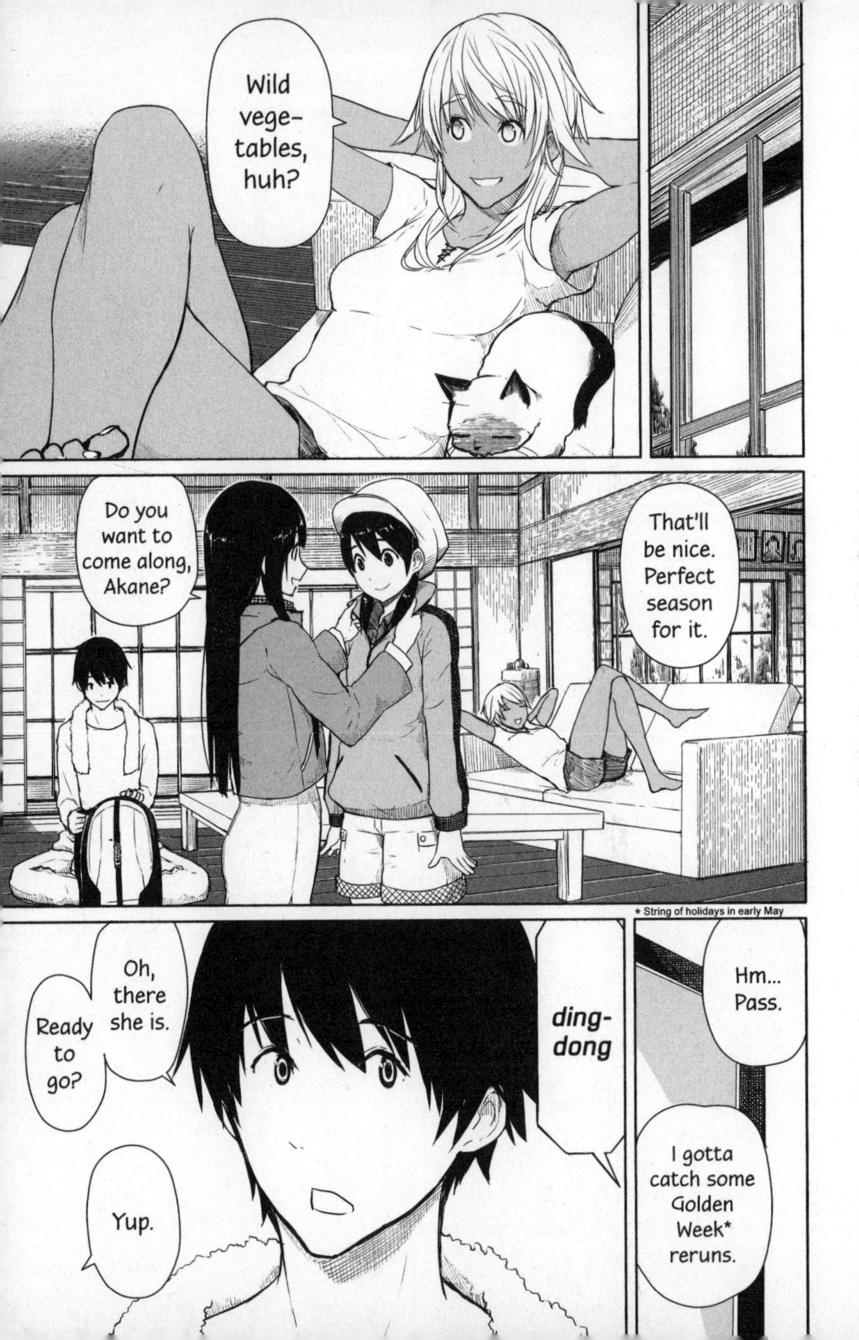
Wild vegetables, huh?
That'll be nice. Perfect season for it.
Do you want to come along, Akane?
Hm... Pass.
I gotta catch some Golden Week* reruns.
ding-dong
Oh, there she is.
Ready to go?
Yup.

* String of holidays in early May

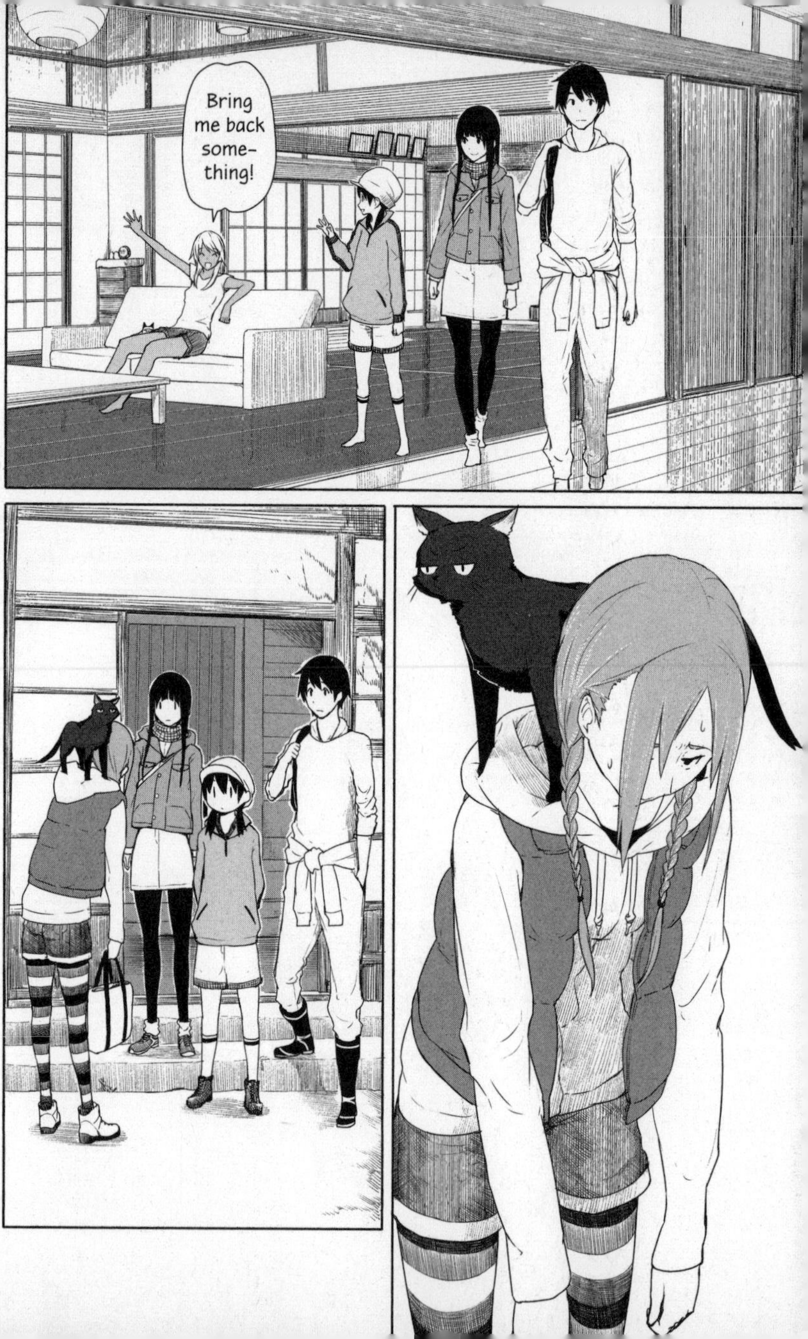
Bring me back some-thing!

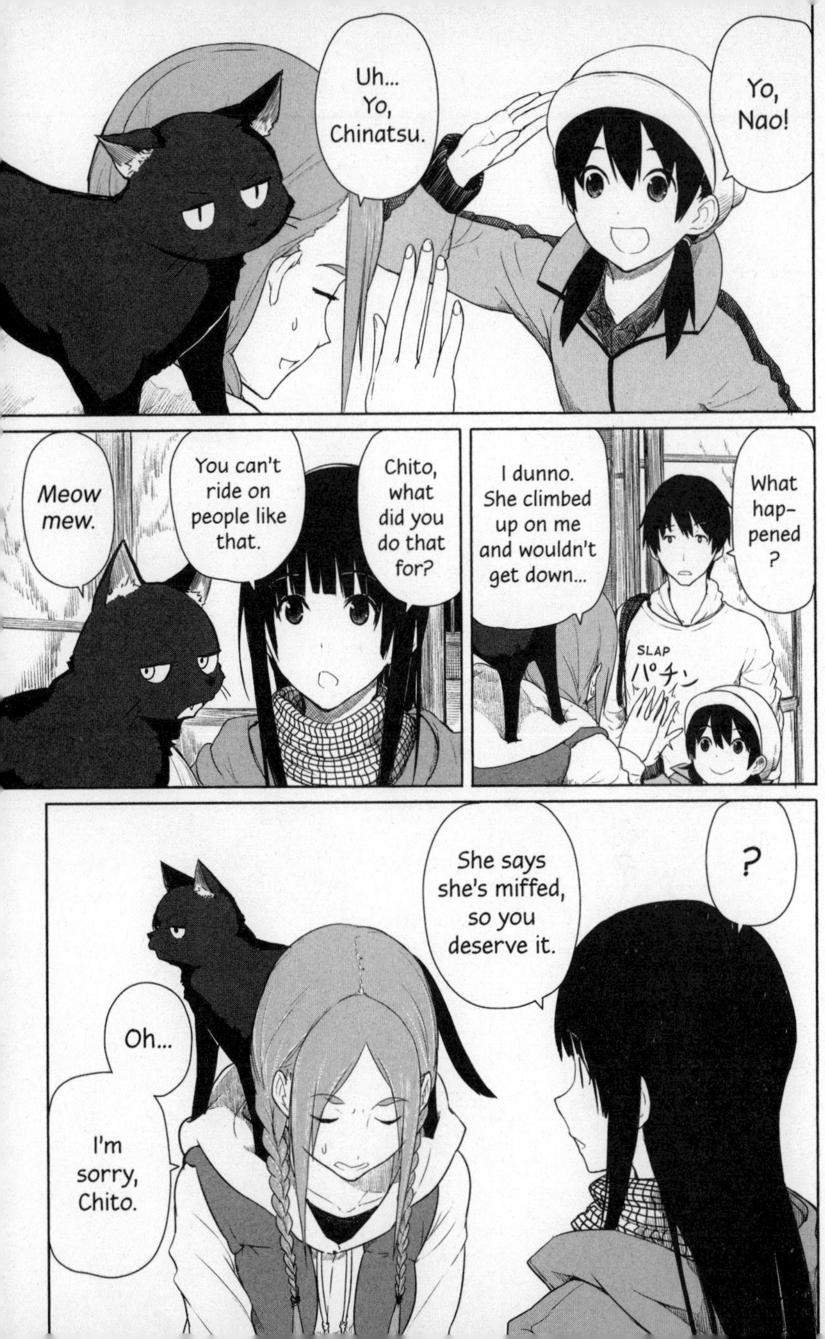
Yo, Nao!
Uh... Yo, Chinatsu.
What hap-pened?
I dunno. She climbed up on me and wouldn't get down...
SLAP
パチン
Chito, what did you do that for?
You can't ride on people like that.
Meow mew.
?
She says she's miffed, so you deserve it.
Oh...
I'm sorry, Chito.

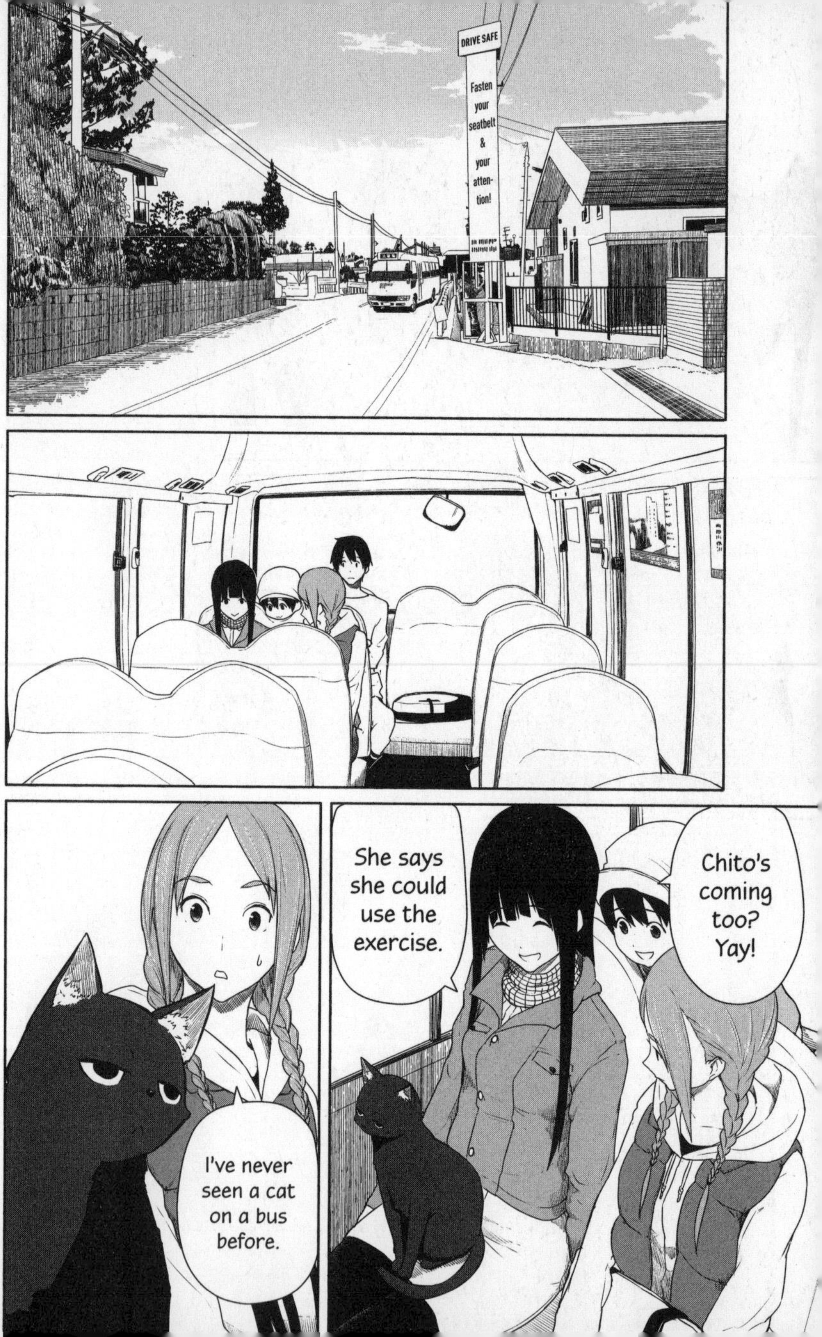
DRIVE SAFE
Fasten your seatbelt & your atten-tion!
Chito's coming too? Yay!
She says she could use the exercise.
I've never seen a cat on a bus before.

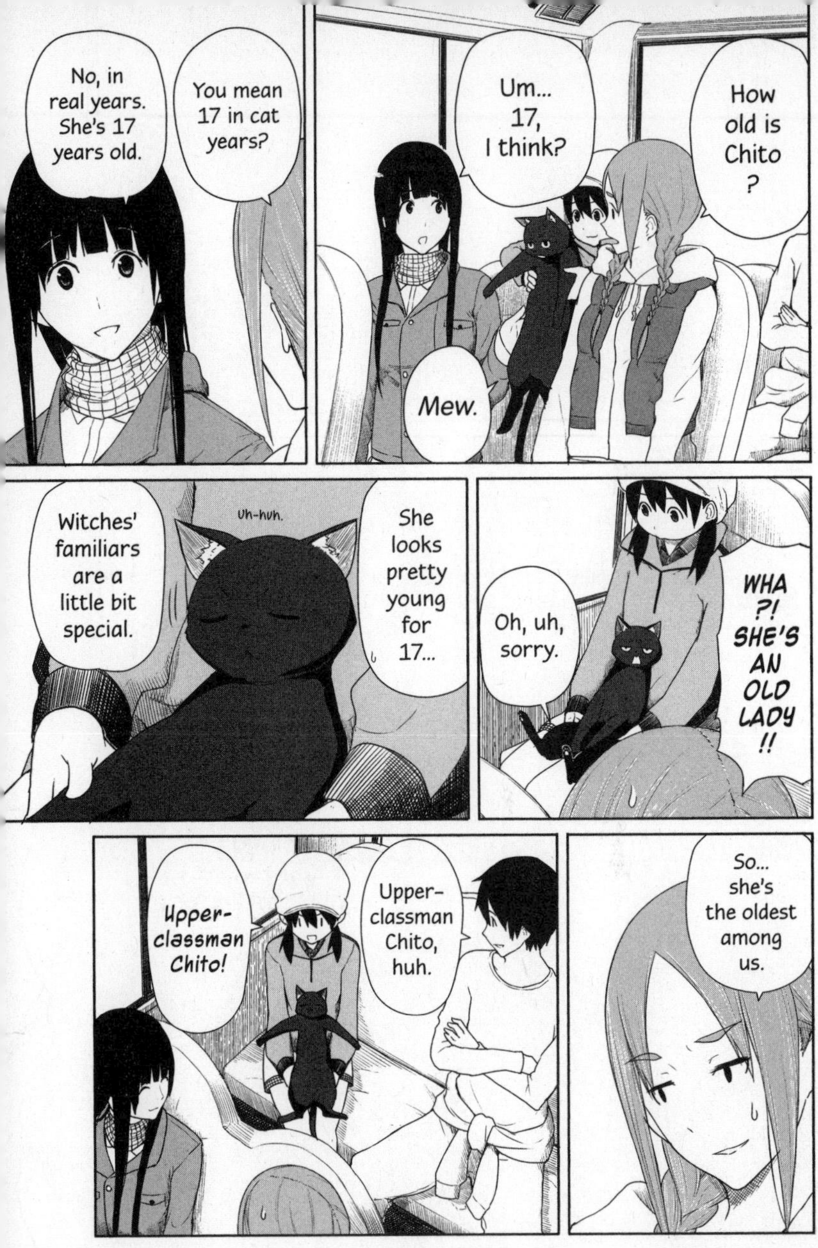
How old is Chito?
Um... 17, I think?
Mew.
You mean 17 in cat years?
No, in real years. She's 17 years old.
WHA?! SHE'S AN OLD LADY!!
Oh, uh, sorry.
She looks pretty young for 17...
Uh-huh.
Witches' familiars are a little bit special.
So... she's the oldest among us.
Upper-classman Chito, huh.
Upper-classman Chito!

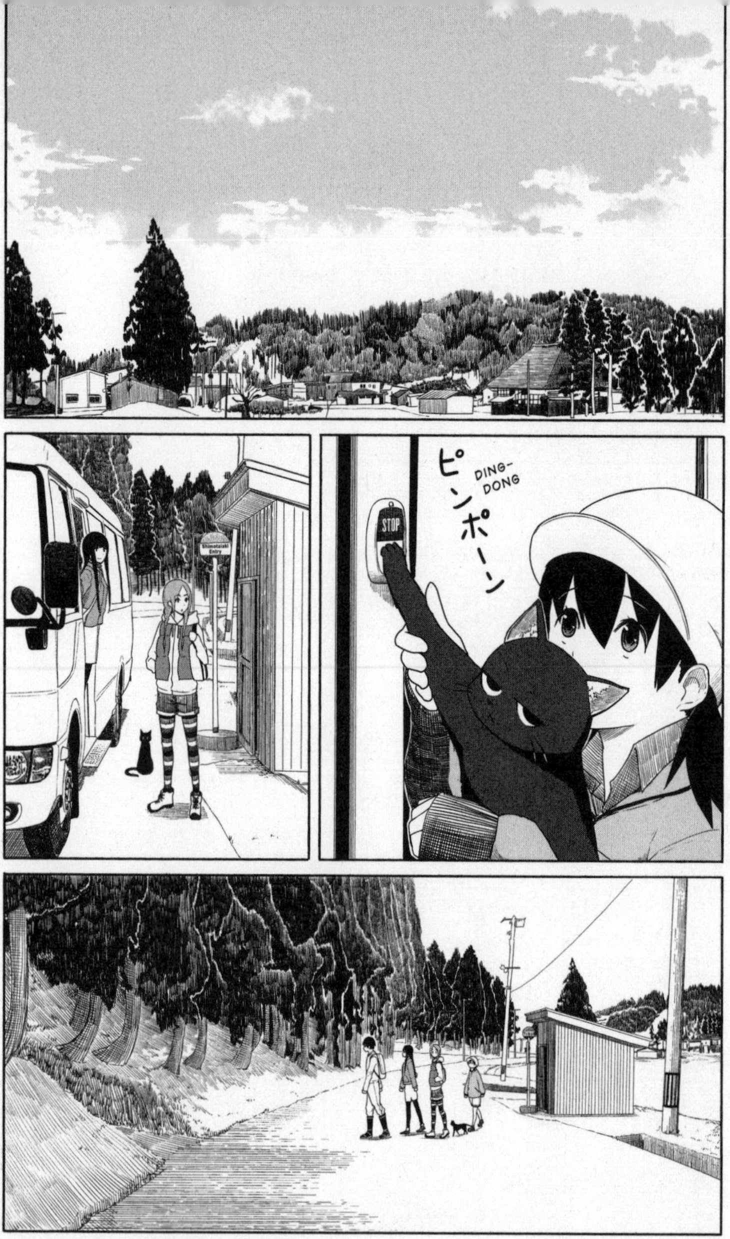
ピンポーン
DING-DONG
STOP
Shimotaiaki Entry

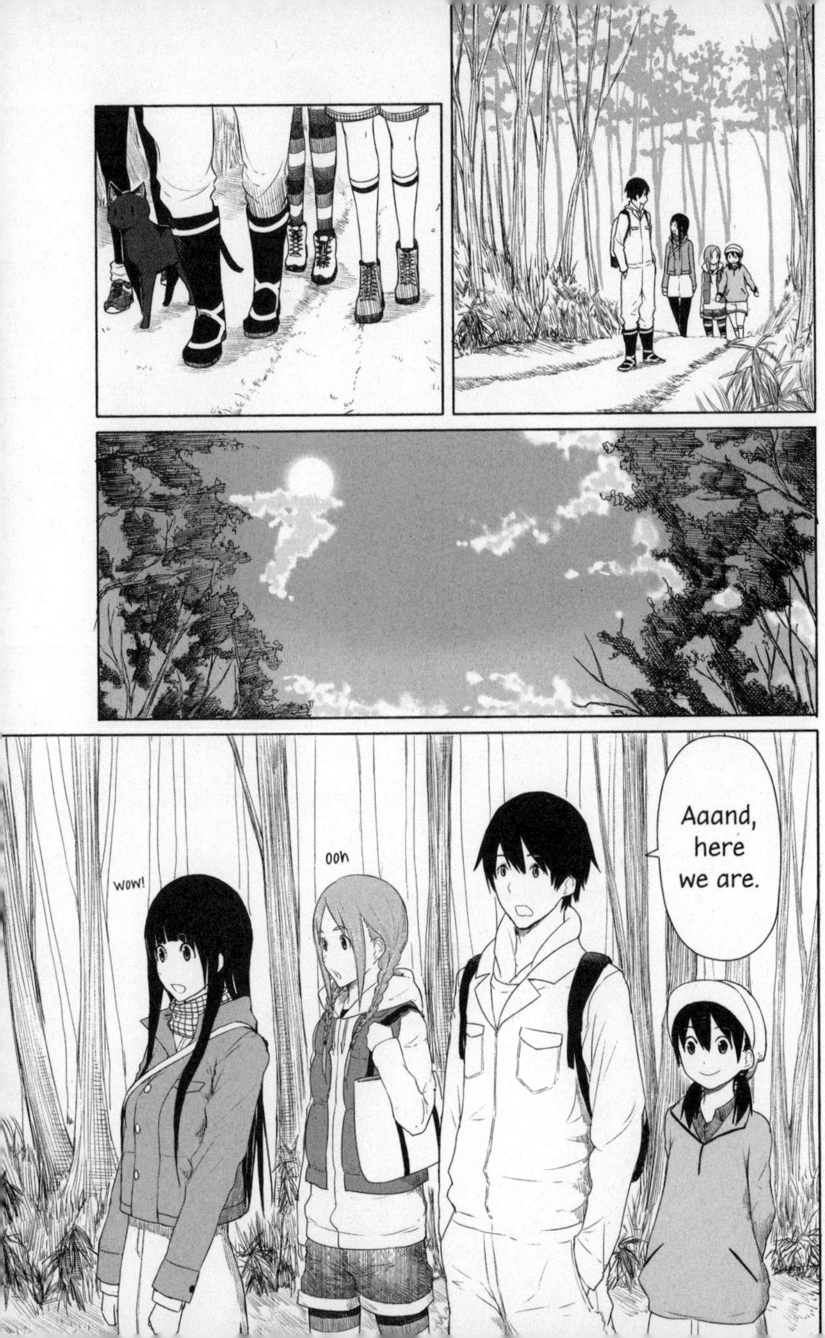
Aaand, here we are.
ooh
WOW!

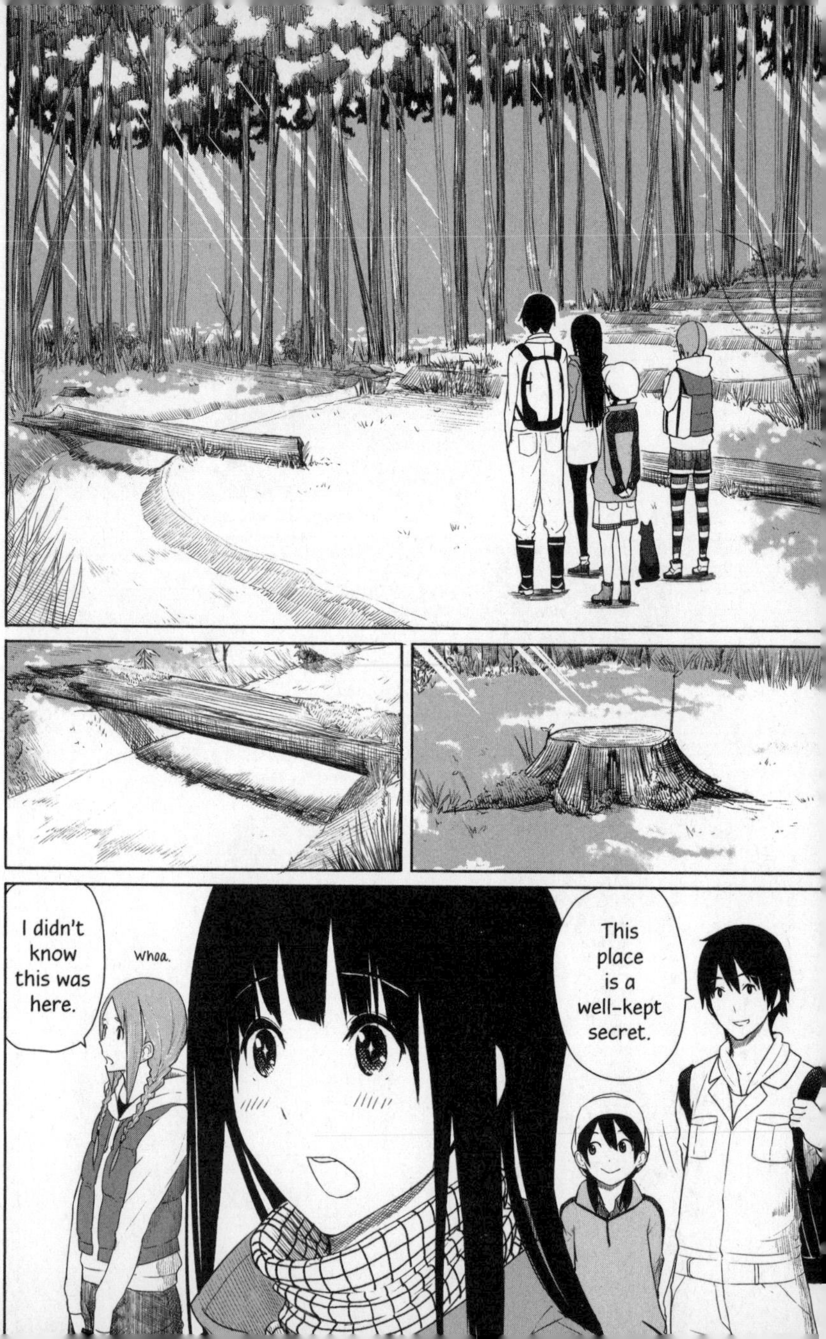
This place is a well-kept secret.
Whoa.
I didn't know this was here.

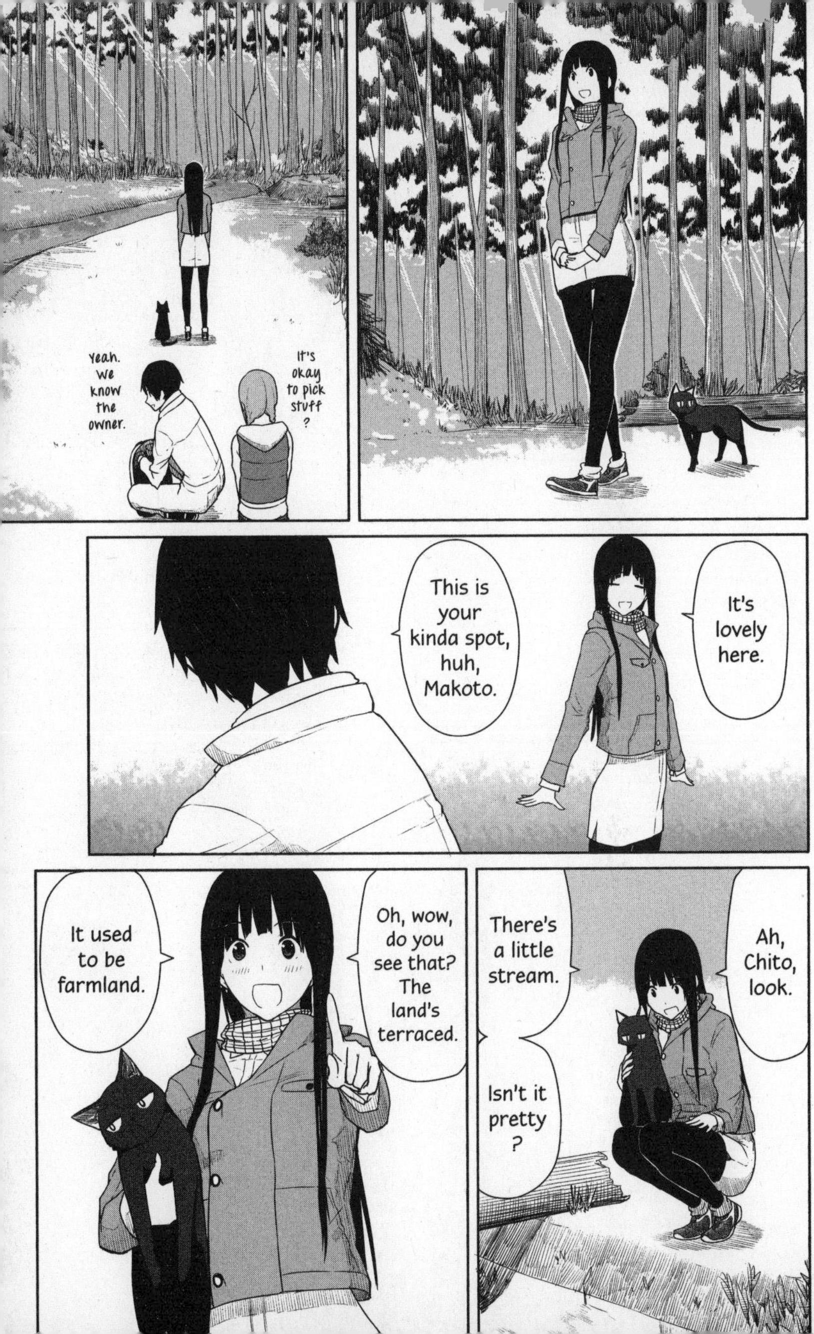
It's okay to pick stuff?
Yeah. We know the owner.
It's lovely here.
This is your kinda spot, huh, Makoto.
Ah, Chito, look.
There's a little stream.
Isn't it pretty?
Oh, wow, do you see that? The land's terraced.
It used to be farmland.

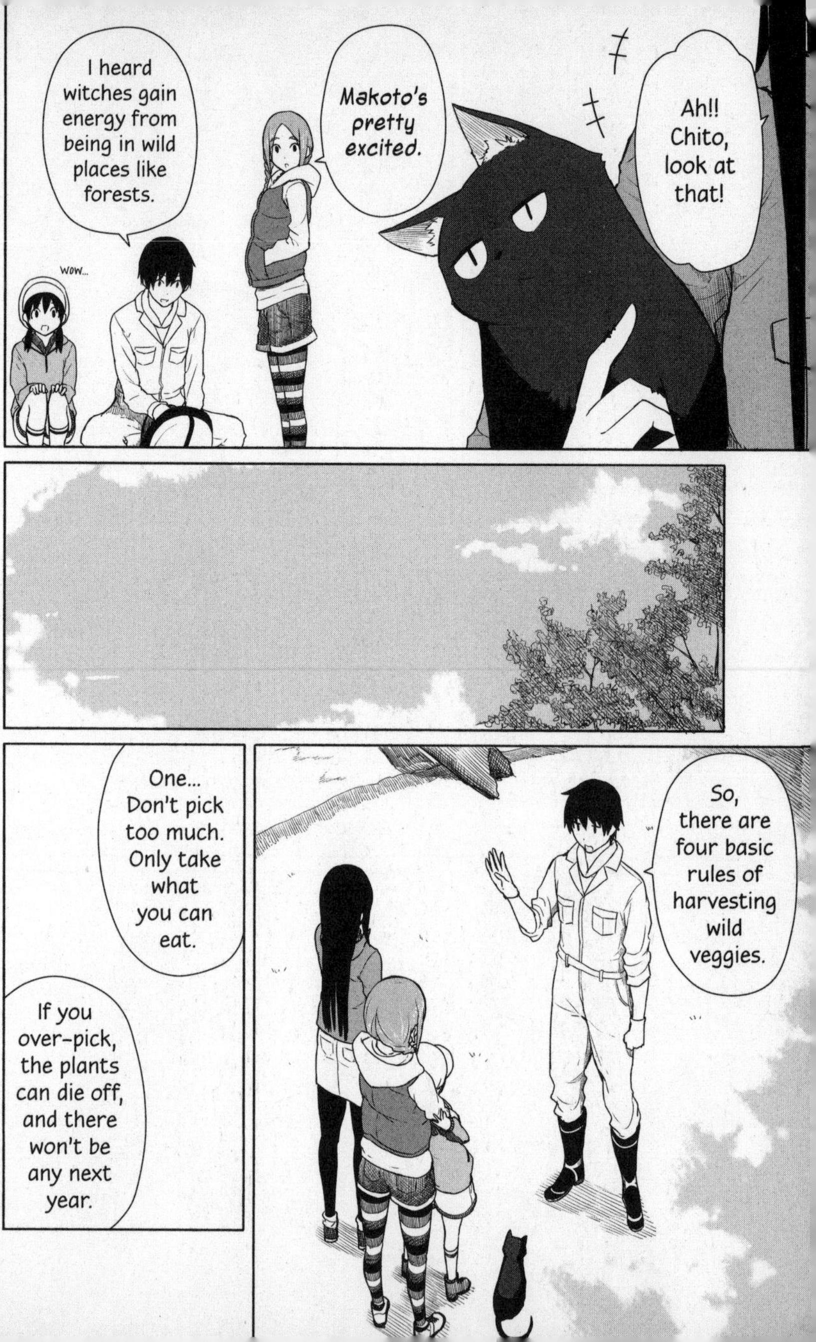
Ah!! Chito, look at that!
Makoto's pretty excited.
I heard witches gain energy from being in wild places like forests.
wow...
So, there are four basic rules of harvesting wild veggies.
One... Don't pick too much. Only take what you can eat.
If you over-pick, the plants can die off, and there won't be any next year.

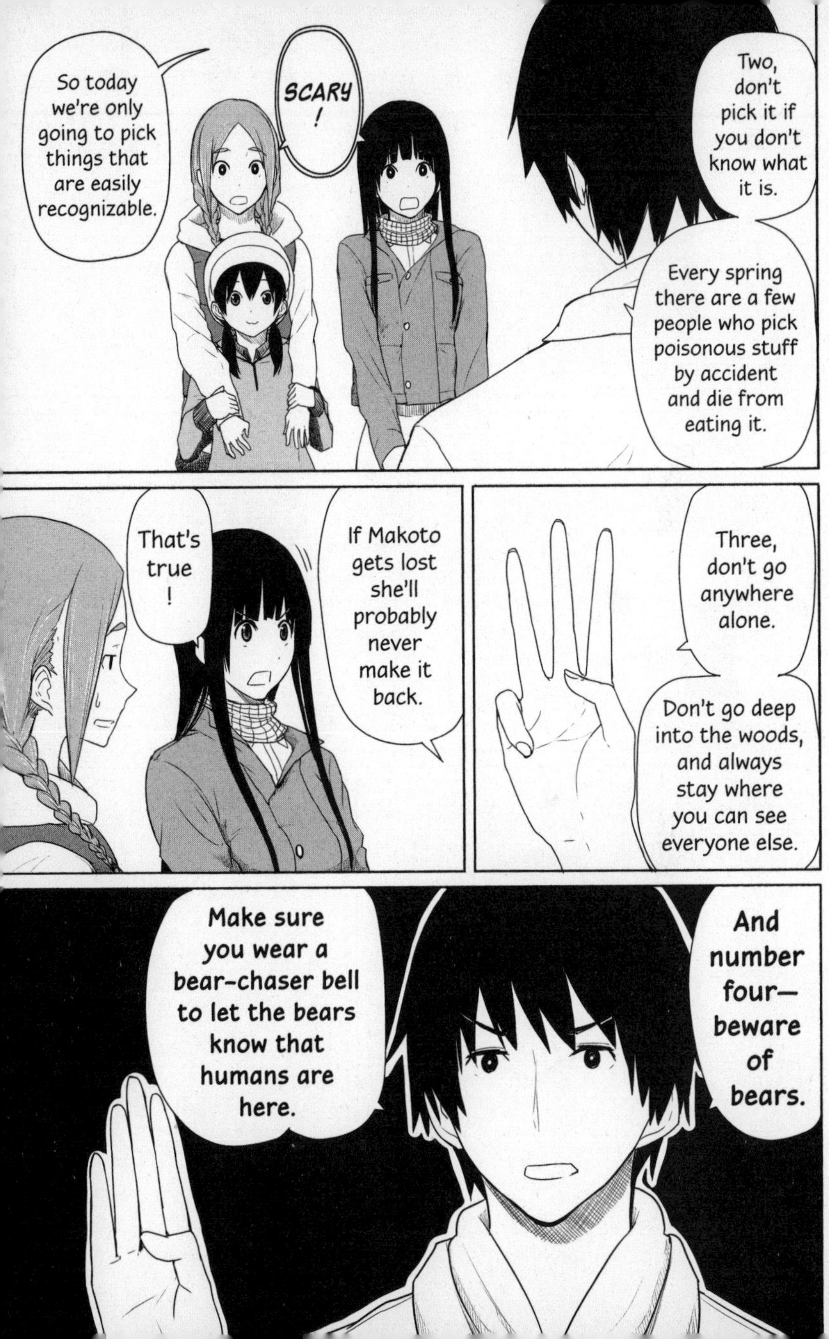
Two, don't pick it if you don't know what it is.
Every spring there are a few people who pick poisonous stuff by accident and die from eating it.
SCARY!
So today we're only going to pick things that are easily recognizable.
Three, don't go anywhere alone.
Don't go deep into the woods, and always stay where you can see everyone else.
If Makoto gets lost she'll probably never make it back.
That's true!
And number four—beware of bears.
Make sure you wear a bear-chaser bell to let the bears know that humans are here.

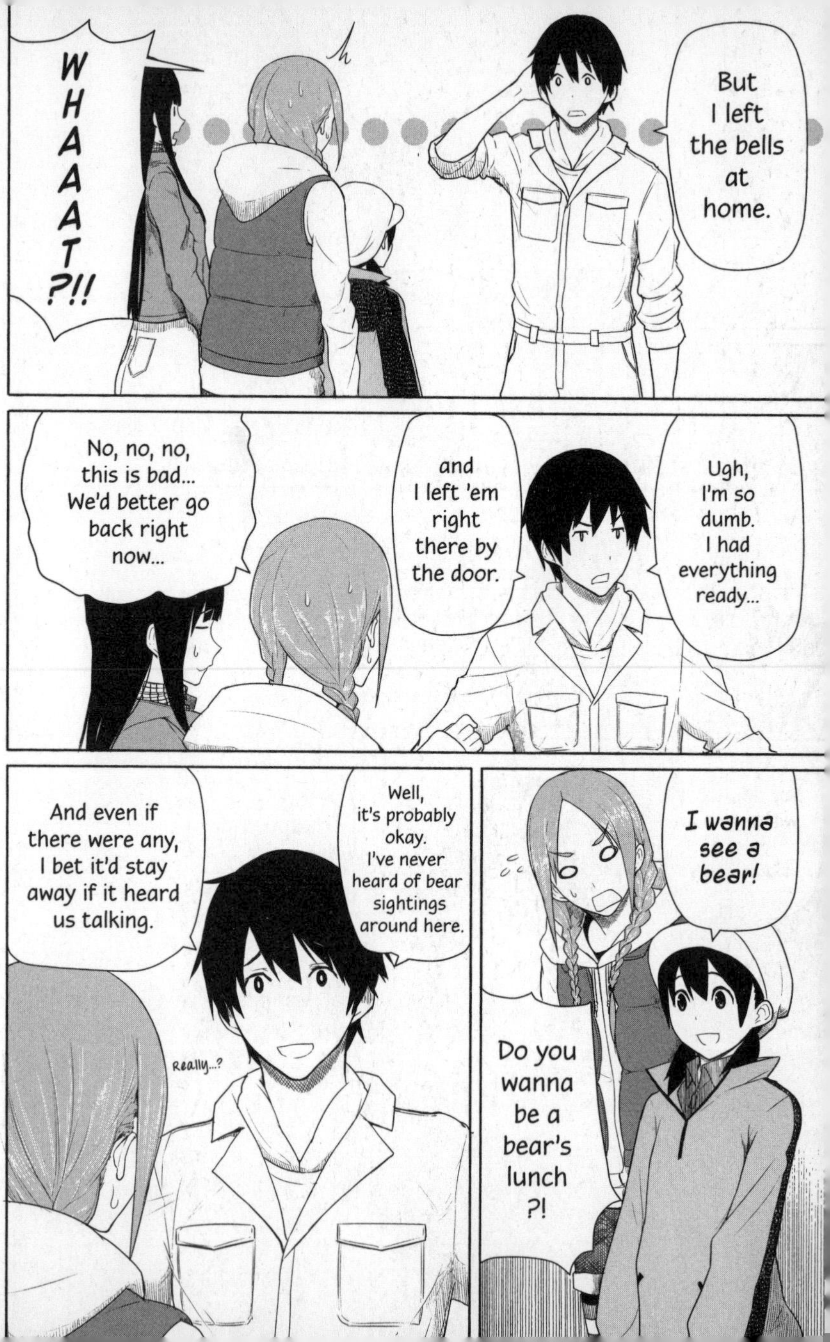

But I left the bells at home.
WHAAAAT?!!
Ugh, I'm so dumb. I had everything ready...
and I left 'em right there by the door.
No, no, no, this is bad... We'd better go back right now...
I wanna see a bear!
Do you wanna be a bear's lunch?!
Well, it's probably okay. I've never heard of bear sightings around here.
And even if there were any, I bet it'd stay away if it heard us talking.
Really...?

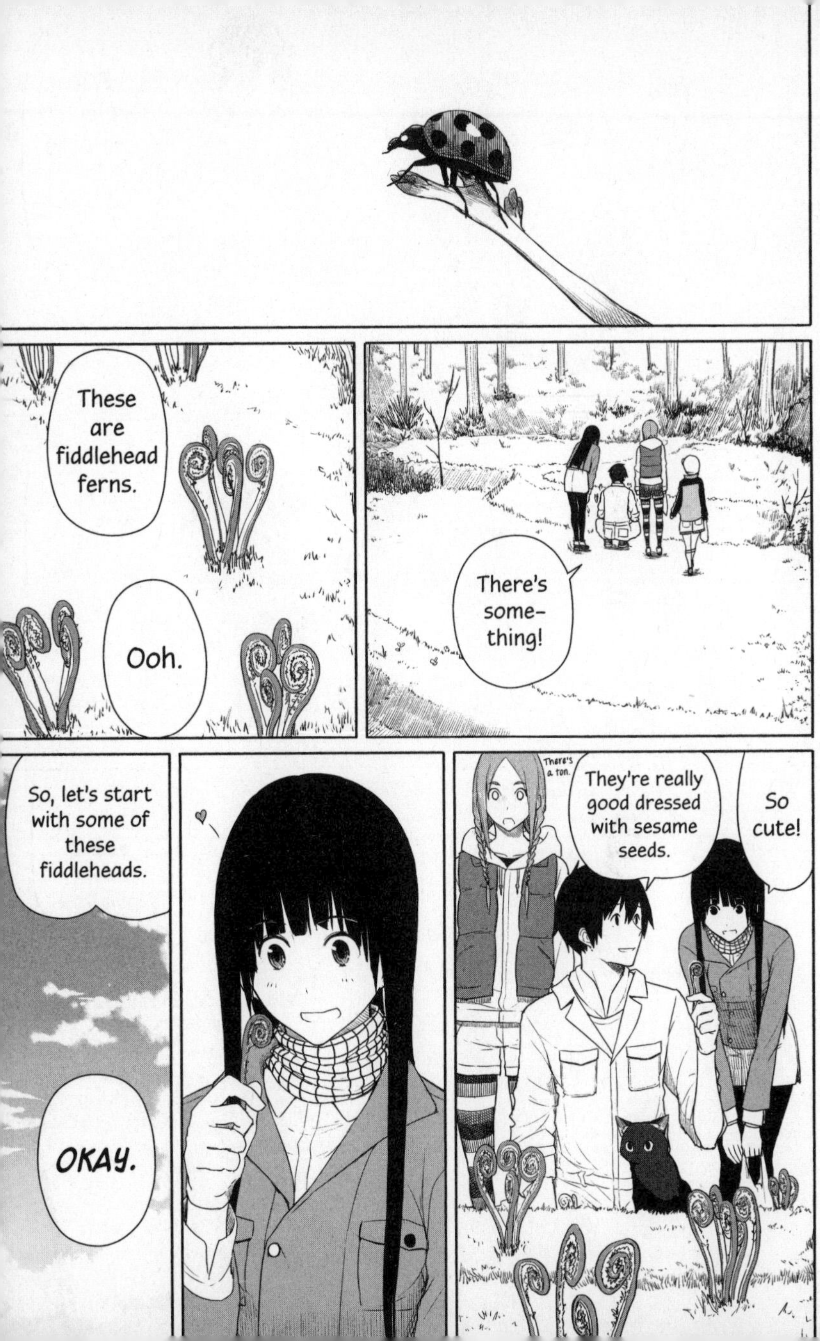
There's some-thing!
These are fiddlehead ferns.
Ooh.
So cute!
They're really good dressed with sesame seeds.
There's a ton.
So, let's start with some of these fiddleheads.
OKAY.

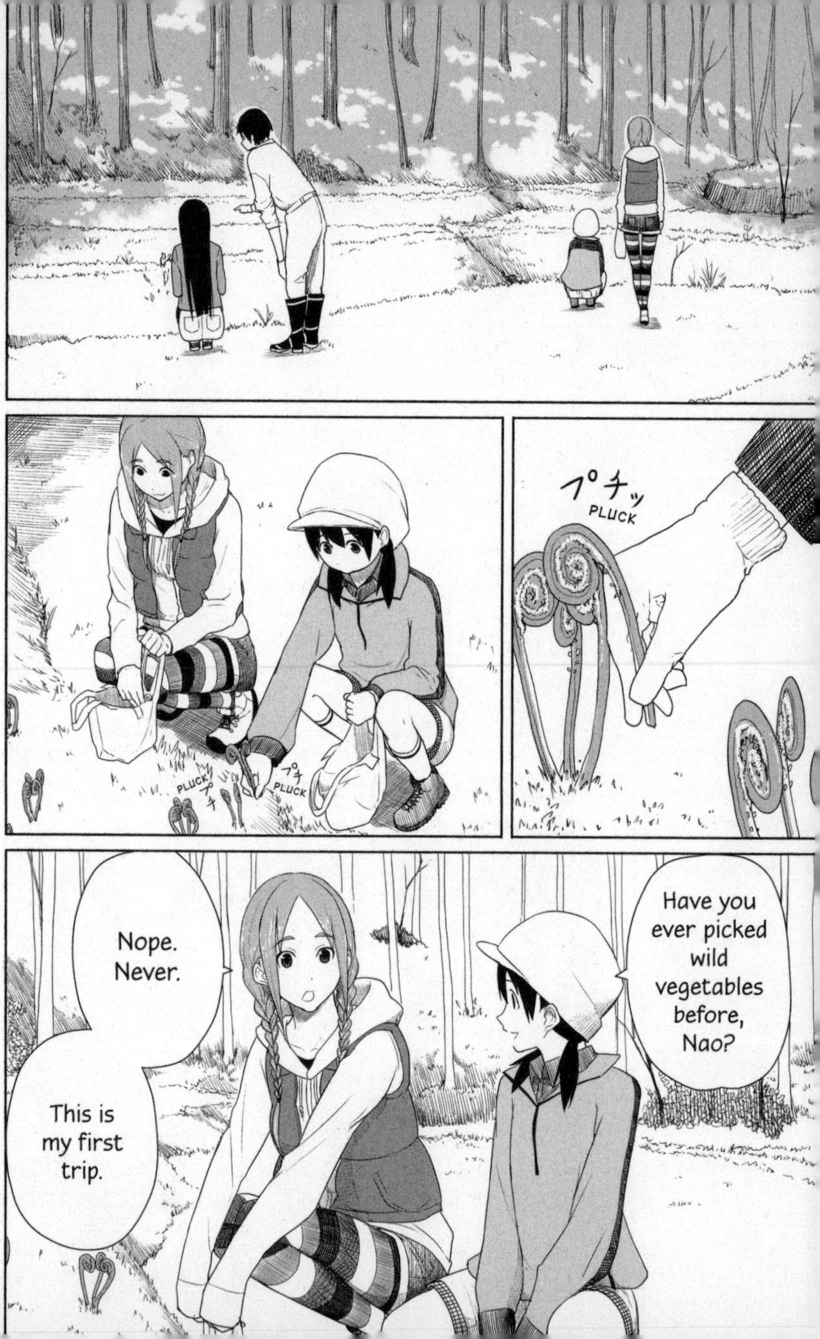

プチッ
PLUCK
プチ
PLUCK
プチ
PLUCK
Have you ever picked wild vegetables before, Nao?
Nope. Never.
This is my first trip.

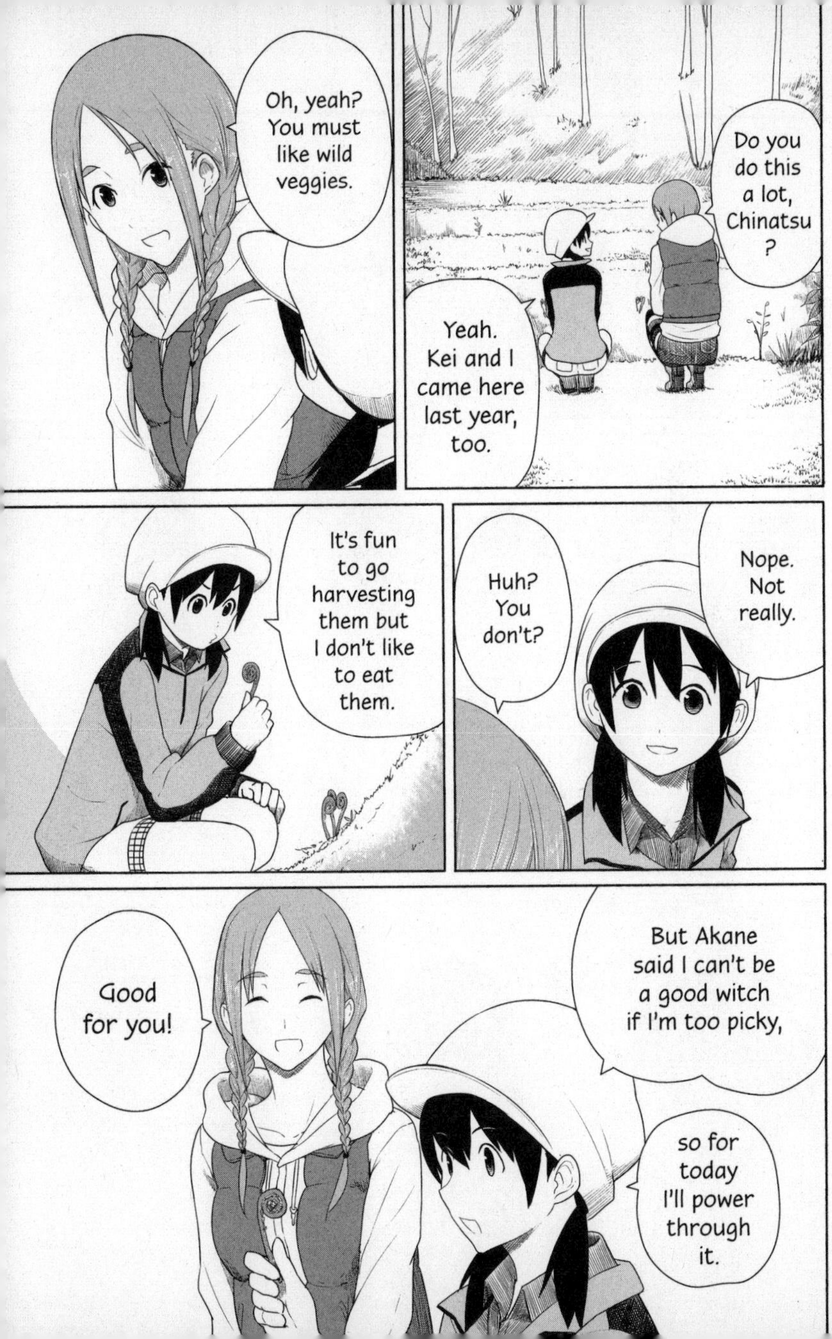
Do you do this a lot, Chinatsu?
Yeah. Kei and I came here last year, too.
Oh, yeah? You must like wild veggies.
Nope. Not really.
Huh? You don't?
It's fun to go harvesting them but I don't like to eat them.
But Akane said I can't be a good witch if I'm too picky,
so for today I'll power through it.
Good for you!

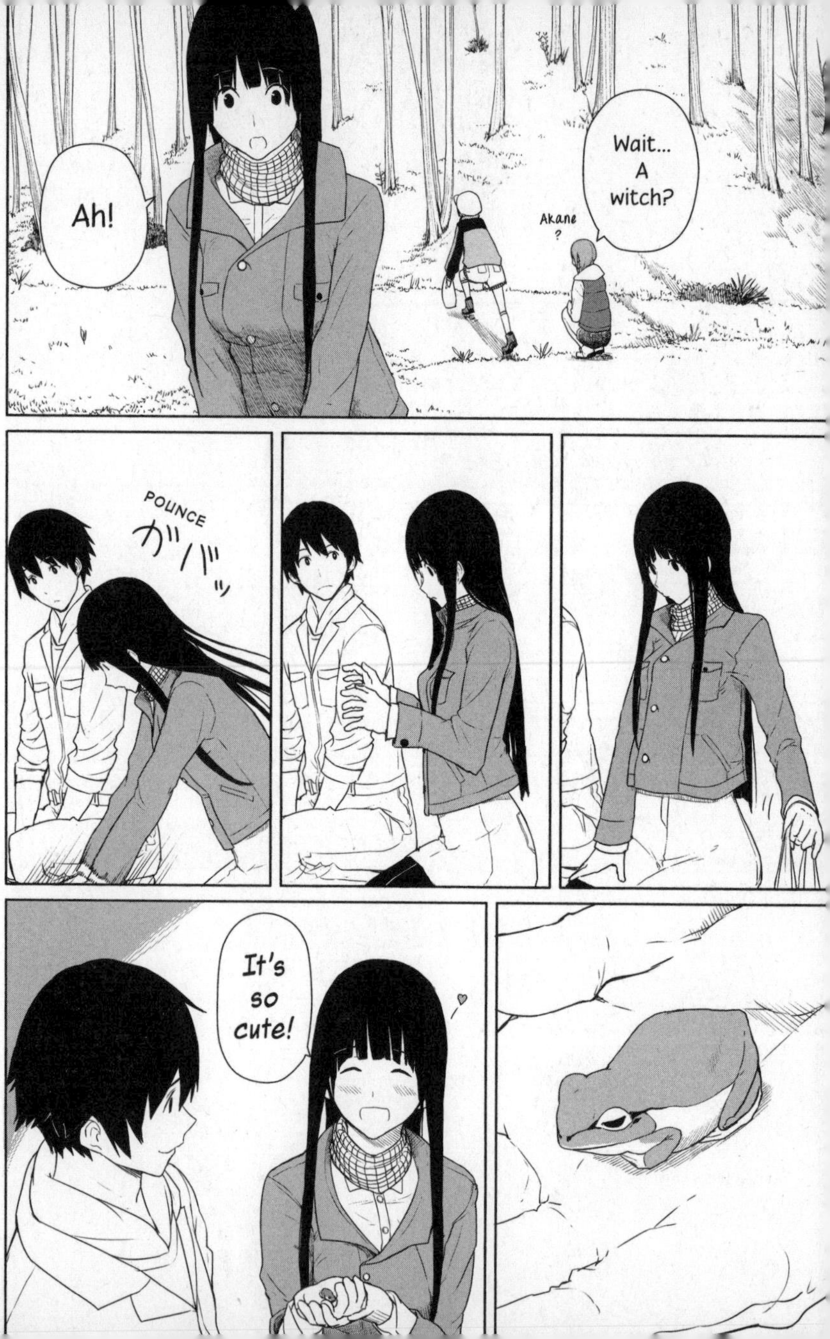
Wait... A witch?
Akane ?
Ah!
POUNCE
ガバッ
It's so cute!

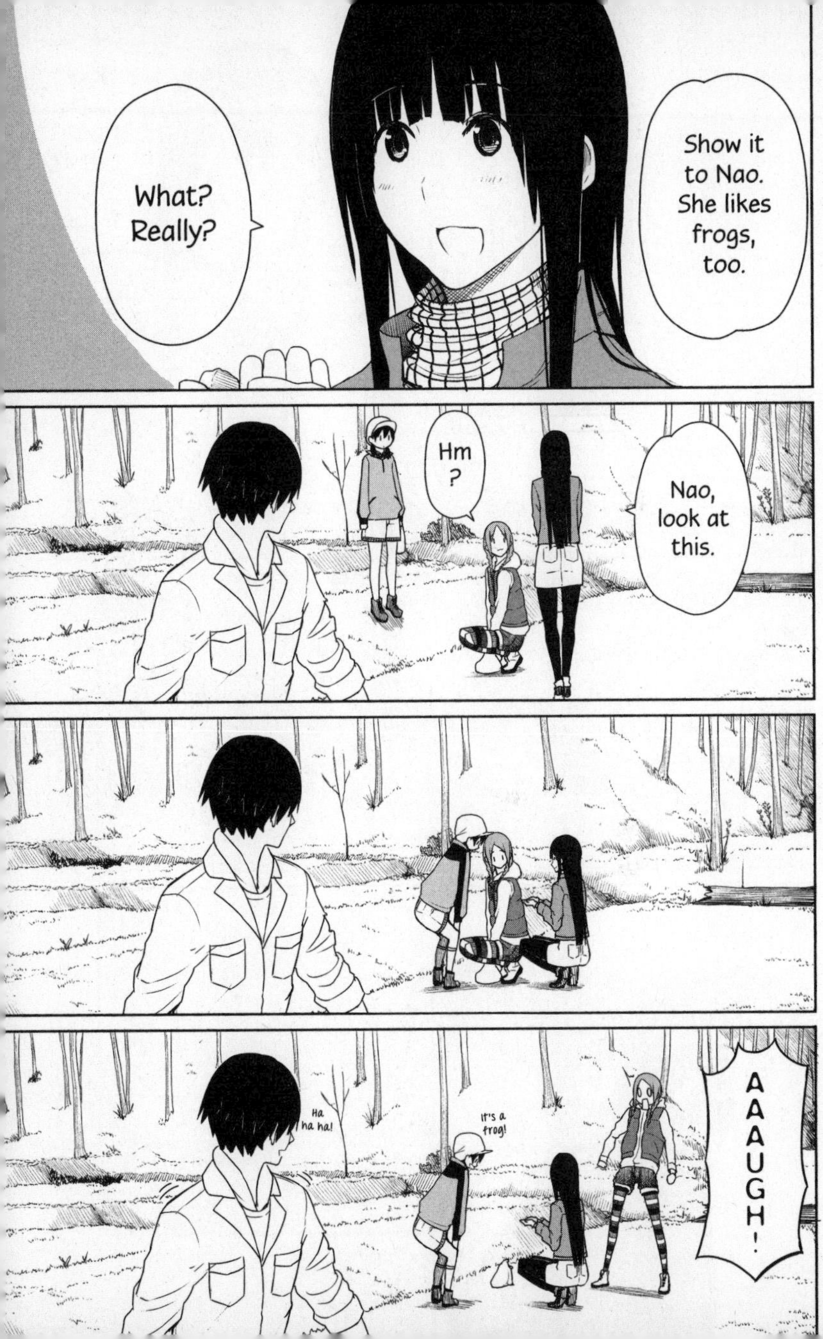
Show it to Nao. She likes frogs, too.
What? Really?
Nao, look at this.
Hm?
AAAUGH!
It's a frog!
Ha ha ha!

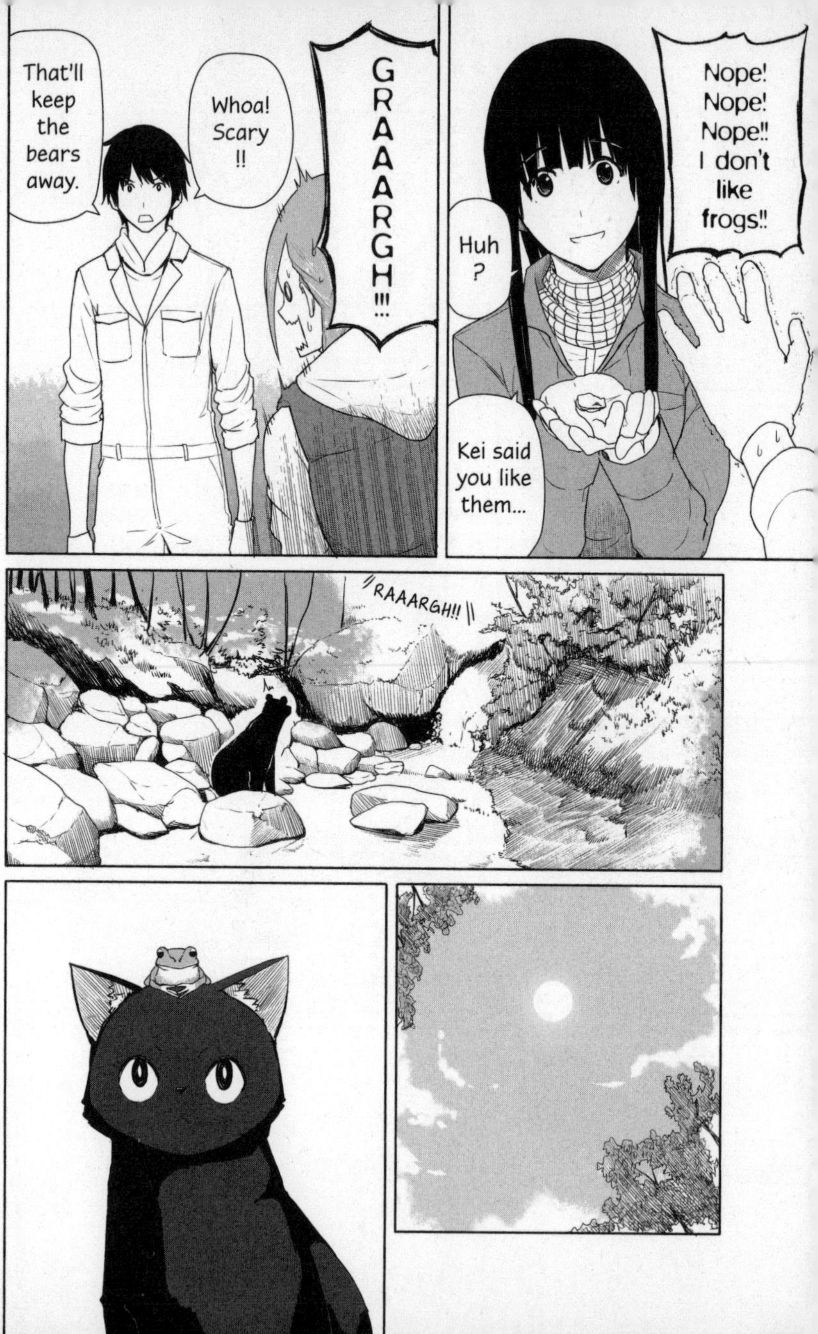
Nope! Nope! Nope!! I don't like frogs!!
Huh?
Kei said you like them...
GRAAAARGH!!!
Whoa! Scary!!
That'll keep the bears away.
RAAARGH!!

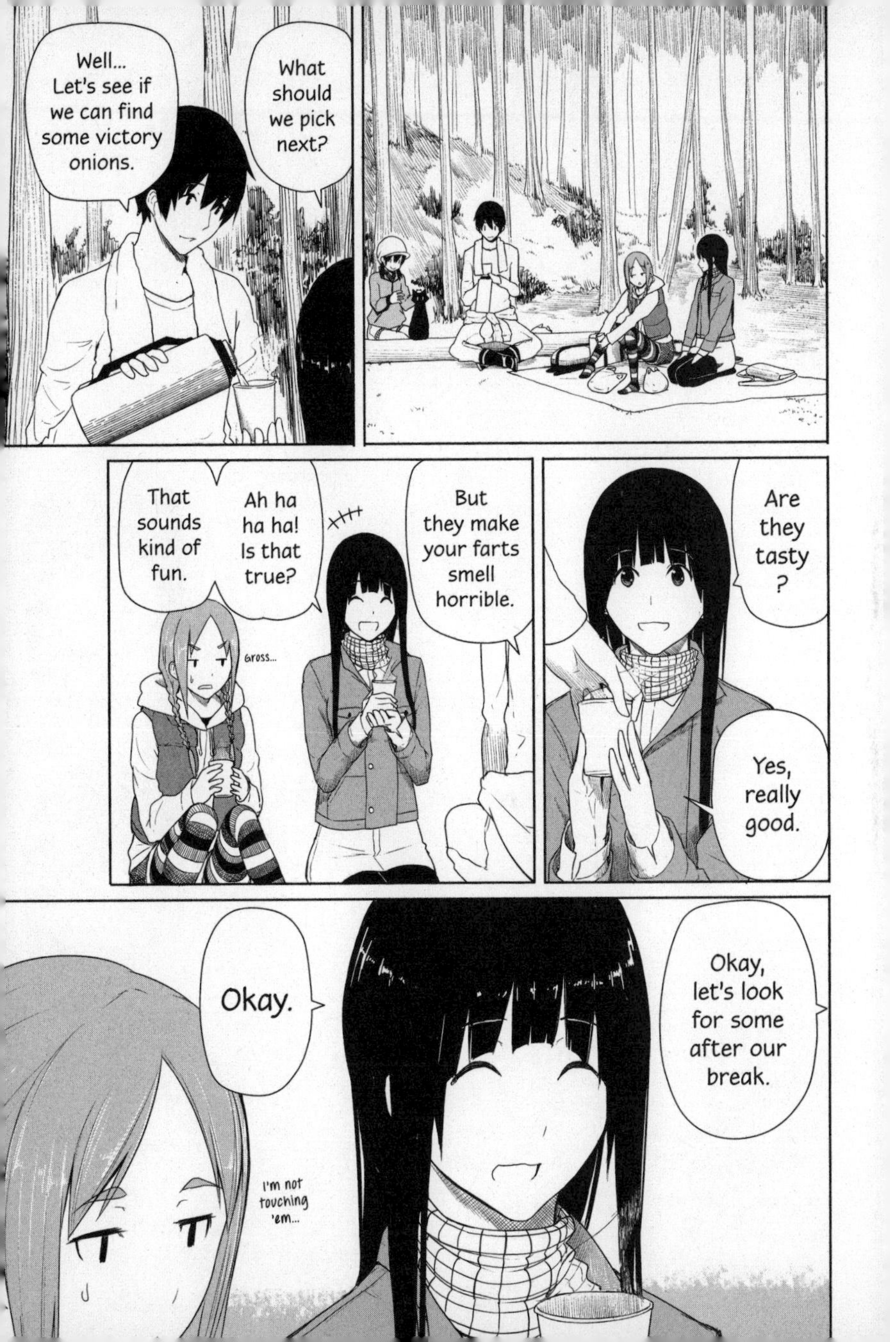
What should we pick next?
Well... Let's see if we can find some victory onions.
Are they tasty?
Yes, really good.
But they make your farts smell horrible.
Ah ha ha ha! Is that true?
That sounds kind of fun.
Gross...
Okay, let's look for some after our break.
Okay.
I'm not touching 'em...

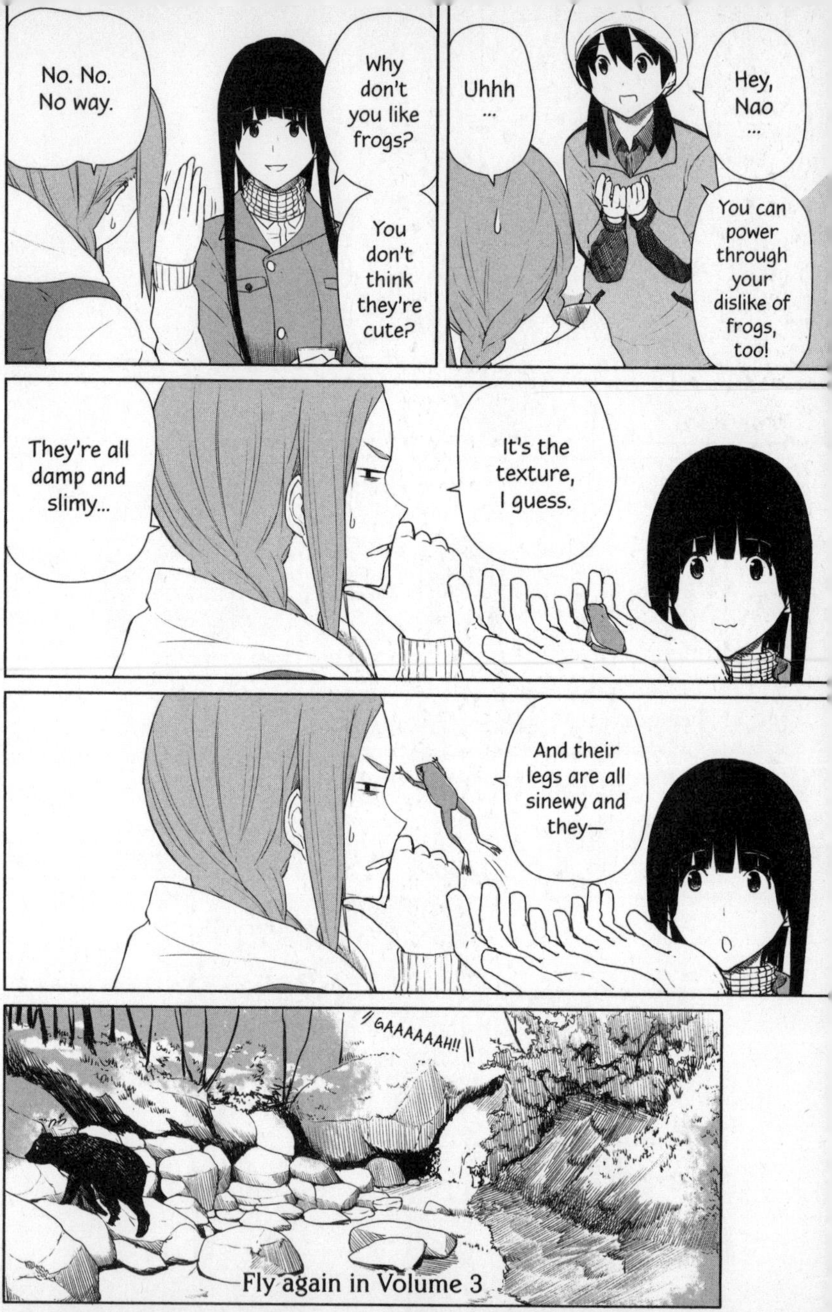
Hey, Nao ...
You can power through your dislike of frogs, too!
Uhhh ...
Why don't you like frogs?
You don't think they're cute?
No. No. No way.
It's the texture, I guess.
They're all damp and slimy...
And their legs are all sinewy and they—
GAAAAAAH!!
Fly again in Volume 3

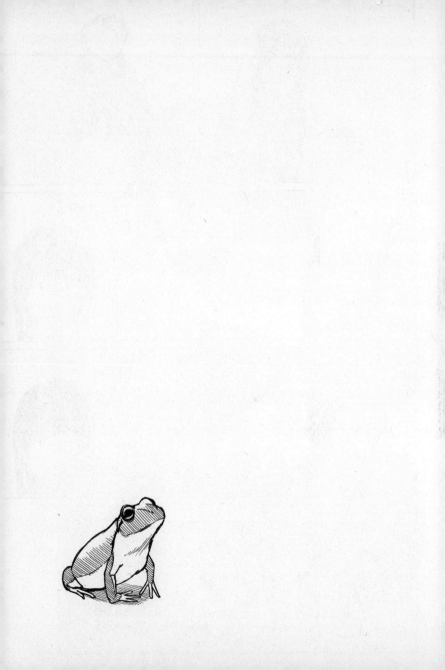

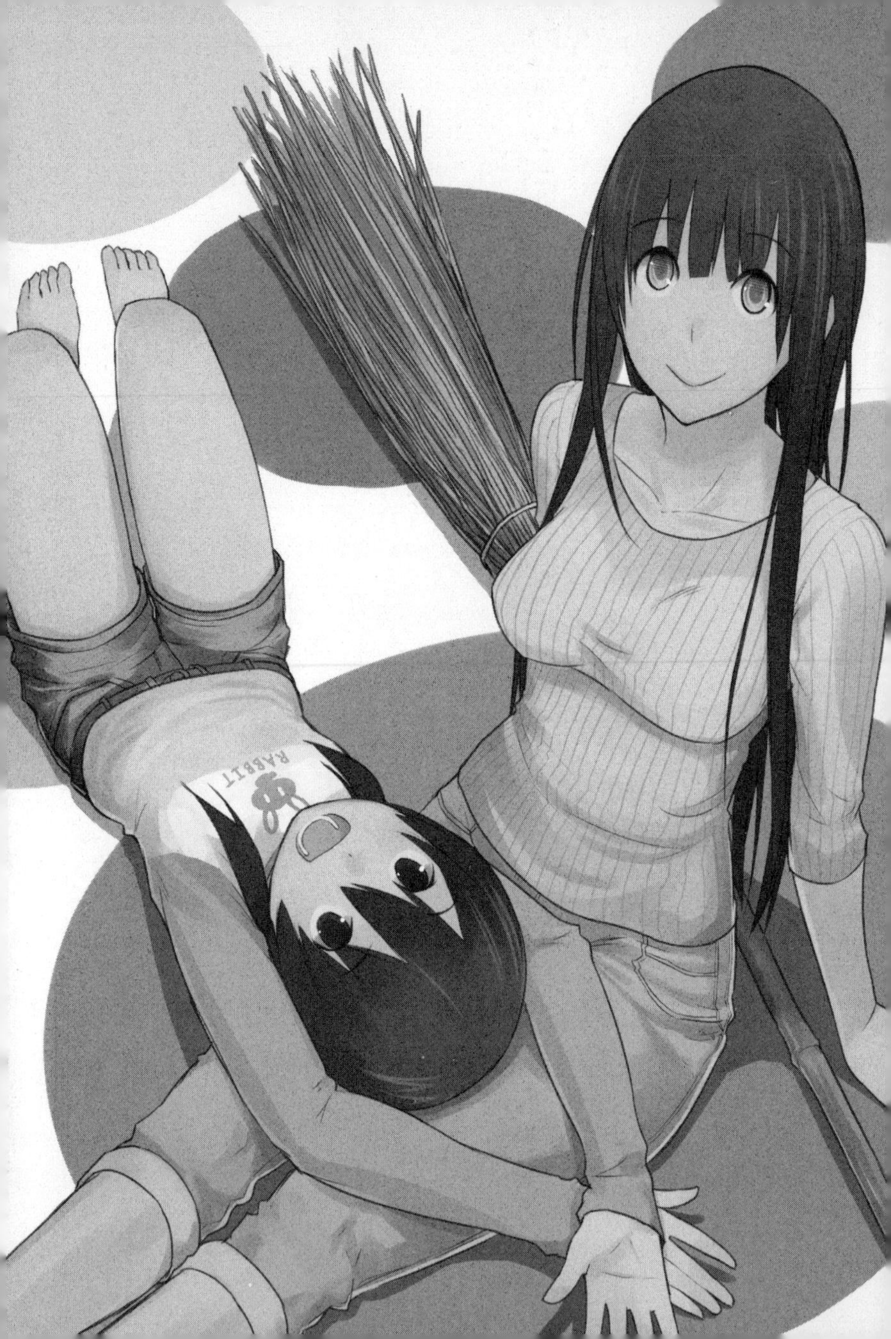
RABBIT

Volume 3 preview

flying witch ☀ kcm flying witch preview for next volume ☀ flying witch ☀ kcm

Volume 3
is coming soon!

Packed full of the
stories of Makoto and
her friends enjoying the
days of early summer
in Aomori.

We hope you enjoy it,
too!

Flying Witch 2

Translation - Melissa Tanaka
Production - Grace Lu
　　　　　　Tomoe Tsutsumi

Copyright © 2014 Chihiro Ishizuka. All rights reserved.
First published in Japan in 2014 by Kodansha, Ltd., Tokyo
Publication for this English edition arranged through Kodansha, Ltd., Tokyo

Translation provided by Vertical Comics, 2017
Published by Vertical Comics, an imprint of Vertical, Inc., New York

Originally published in Japanese as *Flying Witch 2* by Kodansha, Ltd., 2014
Flying Witch first serialized in *Bessatsu Shonen Magazine*, Kodansha, Ltd., 2013-

This is a work of fiction.

ISBN: 978-1-945054-10-5

Manufactured in the United States of America

First Edition

Vertical, Inc.
451 Park Avenue South, 7th Floor
New York, NY 10016
www.vertical-comics.com

Vertical books are distributed through Penguin-Random House Publisher Services.